# How to Get the Teaching Job *You Want*

# How to Get the Teaching Job
*You Want*

## The Complete Guide for College Graduates,
## Teachers Changing Schools, Returning Teachers,
## and Career Changers

### Second Edition

*Robert Feirsen and Seth Weitzman*

STERLING, VIRGINIA

Second edition published in 2004 by

Stylus Publishing, LLC
22883 Quicksilver Drive
Sterling, Virginia 20166

Library of Congress Cataloging-in-Publication-Data

Feirsen, Robert, 1951–
   How to get the teaching job you want : the complete guide for college
graduates, teachers changing schools, returning teachers, and career
changers / Robert Feirsen and Seth Weitzman.—2nd ed.
      p.  cm.
   Includes bibliographical references (p.  147) and index.
   ISBN 1-57922-068-1  (pbk. : alk. paper)
1.  Teachers—Employment—United States—Handbooks, manuals, etc.
2. Teaching—Vocational guidance—United States—Handbooks, Manuals, etc.
3. Job junting—United States—Handbookd, Manuals, etc. I. Weitzman,
Seth, 1958–  II. Title.
LB1780 .F53 2004
371.1'0023'73—dc22

                                                                2003015815

First edition, 2000

ISBN: 1-57922-068-1

Printed on acid free paper

## Dedication

*To JoAnn, Nicole, and Stephanie and to Jill, Jason, and Emily—this book is dedicated to our families with whom we share our dreams and whose love gives us joy.*

# Contents

About the Authors    ix
Acknowledgements    xi

**Chapter 1**            **Why You Need This Book    1**

**Chapter 2**            **Know Yourself    11**

**Chapter 3**            **Finding Job Openings    21**

**Chapter 4**            **Doing Your Homework    43**

**Chapter 5**            **Your Cover Letter    55**

**Chapter 6**            **Your Resume    75**

**Chapter 7**            **Portfolios with Punch    91**

**Chapter 8**            **Getting Ready for the Interview    101**

**Chapter 9**            **The All-Important Interview    109**

**Chapter 10**           **After the Interview    129**

Epilogue    143
Further Reading    145
References    147
Glossary: A Quick Guide to Educationese    149
Index    159

# About the Authors

**Dr. Robert Feirsen** was an elementary school principal and a middle school principal before attaining his current position as Deputy Superintendent in Manhasset, New York. He is also an adjunct professor at Adelphi University. He earned a doctorate in Educational Administration from Fordham University.

**Dr. Seth Weitzman** is the principal of Hommocks Middle School in Larchmont, New York. He has been a principal, assistant principal, and teacher trainer for more than 15 years. He earned a doctorate in Educational Administration from Teachers College, Columbia University.

Prior to their careers in educational administration, the authors had diverse experiences teaching in private and public schools in urban and suburban communities. They are founders of *TeacherEdge,* a consulting firm that equips teachers with job-hunting skills and strategies through workshops and individual counseling.

# Acknowledgments

We extend our appreciation to the teachers, administrators, colleagues, and friends who have taught us many of the principles presented in this book. Their insights, stories, and observations are revealed in every chapter, and we thank them for their willingness to share their ideas. We are also grateful to John von Knorring, editor and publisher extraordinaire, for his invaluable guidance and support throughout this project.

We stand in awe of the boundless enthusiasm and talent we have witnessed in innumerable teacher candidates. We hope this book will build a bridge between their commitment to enriching the lives of children and teaching jobs to which they aspire.

## Chapter One

# Why You Need This Book

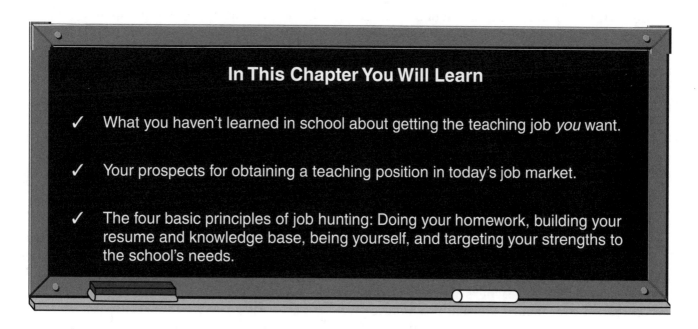

**In This Chapter You Will Learn**

✓ What you haven't learned in school about getting the teaching job *you* want.

✓ Your prospects for obtaining a teaching position in today's job market.

✓ The four basic principles of job hunting: Doing your homework, building your resume and knowledge base, being yourself, and targeting your strengths to the school's needs.

*What do you call a good teacher with poor job-hunting skills?*
*Unemployed!*

Competition for the best teaching jobs is intense. When the schools we serve as a principal and a deputy superintendent of schools advertise vacancies, hundreds of teachers typically apply for a single opening. Ninety percent of the cover letters and resumes we receive go directly to the reject pile because applicants don't use these crucial documents correctly. Of the candidates who advance to the interview round, another ninety percent are disqualified within minutes after they walk in the room. In spite of national statistics portending a shortage of teachers in specific subjects and geographic areas, most candidates feel compelled to take the first teaching job they are offered, not the teaching job they *really* want.

This book provides you with the job-hunting skills and strategies you need to overcome the odds and obtain a teaching job in the type of school, community, and geographic location you favor. In more than thirty-three years of experience reading thousands of resumes and sitting on the opposite side of the interview table, we have discovered that most candidates are ill-prepared for the final, decisive steps necessary to reach their career goals. Time and again, we encounter candidates who achieved superior grades in college and garnered rave reviews while student teaching, but lack the know-how to navigate the unfamiliar territory of the hiring process. We know that in comparison to the innumerable hours teachers have dedicated to learning their craft, they have received scant training in, and sometimes misleading information about, how to obtain the teaching job of their choice.

Jean was one of the finest student teachers Seth had ever known. She earned outstanding grades while enrolled in a renowned teacher preparation program. The cooperating teacher who observed her student teach described her as a natural, and she was loved by students and parents. When the teacher from the classroom next door announced her retirement, good fortune seemed to be smiling on Jean. Her problems began when she formally applied for the teaching position. Many candidates possessed similar qualifications, but several submitted more informative cover letters and resumes geared to the needs of Seth's school. Jean was granted an interview nonetheless, although her application materials did nothing to strengthen her candidacy. A committee designed a series of questions to assess each candidate's knowledge of hands-on teaching techniques. Teachers fondly remembered Jean in the faculty lounge passionately arguing the importance of active learning, and her cooperating teacher attested to Jean's practical skills. Yet, Jean fumbled through the interview and failed to persuade the hiring committee, despite the promise she had shown during her student teaching practicum. Ultimately, the school hired another candidate who communicated a deeper understanding of innovative instructional strategies. Afterward faculty members wondered: Was the superior teacher hired, or was the successful candidate simply more adept at advertising her talents?

We believe there are four explanations why prospective teachers are inadequately prepared for the job-hunting challenge.

1. They do not invest enough time. Candidates naively underestimate the time they must devote to the job search process. The skills needed to land a desirable job are markedly different from mastery of classroom teaching for which candidates prepare assiduously. Richard Nelson Bolles, the author of the best-selling career counseling book *What Color Is Your Parachute?* advises job hunters to consider job searching as a full-time occupation (Bolles, 2000). Yet, aspiring teachers typically tell us they attend only a workshop or two sponsored by their college career placement office, roughly the time they spend studying for a simple test or writing a paper.

2. They listen to the wrong "experts." Much of what candidates learn about job hunting comes from fellow students, college placement offices that do not specialize in classroom teaching jobs, and education professors who are experts in pedagogy but lack an insiders' knowledge of the job search process. To put it simply: You need advice from seasoned school administrators who know exactly what is demanded of prospective teachers and why so many candidates fail.

3. They confuse boardrooms with classrooms. Friends, family members, and countless books offer advice about job hunting from the business world's perspective, but businesses operate much differently from schools. Generic job hunting books really pertain to the business market. People seeking business jobs buy these books, whose authors are definitely not school administrators. The generic books neglect the specialized requirements of job hunting in education and are often responsible for spreading misinformation. For example, every school administrator we know strongly prefers a

---

We know that in comparison to the innumerable hours teachers have dedicated to learning their craft, they have received scant training in, and sometimes misleading information about, how to obtain the teaching job of their choice.

You need advice from seasoned school administrators who know exactly what is demanded of prospective teachers and why so many candidates fail.

resume style known as the chronological resume, yet generic books suggest alternative formats, which could lose you the job you want.

4. They don't recognize that times have changed. Dramatic changes have taken place in job hunting for teachers over the last decade. Computer-designed resumes, interview committees, demonstration lessons, all uncommon in the recent past, have become standard practice. Reams of data about schools are available over the Internet, and candidates have begun posting electronic portfolios on-line. You need counsel from experts within the field who have current, practical knowledge.

An important goal of *How to Get the Teaching Job You Want* is to help you select a school that is right for you. Like a marriage, the relationship between a teacher and a school flourishes when there is a good match. Our book helps you gather crucial information about schools to determine whether there is a close fit between you and a prospective employer. Once you have used the procedure we recommend to identify openings that pique your interest, we help you mount an advertising campaign targeted at demonstrating your ability to meet the needs of these specific schools.

The job-hunting skills we recommend in *How to Get the Teaching Job You Want* are applicable to a wide variety of schools and teaching positions. Elementary, middle, and high schools; public and private schools; parochial schools; international schools; and boarding schools are all discussed. Classroom teachers, guidance counselors, school psychologists, and social workers, indeed, anyone seeking a faculty position in any elementary or secondary school will find the book invaluable.

Candidates for teaching positions come from diverse backgrounds. According to a 1999 U.S. Department of Education study, twenty-seven percent of newly

**BACKGROUND OF NEWLY
HIRED TEACHERS BY PERCENT**

18%

32%

23%

27%

☐ Experienced Teachers Transferring Jobs

◻ Recent College Graduates

◼ Re-entrants Returning to Teaching

■ Career Changers

Source: *Digest of Education Statistics, 2001*

hired teachers were recent college graduates just starting a career. Eighteen percent were novice teachers transferring to the classroom as a second career. A total of thirty-two percent of newly hired teachers were experienced practitioners leaving one school to take a position in another. The remaining new hires, twenty-three percent, were former teachers rejoining the workforce after a break in service, perhaps to raise a family (see the graph on the previous page) (National Center for Education Statistics, 2001). Each of these groups—recent graduates, career changers, transfers from other schools, and teachers returning to the workforce—faces unique challenges when testing the teaching job market, and all three are given special attention in this book.

Career changers, for example, must understand how the hiring process in schools differs from the professions they are leaving. Job-hunting strategies that succeeded when they found employment the first time around may be disastrous in education. Consider the plight of former engineers who worked for Grumman Corporation, a major employer in Long Island's (New York) once-thriving aerospace industry. When the plant doors closed permanently in the early 1990s, numerous Grumman workers attempted to parlay years of engineering experience into a second career as a mathematics or science teacher. However, most of the former Grumman employees could not make the transition from the business world to the classroom. *How to Get the Teaching Job You Want* offers advice to meet the needs of people changing careers and those who always knew they wanted to be teachers.

In a school district in which one of us formerly worked, administrative policies gave preference to hiring teachers reentering the classroom because they were more experienced than recent college graduates. Despite this preferential treatment, the more seasoned applicants, many of whom had taken a hiatus to raise their families, frequently disqualified themselves because they were unable to demonstrate that they had remained current in the field. Our book offers practical advice to help teachers returning to the workforce overcome this common obstacle to resuming a successful teaching career.

This new edition of *How to Get the Teaching Job You Want* also provides invaluable assistance to two other groups of job seekers: those who are trying to move from one school (or district) to another, and those who are entering the teaching profession through one of the increasingly popular alternative routes to certification. In the former case, candidates must demonstrate that they are literally worth the investment, that is, the extra salary that will be required to pay an experienced instructor. In the latter instance, applicants must show that they are able to provide quality instruction without having completed the coursework and preparatory activities associated with a traditional university "teacher prep" program.

Our book is guided by four basic principles of job hunting.

## Basic Principle #1: Do Your Homework

As we mentioned before, job hunting should be considered a full-time occupation. *How to Get the Teaching Job You Want* describes strategies for finding job vacancies, writing effective cover letters and resumes, compiling an employment portfolio, and demonstrating your abilities in an interview; each of these tasks requires considerable effort. Remember, the best-prepared candidate has the competitive edge in a job search.

## Basic Principle #2: Build Your Resume and Knowledge Base

Your preparation begins here. You must strive to become the ideal candidate that your target school is looking to hire. Identify your strengths as a prospective teacher, assess your weaknesses, and work continually to improve your qualifications. Some practical strategies include:

- If you are uncertain how you would answer an interview question about a specific teaching technique, prepare yourself by reading a book or journal article in advance.
- The greatest deficiency of a young candidate just out of college is lack of experience. If this is your situation, volunteer at a school or tutor children at the grade level you want to teach.
- On the other hand, the biggest drawback for a parent returning to the teaching force after

raising a family may be lack of knowledge about changes in the field since she last taught. If this applies to you, take education courses online or at a local college and subscribe to a professional journal.

### Basic Principle #3: Be Yourself

This book advises you repeatedly to be yourself and express your beliefs passionately. You are a special individual with a unique personality, background, and educational philosophy to offer the teaching profession. Nobody has the same experiences, abilities, or ideas that you have. Your task when applying for a teaching position is to shine a spotlight on your special qualities. You must reveal your extraordinary qualities or you will join most of the other job seekers in the reject pile. Failure to stand out from the crowd is the most common mistake unsuccessful teacher candidates make.

### Basic Principle #4: Target Your Strengths to the School's Needs

Each candidate is unique, and the needs of each school are unique. Administrators recruiting teacher candidates are not searching for a generic "good teacher"; they are looking to address specific needs in their schools. The mission of your job hunt is to identify the qualities your targeted school is seeking, and then demonstrate that you are the one to solve the school's problems or enhance its programs. Consider these illustrations:

- A traditional junior high school converting into a contemporary middle school aims to hire teachers who understand the developmental needs of young adolescents.
- A school district that recently passed a multimillion-dollar bond issue to purchase computers needs teachers who can easily integrate technology into their lessons.

Subsequent chapters explain how you can determine the school's needs and present yourself as the most suitable candidate.

Chapter 2, titled *Know Yourself*, incorporates exercises to recognize the unique constellation of talents you offer the teaching profession and reminds you of the education and work experiences that have prepared you to become a teacher. These activities lay the groundwork necessary to write a cover letter and resume, prepare for job interviews, and create an employment portfolio. Chapter 3, *Finding Job Openings* suggests a variety of traditional and nontraditional resources you can mine to locate job opportunities. Too many candidates rely exclusively on a single avenue, such as newspaper advertisements, thereby limiting their chances of discovering vacancies. *Doing Your Homework*, the next chapter, recognizes that job hunting is a two-way street. It is just as important to learn about the school to which you are applying as it is for the school to learn more about you. This chapter tells you how to acquire information about a school's educational philosophy, curriculum, student population, test results, administrative staff, and the community it serves. This information has two purposes: First, it will help you decide whether the school is right for you, and, second, you can use the information to help determine what the school is looking for, so you can target your presentations to meet the school's particular needs. The fifth and sixth chapters, *Your Cover Letter* and *Your Resume*, respectively, explain how to grab an administrator's attention so you stand out from the rest of the applicants. Sample cover letters and resumes are included, geared to the specific circumstances of recent college graduates, career changers, and mature teachers returning to the workforce. As educators began experimenting with alternate assessment techniques in classrooms, portfolios were introduced into the hiring process as a means of evaluating candidates. *Portfolios with Punch*, Chapter 7, provides up-to-date advice regarding the content and organization of portfolios and how to use a

---

Failure to stand out from the crowd is the most common mistake unsuccessful teacher candidates make.

portfolio to your best advantage. The most anxiety-provoking step of a job search, the interview, is covered over two chapters. Chapter 8, *Getting Ready for the Interview,* presents helpful suggestions to ready yourself for the demands of the interview even before you enter the room. Topics include dressing for success, handling stress, and identifying key points you would like to cover. In Chapter 9, *The All-Important Interview,* you learn how to make a favorable first impression and answer questions knowledgeably and confidently. You also become acquainted with various interview formats and their purposes. The final chapter, *After the Interview,* discusses second-round interviews, demonstration lessons, salary negotiations, and all the other steps leading up to signing a teacher's contract. The glossary at the end of the book provides concise definitions of many terms you may encounter while you are job hunting. These terms are also printed in bold type in the text.

## The Teaching Job Market

Every year, approximately ten percent of the teacher workforce consists of newly hired teachers. In 1999, the U.S. Department of Education forecast that 2.4 million new teachers would be hired over the next decade to educate 53.8 million elementary and secondary school students, almost the largest population of students and teachers in U.S. history (Hussar, 1999). To meet the demand for new teachers, more than 1.2 million students were enrolled in undergraduate and graduate education programs, and nearly a quarter million undergraduate and graduate degrees in education were conferred, more than any field except business (National Center for Education Statistics, 2001). Exacerbating the need for new teachers has been the graying of the teacher workforce. Nearly three-quarters of a million teachers working today are expected to retire by 2009 (Hussar, 1999). Looking at public school student enrollment in each state, the National Center for Education Statistics forecasts the greatest growth in Western states over the

next decade. Student enrollment in Midwestern and Southern states is mixed. In the Northeast, enrollment is expected to decline (National Center for Education Statistics, 2001). Additional information about trends can be found in the charts and graphs on the following page.

The availability of teaching jobs also depends on a candidate's area of certification. The good news is: No field of education is expected to have many more qualified candidates than available jobs, according to a study sponsored by the American Association for Employment in Education (2001). Health education and physical education will have some surplus of candidates. Teachers preparing to instruct students with behavioral disabilities, bilingual backgrounds, and speech and language disorders, and prospective mathematics, chemistry, and physics teachers will enjoy a surfeit of vacancies. Other fields will have moderate shortages of applicants or balanced supply and demand, as indicated in the chart on page 8.

Interest in teaching careers has reached new heights. Enrollment in teacher education programs increased steadily during the 1990s, in contrast to admissions to business, law, and medical schools, which saw no growth. The number of college freshmen expressing an interest in teaching careers has doubled since 1983. There are more graduate and undergraduate students attending schools of education than any other preprofessional field today except business (see page 9). In addition, the ranks of job seekers are now swelled by participants in **alternative certification** programs; these prospective educators are generally allowed to bypass student teaching and begin work in a classroom in certain districts or academic fields without having completed college coursework in pedagogy. In the New York metropolitan area, the authors have interviewed a surge of prospective teachers who state they reevaluated their career choices since September 11, 2001, opting to change career paths to make a meaningful contribution in America's classrooms.

How will the job market affect you? While the market is subject to the forces of supply and demand, there will continue to be an excess of

## U.S. TEACHERS
Elementary and Secondary,
in Thousands
(1) Projected

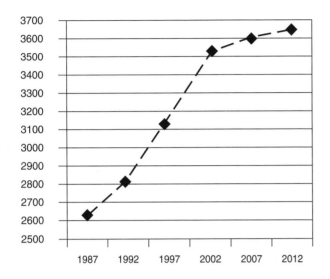

## U.S. STUDENTS
Elementary and Secondary,
in Thousands
(1) Projected

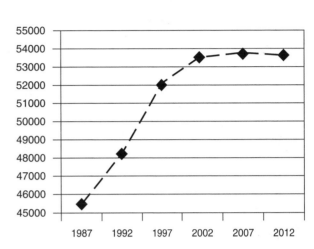

Source: National Center for Education Statistics, 2001

## PROJECTED STUDENT ENROLLMENT BY STATE
Percent Change in Grades K–12 Enrollment in Public Schools, by State: Fall 2000 to Fall 2012

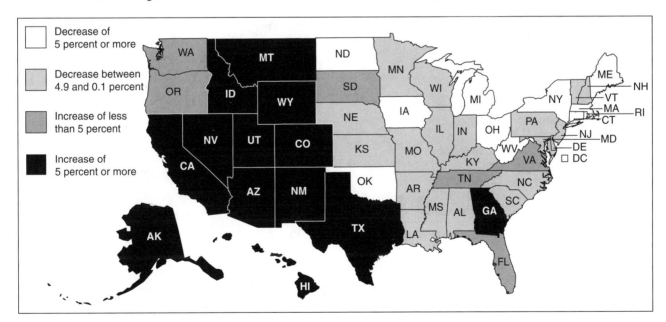

Source: U.S. Department of Education, National Center for Educational Statistics, Common Core of Data Surveys; and State Public Elementary and Secondary Enrollment Model

**TEACHING SUPPLY AND DEMAND
BY CERTIFICATION AREA**

| Many More Jobs than Candidates | More Jobs than Candidates | Balanced Supply and Demand | More Candidates than Jobs | Many More Candidates than Jobs |
|---|---|---|---|---|
| Behavioral disorders | Agriculture | Art | Health education | None |
| Bilingual education | Audiologist | Business education | Physical education | |
| Chemistry | Biology | Classics | | |
| Computer science | Early childhood special education | Driver education | | |
| Developmentally disabled | Earth science | Dance | | |
| Emotional disorders | Elementary principal | Elementary education | | |
| Hearing impaired | English as a Second Language (ESL) | English/Language arts | | |
| Learning disabilities | French | General music | | |
| Mathematics | General science | German | | |
| Physics | Gifted/Talented | Journalism | | |
| Visually impaired | Guidance counselor | Occupational therapist | | |
| | High school principal | Physical therapist | | |
| | Home economics | Nurse | | |
| | Instrumental music | Social Studies | | |
| | Japanese | Speech education | | |
| | Librarian | Theater/Drama | | |
| | Middle school principal | | | |
| | Physical science | | | |
| | Psychologist | | | |
| | Reading | | | |
| | Social worker | | | |
| | Spanish | | | |
| | Speech pathologist | | | |
| | Technology education | | | |
| | Vocal music | | | |

Source: American Association for Employment in Education, 2001

well-qualified candidates competing for the most desirable positions. Friends may say you're lucky when you land a teaching job, but like all professional achievements, we believe little luck is involved. Getting the teaching job you want depends on acquiring essential job hunting knowledge and skills.

To prepare for your job search, Chapter 2 prompts you to reflect on the road you have already traveled.

**ENROLLMENT IN POST–SECONDARY INSTITUTIONS**
in Thousands

| Field of Study | Undergraduate | Graduate | Total |
|---|---|---|---|
| Business | 1439 | 393 | 1832 |
| Education | 674 | 566 | 1240 |
| Computer science | 439 | 85 | 524 |
| Engineering | 418 | 94 | 512 |
| Health | 653 | 255 | 908 |
| Law | 63 | 132 | 195 |
| Liberal studies | 387 | 59 | 446 |
| Life/physical sciences | 501 | 109 | 610 |
| Mathematics | 64 | 25 | 89 |
| Psychology | 349 | 74 | 423 |
| Public administration/social work | 105 | 51 | 156 |
| Social sciences | 549 | 92 | 641 |

Source: National Center for Education Statistics, 2001

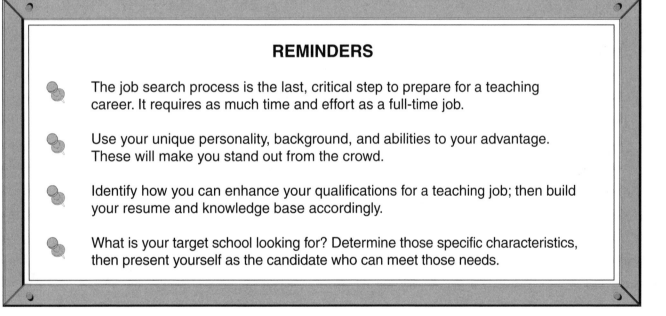

## REMINDERS

The job search process is the last, critical step to prepare for a teaching career. It requires as much time and effort as a full-time job.

Use your unique personality, background, and abilities to your advantage. These will make you stand out from the crowd.

Identify how you can enhance your qualifications for a teaching job; then build your resume and knowledge base accordingly.

What is your target school looking for? Determine those specific characteristics, then present yourself as the candidate who can meet those needs.

# Chapter Two

# Know Yourself

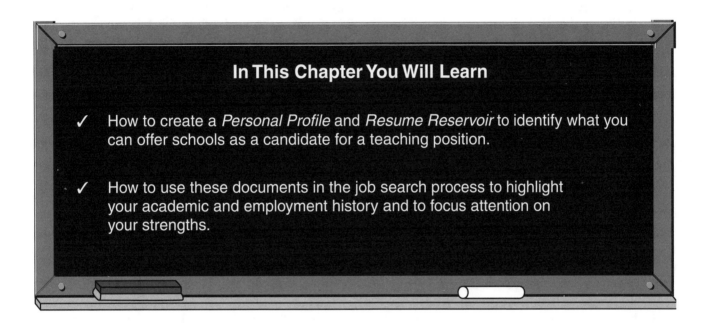

## In This Chapter You Will Learn

✓ How to create a *Personal Profile* and *Resume Reservoir* to identify what you can offer schools as a candidate for a teaching position.

✓ How to use these documents in the job search process to highlight your academic and employment history and to focus attention on your strengths.

*How have your educational background and work experiences prepared you for a teaching position?*

This question, or a variation of it, begins almost every interview. It is designed to be a confidence builder. The query focuses on the candidate's successes from the outset and breaks the ice in a nerve-racking situation. To provide an extraordinary answer, candidates must possess a steadfast sense of who they are and confidence in their ability to meet the educational needs of students. This chapter shows you how to identify the individual skills, knowledge, training, and experience you have to offer the teaching profession. You will rely on this information later when you write a cover letter and resume, prepare for an interview, and create an employment portfolio. In the words of an employment counselor we know, "You can't convince an employer of what you have to offer until you know yourself."

"You can't convince an employer of what you have to offer until you know yourself."

> What differentiates candidates is how they describe what they learned in the process.

When we bring home stacks of resumes to read at night, the profiles of prospective teachers seem almost identical. To meet state certification requirements, every applicant's college transcript reflects similar education courses, and everyone has completed a student teaching **practicum.** The majority of candidates are recent college graduates who have participated in extracurricular clubs and sports, and spent summers, afternoons, and weekends serving children in such familiar capacities as camp counselors, tutors, soccer coaches, and other roles. The activities themselves are often indistinguishable. What differentiates candidates is how they describe what they learned in the process.

**Q:** "Tell me about yourself."
**A:** "There isn't a lot to say."

We have actually heard this from a number of candidates in interviews. Too many candidates offer pat, mundane answers, and fail to present themselves as the fabulous teachers that administrators are looking to hire.

One afternoon Seth was interviewing at a college-sponsored recruiting fair where all the candidates seemed cut from the same cloth—they all attended the college where the fair was held, completed the same introductory-level courses, even espoused similar jargon. Several hours later, a young woman's extraordinary responses kindled Seth's interest. In reviewing her resume a second time, he noticed an odd coincidence: the promising candidate's address, college, even her last name were exactly the same as another woman he had met earlier. Indeed, the two women were sisters, and their preparation took nearly identical paths. The difference between them was not to be found in the education or experiences listed on their resumes. Instead, it was the younger sibling's rich description of how she proposed to meet the needs of Seth's school that made her stand out.

Another example of the importance of candidates knowing what they have to offer is apparent when we interview mothers returning to the workforce. Asked what they were doing since they last held a job, the typical answer is, "I raised my family." One day, Rob heard a better response. An applicant for a kindergarten position explained how she had been using her time. "I've been learning about the developmental needs of young children while watching my children grow." She proceeded to state theories of preschool maturation and learning worthy of a master's thesis.

You *are* special, of course, but the people you meet along the road to a job won't know that at first glance. To get the teaching job you really want, you have to wage a targeted marketing campaign to sell yourself. You have to create the impression that you are the only one who can do the job the way the school wants it to be done. And you have to do it by making the most of the brief opportunities you will be given to prove yourself. It is your job to show how your experiences have prepared you for the position. To the extent that you know yourself and express your individuality, you will stand out from the crowd of candidates applying for teaching jobs in competitive schools.

To prepare your best case for employment, we recommend that you catalog your life experiences and your ideas about teaching in data banks that you can draw on to design a cover letter and resume or to prepare for an interview. The process is much like a funnel, with the open-ended side representing your accumulated experiences, your general career goals, and your beliefs about the educational process, and the narrow end serving as the filter through which you select the details most relevant to a particular classroom position. To accomplish this task, we will help you create two documents: your *Personal Profile* and your *Resume Reservoir.*

## Your *Personal Profile*

The *Personal Profile* enables you to take stock of yourself. In our culture, we rarely perform this kind of self-inventory, but it is essential in the job-seeking process. It helps you to identify your

---

**Your Job Find Friend and Job Find File**

We recommend you find a *Job Find Friend* who will support you in your efforts to secure a teaching position. Someone must edit your cover letter and resume and rehearse interview questions with you. Just as important, your *Job Find Friend* will serve as a sounding board for your ideas, encourage you when you open the inevitable rejection letters, and celebrate with you once you are hired. Your *Job Find Friend* may be a spouse, a fellow student teacher, a trusted friend, or a parent. No experience in the field of education is necessary (although this might be especially helpful for those entering the field without an education degree or student teaching experience), but your *Job Find Friend* should have facility with written and spoken English. Be certain to review your *Personal Profile* and your *Resume Reservoir* with your *Job Find Friend*.

Your *Job Find File* is a place to store all your job search records. This will hold copies of advertisements, cover letters and resumes you send out, research you collect about individual schools, and notes from telephone conversations and interviews. To start your *Job Find File*, visit an office supply store and purchase a four-inch accordion file. You will also need one 8 1/2- by 11-inch manilla folder for every application you submit, so buy several dozen of these items, too.

Careful, organized record keeping is vital to an active job hunt, because there will be a great deal of data to keep straight in your mind. When you return home from the office supply store, place your *Personal Profile* and *Resume Reservoir* in the front of your *Job Find File* for easy reference later on.

---

individual talents and most important accomplishments. Armed with this self-knowledge, you will be able to write a cover letter and resume that are sure to highlight your strengths and launch your "sales" campaign in a most effective manner.

The *Personal Profile* is designed to help you summarize your background, identify your unique characteristics, and think about your views on teaching (see pages 14–15). If you've done the job carefully and honestly, you should have a better sense of who you are and what you want as a person *and* as an educator. For those with little or no experience as teachers, in particular, the completion of the *Personal Profile* may mark the first instance in which views about the nature of teaching has been systematically recorded. With these understandings in place, you can move ahead to your *Resume Reservoir,* in which you will record the details of your training, job history, life experiences, and achievements. Constructing a detailed *Personal Profile* takes time. Don't wait until a job opportunity arises to begin this critical task. Instead, do it when you have enough time to concentrate on the assignment in a careful, analytical fashion.

## Your *Resume Reservoir*

The *Resume Reservoir* is just what the title implies—a place to store data. No resume that you send to a school or district will ever contain all the material contained in this file. With your *Resume Reservoir* at your fingertips, you will be able to select the information that best matches the needs of a particular school in a matter of minutes. Then you can write an effective resume and get it into the hands of an appreciative reader in a timely manner.

We have provided you with a generic form (see pages 16–19). Novice teachers and those involved in **alternative certification** programs should try to complete all relevant sections at this early stage in their careers, while those with more experience in the workforce may not need to dwell on high school histories, summer jobs, etc., from the distant past. Remember: The work you do now, when you have the opportunity to be thorough and accurate, will save you a great deal of anxiety and time when you have a deadline to meet.

## Everyone Has Strengths . . . and Weaknesses

Sarah was an outstanding high school social studies teacher. Her department chairperson and principal raved about the creative, stimulating methods she used in her classroom and the relationships she fostered with difficult teenagers. When her children were born, she resigned her teaching position so she could devote herself full-time to motherhood until her youngest child entered kindergarten. Seven years later, with more time on her hands and the family's savings

---

**Personal Profile**

When and why did you decide to become a teacher?

_____

_____

_____

What impact do you hope to have on your students?

_____

_____

_____

What life experience can you use in your teaching?

_____

_____

_____

What have you learned from your teacher training program to make you a better teacher?

_____

_____

_____

_____

What are your greatest strengths as a teacher?

_____

_____

_____

---

dwindling, Sarah began applying for secondary school social studies teaching positions. She felt hopeful and excited when she noticed an advertisement for a job in a neighboring town—an ideal location since she could pick up her young children immediately after school let out. Sarah attached a glowing letter of recommendation from her former principal and superior classroom observation reports written by her department chairperson. Sarah's impressive teaching background and references landed her an interview, but she lacked the up-to-date qualifications that the school wanted. Queries from the interview panel focused on unfamiliar topics, such as document-based questions and lessons using the Internet in the wake of a $35 million bond referendum approved by district voters.

James enjoyed a successful career in financial services until he was bitten by the teaching bug. In the midst of a mid-life crisis, he enrolled in courses to become a mathematics teacher, a dream he had harbored since college, but had never acted on. During interviews, he spoke passionately and convincingly about a burning desire to teach. Interview committee members had similar reactions to James's presentation. He displayed laudable idealism and valuable life experiences, but a competing candidate had a proven ability to relate to students. Understandably busy raising a family and holding a challenging job, James's child care experience over the last 15 years was limited to parenting his own children. In contrast, the other finalist served as a camp counselor, tutor, and soccer coach. The

What have been your main accomplishments? (Don't limit yourself here—consider all that you have achieved before writing your answer.) How might these help you in teaching?

_____

_____

_____

_____

What special talents or abilities do you have? Play an instrument? Little League coach? Great memory? How can you apply these to teaching?

_____

_____

_____

_____

When you think about yourself, what adjectives come to mind?

_____

_____

_____

_____

Describe your ideal teaching job.

_____

_____

_____

_____

Use the answers you wrote for the previous questions to respond to the following: What can you offer as a teacher that makes you special?

_____

_____

_____

_____

school refused to take a chance on James, a completely untested candidate.

Nothing is more frustrating when you apply for your dream job than to realize that you are inadequately prepared for the position. Despite Sarah's meritorious experience and James's commendable motivation, they failed to prepare themselves for today's job market. Sarah, for example, could have taken computer literacy courses or studied the state's curriculum changes by surfing the state education department's Web site. James had the opportunity to compensate for the deficiencies of his candidacy by volunteering for the finance company's "Helping Hands" lunchtime tutoring program in the local public school, coaching his daughter's softball team, or teaching Sunday school classes. By the time they mailed out cover letters and resumes, and entered interview conference rooms, it was too late to redress their inadequacies.

There is a lesson to be learned from the above anecdotes. Remember one of the basic principles of this book and work unceasingly to build your resume and knowledge base. Numerous sources of information are available to help you achieve this goal. Start with the written record: Review papers you wrote in education courses, tests you have taken, written evaluations of your student teaching practicum, and year-end evaluations and classroom observations if you have taught before. Next, seek knowledgeable mentors. Ask other teachers, school administrators, professors, and perhaps

---

**Resume Reservoir**

**Your Education**

**High School**

Name _____    City, State _____

Year of Graduation _____    Honors _____

Co-curricular, Service, Athletic Activities

_____

Other noteworthy accomplishments

_____

**College(s)** Photocopy page for each additional college attended.

Name _____    City, State _____

Year of Attendance _____    Degree Earned _____

Major _____    Minor _____

Overall GPA _____    GPA in Major Field _____

Honors

_____

Co-curricular, Service, Athletic Activities

_____

Other noteworthy accomplishments

_____

**Graduate School(s)** Photocopy page for each additional graduate school attended.

Name _____    City, State _____

Year of Attendance _____    Degree Earned _____

Major _____    GPA _____

Honors

_____

Other noteworthy accomplishments

_____

**In-Service Training** On a blank piece of paper, list in chronological order all in-service training workshops, minicourses, seminars, certificate programs, staff development initiatives, etc. Note the year you attended.

---

your *Job Find Friend* to make three suggestions that will make you a better teacher. Read professional journals and visit Web sites of professional associations and state education departments to learn about "hot topics" that have gained currency in the field. Finally, survey your *Personal Profile* and

*Resume Reservoir* to determine your relative strengths and weaknesses. Set a goal to learn something new every day or expand your repertoire of experiences.

We know this seems like a lot to do. The effort you put into creating your *Personal Profile*

---

**Your Employment in Schools**

**List schools in reverse chronological order. Photocopy this page as needed. List all education-related jobs, including student teacher, paraprofessional, substitute teacher, tutor, etc. Volunteer work may be cited.**

School Name _____    City, State _____

Dates of Employment _____    Supervisor _____

Reason of Leaving _____    Grades/Subjects Taught _____

(If Secondary) Courses Taught _____

What were your major accomplishments (use powerful, descriptive verbs and adjectives)?

_____

_____

_____

_____

Honors, special achievements, involvement in co-curricular activities or special projects

_____

_____

School Name _____    City, State _____

Dates of Employment _____    Supervisor _____

Reason for Leaving _____    Grades/Subjects Taught _____

(If Secondary) Courses Taught _____

What were your major accomplishments (use powerful, descriptive verbs and adjectives)?

_____

_____

_____

_____

Honors, special achievements, involvement in co-curricular activities or special projects

_____

_____

**Teaching Certifications**

Name of Teaching Certificate(s) _____

State(s) Issued From _____    Year(s) Issued _____

---

and *Resume Reservoir,* however, will pay great dividends when time is at a premium—that is, when you need to create a riveting cover letter, design a dynamite resume, and get them into an administrator's hands before anyone else can turn on a computer. Then, your efficiency and effectiveness as a writer may result in an interview, while your competition will be consigned to the bottom of the resume heap. Get started! The job vacancy of your dreams will be advertised any day!

**Other Employment History**

**List employers in reverse chronological order. Photocopy this page as needed.**

Name of Employer _____     City, State _____

Years of Employment _____     Job Title _____

Supervisor _____     Reason for Leaving _____

What were your major accomplishments (use powerful, descriptive verbs and adjectives)?

_____

_____

_____

Honors, special achievements, involvement in co-curricular activities or special projects

_____

Name of Employer _____     City, State _____

Years of Employment _____     Job Title _____

Supervisor _____     Reason for Leaving _____

What were your major accomplishments (use powerful, descriptive verbs and adjectives)?

_____

_____

_____

Honors, special achievements, involvement in co-curricular activities or special projects

_____

**Organization Memberships**

Educational organizations

_____

Offices held, special recognition received, major accomplishments

_____

Civic or service organizations

_____

Offices held, special recognition received, major accomplishments

_____

Other organizations

_____

Offices held, special recognition received, major accomplishments

_____

**Other Creditable Experiences**

Refer to list on page 00.

_____

_____

_____

**References**

Whom can you rely on to provide clear, detailed information about your accomplishments, talents, or character? References within the last three years are preferable.

Name of Reference _____   Title of Reference _____

Address _____   Telephone Number _____

Fax _____   E-mail address _____

How do you know this person? _____

How long have you known this person? _____

How long ago did you have regular contact with this person? _____

What specific things would you like this person to discuss in her/his reference?

_____

Name of Reference _____   Title of Reference _____

Address _____   Telephone Number _____

Fax _____   E-mail address _____

How do you know this person? _____

How long have you known this person? _____

How long ago did you have regular contact with this person? _____

What specific things would you like this person to discuss in her/his reference?

_____

Name of Reference _____   Title of Reference _____

Address _____   Telephone Number _____

Fax _____   E-mail address _____

How do you know this person? _____

How long have you known this person? _____

How long ago did you have regular contact with this person? _____

What specific things would you like this person to discuss in her/his reference?

_____

## Creditable Experiences

These experiences serve a dual purpose. They look terrific on your resume and they prepare you to be a better teacher. Here are some things you can do *today.*

- Take college courses
- Find a job as a **paraprofessional**
- Subscribe to professional journals
- Find a job related to education
- Volunteer at a school
- Join a professional teachers' association
- Participate in a faculty committee while you are student teaching
- Attend conferences
- Tutor for a community service agency
- Develop a job-related hobby
- Travel to interesting places
- Attend workshops offered by the school district while you student teach
- Practice with software you might use in your classroom
- Surf the Internet to find information about your field
- Take a course on the Internet
- Help sponsor an extracurricular club while student teaching
- Visit the local library to study an educational issue or a new teaching method

## REMINDERS

Your *Personal Profile* and *Resume Reservoir* are essential parts of your campaign to get your desired teaching job. Complete each part thoroughly—a lot is riding on it!

Use the material in these documents to design your cover letter, draft your resume, and prepare for interviews.

Build your resume and knowledge base today to strengthen your candidacy, using the creditable experiences listed in this chapter.

Find your *Job Find Friend* and start your *Job Find File,* two vital supports you will need to launch a successful job hunt.

# Chapter Three

# Finding Job Openings

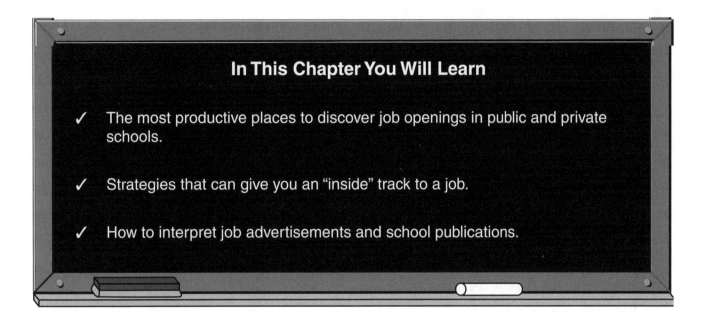

## In This Chapter You Will Learn

✓  The most productive places to discover job openings in public and private schools.

✓  Strategies that can give you an "inside" track to a job.

✓  How to interpret job advertisements and school publications.

*Dynamic school district seeks innovative teacher who understands and applies effective teaching strategies, is well-versed in a variety of assessment methods, contributes to co-curricular activities, demonstrates outstanding communication skills, and is knowledgeable about content area.*

—Newspaper advertisement

*The best advice I can offer a prospective teacher is to leave no stone unturned when you search for job openings.*

—College placement officer

Now that you have crystallized your unique background and what you have to offer to students, it's time to take the next step on the road to a wonderful teaching job. How do you find job openings? You've probably heard at least one or two stories about someone who "lucked out" when trying to find a teaching job: the job really found the person, rather than the other way around. Needless to say, such events are rare, indeed. The reality is that you can't count on luck to lead you to your ideal teaching job. Fortunately, there are effective strategies for discovering openings, and this chapter shows you how to apply them.

In our experience, the biggest mistake candidates make is limiting their search to one or two sources. Good teachers come to the attention of schools in a variety of ways. For example, many school districts advertise vacancies in national publications such as the *New York Times* and *Education Week,* as well as local newspapers. Job announcements, sometimes referred to as "job postings," may also be forwarded to colleges of education. In addition to these traditional methods of announcing job vacancies, there are other sources. Principals often receive referrals from colleagues in neighboring schools who have become acquainted with promising student teachers, but do not have jobs to offer. Internet postings are becoming increasingly popular. Parents sometimes hand us envelopes containing the resumes of family members, friends, and neighbors whom they would like us to consider. Sometimes candidates emerge from even more unusual places. After searching through more than a thousand resumes and not finding a suitable candidate, Seth hired a teacher who was recommended by a faculty member. The two had met each other while they were walking their Irish terriers early one morning.

A review of our hiring records over the last few years demonstrates that successful applicants come from a variety of sources. The results of our informal survey are in the chart below.

Your chances of finding an opening are greater if you use many methods to bring your name to the attention of decision makers. Let's examine these in greater detail.

## Print Possibilities

Let's start with one of the most traditional methods of job hunting: using major metropolitan area newspapers. Each Sunday, for example, the *New York Times* posts pages of educational job openings in the "Week in Review" section. Indeed, for many districts and private schools in the Northeast, an advertisement in the *Times* or similar paper is the primary avenue for accumulating the resumes needed to start the hiring process. Although advertisements are published throughout the year, vacancies for the following school year first appear in January and increase every week, reaching a crescendo from April through early August. Other major metropolitan newspapers that post teaching jobs in a Sunday edition include the *Atlanta Journal-Constitution, Boston Globe, Chicago Tribune, Los Angeles Times, Philadelphia Inquirer, San Francisco Chronicle,* and *Washington Post.*

Many people underestimate the value of searching through advertisements in the *Times* or similar papers. Let's correct some common misconceptions about newspaper ads. First, major metropolitan newspapers have a nationwide circulation. Although these papers predominantly contain advertisements announcing vacancies in their geographic areas, they often include job postings from a wider region, too. The *New York Times* contains advertisements from schools all around the country and even overseas. To save costs, advertisements frequently list all vacancies anticipated in a school district, a boon to job seekers who are certified in more than one discipline.

One advertisement in a major daily can generate scores of responses, and the sponsors of the ads give serious consideration to each of the resumes received. For example, a 3 1/2-inch-square advertisement in "The Week in Review"

| Source | Percentage of Teachers Hired |
| --- | --- |
| Newspaper Advertisements | 34 |
| Inside Candidates: Student Teachers, Substitutes, etc. | 18 |
| Networking: Referrals from Staff, Parents, etc. | 14 |
| Job Fairs | 13 |
| Campus Recruiting | 10 |
| Unsolicited Resumes from E-mail, Bulk Mailings, etc. | 6 |
| Web-Based Referrals | 5 |

section of The *New York Times'* Sunday edition costs approximately $6,000. Schools are willing to make the costly investment of a newspaper advertisement because they have recruited promising candidates this way before. Many people get jobs through newspaper ads (including the authors). Our advice: Make these publications part of your job search routine, and be ready to respond quickly to advertisements that appeal to you.

Another popular source of job vacancy information is the periodical, *Education Week.* This newspaper reaches a national audience of school administrators, and its back pages are filled with advertisements from districts around the country, private schools of all different types, and schools located around the world. Many of the advertised positions are administrative, but a considerable number of teaching openings are listed in each edition. (See Further Reading.)

Nor should you overlook the community newspapers published in counties, towns, villages, and even small neighborhoods. These papers often contain vacancy notices, frequently for part-time or long-term substitute jobs that are well suited to applicants seeking a first position or those returning to the profession after a leave. If you don't live in the area in which these local publications are circulated, don't give up hope. You can subscribe by mail or visit the local library in the community of interest to review current and back issues.

## Interpreting an Advertisement

Job announcements contain valuable clues for the job hunter. At a minimum, advertisements provide information about the school or district in which the vacancy occurs, a listing of available jobs, and application procedures. An advertisement may also inform candidates of a school's instructional objectives and the salary and benefits package offered to new teachers.

Advertising space is expensive, so schools choose their words carefully when they write advertisements. Let's take a guided tour of advertisements from two fictitious employers: New Frontier County Schools, a public school system, and Academy Prep, an independent school. These advertisements (illustrated on page 24) offer a wealth of information to guide potential candidates.

## About the School or District

What does the New Frontier School District want you to know about the community it serves? What can you tell about Academy Prep?

*Location*

New Frontier's location near the state capital and its suburban environment are considered to be selling points. If you're not sure where New Frontier is, refer to the address at the bottom of the ad and look up the location on <**www.mapquest.com**>, a Web site often used by travelers. Academy Prep is proud of its picturesque campus, active community, and 80-year-old traditions; it behooves candidates to learn more about that legacy.

*Size*

A school district the size of New Frontier probably employs several hundred teachers and experiences considerable turnover from year to year. Thus, there's a good chance that the school district plans to hire a number of new teachers for the coming school year. Academy Prep serves only 600 students, so it is likely to employ fewer teachers. Like many independent schools, Academy Prep may also feature small classes.

---

Job announcements in newspapers *always* contain the following information:

- Information about the school or school district
- Listing of available jobs
- Application procedures

In addition, job announcements *may* contain the following information:

- The school's instructional goals
- Salary and benefits offered to teachers

**NEW FRONTIER COUNTY SCHOOLS
"EXCELLENCE FOR ALL"**

Suburban district located ten miles from the state capital, New Frontier serves 8,000 multicultural students in five elementary schools, two middle schools, and one high school. The school district emphasizes instructional technology and the state's Learning Standards. The district is accepting resumes for the following positions:

About the school district

Instructional priorities

<u>Immediate Vacancies</u>
Reading K–6 (leave replacement)
Physical education .4

<u>Anticipated Vacancies</u>
Elementary, all grades
MS/HS science
Foreign language, Spanish and French
Special education inclusion, dual certification required.

Available jobs

Interested candidates must submit letter of interest, resume, college transcripts, and copy of certification. No phone calls.

How to apply

Human Resource Office
New Frontier County Schools
101 Covered Wagon Circle
Anytown, USA 00001
AA/EOE

**ACADEMY PREP**

Independent, 80-year-old, coed, college preparatory school. Dynamic community on beautiful campus serving 600 students in upper and lower divisions. Resumes are being accepted for the following positions for next school year:

About the school and its instructional priorities

English—Upper Division
Latin and Spanish—Upper and Lower Division
Classroom Teachers—Lower Division

Available jobs

Excellent salary and benefits. Respond to:

How to apply

Headmaster
Academy Prep
Anytown, USA 00001
www.academyprep.edu
AA/EOE

*The Student Body*

The New Frontier school district is looking for teachers who can work with students from diverse backgrounds, although the advertisement does not tell you the specific demographic makeup of the community. You will want to do some research to learn more about the district so you can present yourself as a candidate who understands the needs of New Frontier students. The only clue provided by the Academy Prep advertisement is the reference to its coeducational program, a characteristic that separates Academy Prep from some other private schools.

*Instructional Priorities*

Every school or school district has educational goals and priorities. This section of the advertisement supplies you with information about specific skills and knowledge that new teachers are expected to have. The New Frontier slogan, "Excellence for All," implies that the district desires all students to reach high levels of performance. "All children can learn," "It takes a village to raise a child," and "21st-century Schools" are other common mottos adopted by schools to communicate their basic educational ideals. To be successful, job hunters need to learn how educational philosophy is translated into classroom practice. In the case of New Frontier, candidates must demonstrate an ability to meet the varied needs of a diverse student body.

New Frontier wants to hire teachers who are technologically savvy, since that is highlighted in the advertisement. Candidates should design their cover letters, resumes, portfolios, and interview strategies to convey their ability to use computers in the classroom.

New Frontier emphasizes learning standards, as mandated by the state. Learning standards are statements of what students "should know and be able to do." If you are unfamiliar with learning standards in the state where New Frontier is located, you need to find out more before you submit your application. The Internet is an excellent resource for this research. State curriculum requirements are often described on the Web sites of each state's Education Department.

At Academy Prep, teachers are expected to deliver a high-powered curriculum designed to help students prepare for college admission. More research is needed to discover particulars of the instructional programs of both schools.

## Listing of Available Jobs

Vacancy announcements list specific jobs available. These postings can be divided into two broad categories: immediate and anticipated.

Immediate vacancies are those that need to be filled at once. Openings of this type can and do occur at any time of the year. They arise from a variety of circumstances—for example, maternity leaves, extended illness of a teacher, the opening of new classes due to higher-than-anticipated enrollments, and the adoption of new programs after the school year has begun. School districts are anxious to fill immediate vacancies, so there is an advantage to submitting your cover letter and resume as rapidly as possible.

Rob remembers a teacher calling from home to notify him that she was confined to bed rest for the remainder of her pregnancy. Attempting to fill this immediate vacancy, the school advertised in a newspaper the following Sunday. By Monday morning, a fax had already arrived from one promising candidate. An interview was arranged for the same afternoon. By week's end, before most candidates had mailed their application materials to the school, this ambitious, outstanding candidate was hired.

Anticipated vacancies are projected to occur in the months ahead, in contrast to immediate vacancies. Under the theory, "the early bird gets the worm," school administrators begin to develop their staffing plans for the next school year during the winter, and place job advertisements in the newspaper as early as possible to attract the best candidates. The first vacancy notices appear in January, and they continue throughout the spring and summer. Our advice, therefore, is to keep reading the want ads, even if your first attempts to find a job have not proved productive.

Whenever you apply for a job, clip out the advertisement to which you have responded, put it in a folder labeled with the name of the school or district, and file it alphabetically in your *Job Find File*. You will need the advertisement later when you write your cover letter and resume, prepare for an interview, and create your employment portfolio.

---

**Job Vacancy Shorthand**

With space at a premium, vacancy announcements often use a specialized language to provide information. Here is an introduction to the jargon and abbreviations used in educational advertisements.

AA      Affirmative Action
A policy that encourages the hiring of minority candidates.

Cert    Certification Required
You must have a teaching license in the advertised field to secure the job.

CV      Curriculum Vitae
A modified type of resume often used to attain college employment.

Dual (or Multiple) Certification
The position requires the teacher to hold a license in at least two curriculum areas. For example, secondary schools often look to hire foreign language teachers who are certified to teach more than one language—e.g., Spanish and French.

EOE     Equal Opportunity Employer
The school does not discriminate in its hiring practices in accordance with federal and state laws.

FTE     Full-Time Equivalent
In spite of its name, Full-Time Equivalent uses the decimal system to indicate hours and compensation associated with part-time positions. A 1.0 FTE is a full-time position, .5 FTE is half-time, etc. For example, the physical education job in New Frontier is slightly less than half-time.

Leave Replacement or Term Position
A job replacing a teacher who has left after the school year has begun, or who will return to teaching before the school year ends. Reasons for a teacher leaving include child care, illness, and sabbatical. Leave replacement positions terminate when the employee returns, and there is no assurance of continued employment. New Frontier, for example, is seeking a leave replacement reading teacher.

Minority Candidates Encouraged to Apply
The district is seeking a diverse teaching staff.

P/T     Part-Time Position

Per Diem Substitute
A substitute employed on a day-by-day basis. Per diem substitutes are not paid for holidays, vacations, or days when they are not needed.

Permanent Substitute
A long-term substitute position in which a substitute teacher is assured of daily employment. The teacher substitutes in the same classroom for an extended period of time or works in a variety of classes in one school. Permanent substitutes are usually paid on a lower salary scale than teachers.

Probationary Position
In public school lingo, a regular teaching position leading to tenure after a trial period.

---

## How to Apply

This section tells you how to get your cover letter and resume in the hands of your prospective employer. Follow the directions exactly. For instance, if the advertisement tells you to fax your cover letter and resume, do so. (Always follow up with a "snail mail" copy, however.) Since the directions often require you to show proof of your teaching license, make sure you have a copy of your certificate available to submit with your application materials. Many candidates ask us what they should do if they have completed the requirements for teaching certification, but the state department of education has not yet sent an official copy of the license. Don't worry, this is a common problem. We recommend that you ask the school of education at your college to write a letter stating that you have fulfilled the requirements for certification and are waiting for the state education department to process the form. Make several copies of the letter and use it until your license arrives in the mail.

It's a good idea to maintain an active placement file at your college's career services office so that you can forward it readily to a prospective employer if a job advertisement demands it. Your placement file should include an unofficial transcript of all undergraduate and graduate courses as well as confidential references. If you do not have an unofficial transcript, contact the college registrar's office to obtain a copy. There is generally a one- or two-week delay in securing an unofficial transcript and starting a placement file, so plan ahead.

Seth knew an administrator who said, "I automatically reject any candidate who fails to include all the information requested in the advertisement. I assume applicants who do not follow procedures when they have a job on the line, probably never follow directions." The administrator's statement demonstrates the necessity of complying fully with the application procedures set forth in a job advertisement.

Is it permissible to send a school *more* information than it requests? Our school districts request four or five sheets of paper from applicants: a cover letter, resume, transcripts, and a copy of the candidate's teaching license, yet we sometimes receive 20-page packets containing stacks of references, samples of student work, and other items. We advise candidates to submit only the information the school requests until they secure a second-round interview, unless they have a truly extraordinary reference. For example, Seth's decision to interview and subsequently hire one teacher was influenced by a recommendation she attached to her application packet from an esteemed educator who was the president of a national association.

In the computer age, more and more candidates apply by e-mail. If you are sending application materials via e-mail, two notes of caution are in order: First, send your cover letter and resume as an attachment and note in the body of the e-mail the name of the word processing software you used. Second, unless directions prohibit it, always follow-up cover letters and resumes submitted via e-mail with an identical "snail mail" version in case the file does not transmit properly or the administrator is not computer literate.

Increasingly, districts are requesting or requiring candidates to submit their applications over the Internet. In such cases, you will see instructions for submissions somewhere in the body of the vacancy announcement, as in "On-line application required," or, "Reply to this announcement at **<www.anydistrict.org>**." We strongly suggest that you use the Internet even if the advertisement merely says "on-line applications *preferred*"; at the very least, you will be making the point that you are comfortable with computers.

When applying through a Web site, you will be first asked to create a log-in (or user) name and password; complying with these directions will give you access to the full site. Use your name or a variation, for example, your first initial and last name, as your log-in, so that you will not have problems remembering it if you access the site at a later date. Similarly, your password should be something you can recall with ease. Once admitted to the site, you will be able to view a list of openings. You will also be prompted to complete an employment application. Generally, these applications require information similar to that included on your resume. However, each on-line application is different; for that reason, we recommend that you keep your *Personal Profile* and *Resume Reservoir* handy as you work. Some , but not all, districts allow you to return to your application at another time to update information— make sure you check the rules regarding modifying your submission and proofread your responses before clicking the "send" button. We also advise you to keep a copy of your application, if possible, and return to the district's Web site on a regular basis to see if additional job announcements or information have been posted.

## The Power of the Press

Even if reading the national or local press in a given week doesn't yield any advertisements of interest, you can still profit from the time you invest. Take note of all the articles related to education in general and local schools in particular. (Local community papers often print press releases and photographs

Decoding a newspaper advertisement is like a detective solving a mystery. In Chapter 4, you learn to follow up on the leads provided in an advertisement by conducting research about the school, its instructional priorities, and key decision makers.

issued by the schools themselves.) After a short time, you'll begin to develop an understanding of trends and developments that may affect your job search strategies. For example, you may learn that a local district has just launched a wide-ranging technology initiative, an indication that it is looking for candidates who have a strong background in computers and familiarity with computer-assisted instruction. Alternatively, you may discover that an **inclusion** program requires teachers to be dual-certified in special education and an academic discipline. On a national level, you may learn about federal funding increases to support special programs, or you may become more informed about demographic trends that affect the hiring of teachers in different areas of the country. At the very least, you will gain knowledge that will help you shape your cover letter and resume to match specific school needs, and you will be more prepared for some of those tough interview questions.

Newspapers can provide you with some of your best leads for teaching positions. If you read the papers regularly, you are almost certain to come across appealing career opportunities.

## Your Ally: The College Placement Office

Friends are always important, and sometimes there is no better friend than a counselor in your college placement office. A good placement office puts the highest priority on staying abreast of trends in the employment sector, working with you to develop your job-hunting skills, and providing you with specific, timely information about openings in your field. A college placement file, moreover, provides you with a ready-made place to store confidential references so that you'll be able to provide a prospective employer with recommendations promptly.

We suggest you visit your college placement office regularly. When you drop in, check the bulletin board for job postings. In addition, cultivate relationships with the counselors so they come to know your interests and your strengths. Ask them for advice about cover letter and resume writing and let them critique your drafts. College career placement offices offer many other invaluable services. Attend their informative workshops to develop your interview skills and let them help you perfect your job search strategies and communication style. In this way, you will become a more effective candidate, and your name will be on the tip of the counselors' tongues when they hear of vacancies. Your visits will also alert you to recruiters from schools looking to hire teachers who are visiting the campus.

Our advice does not apply only to current students. Alumni also can make use of the placement office; whenever possible, they should follow the same strategy for establishing strong relationships with the placement counselors and for taking advantage of the individualized services they offer.

We envision that placement office services will be conducted with greater frequency via the Internet. Make sure you know the URL, or Internet address, of your college placement office, and check it regularly to learn about programs, opportunities to consult with counselors, and job listings. Many career service Web sites post helpful advice about job hunting. Your career placement office may already belong to *Job Connect,* a Web-based service that connects colleges and universities to schools looking for teacher candidates. Ask your counselor whether your placement office subscribes.

Career professionals in the college placement office are knowledgeable, friendly, and eager to help. Best of all, these beneficial services are provided free of charge.

There is no better friend than a counselor in your college placement office.

## Job Fairs

Job fairs for teachers are becoming more and more popular. They provide an efficient way for schools, school districts, or consortia of school districts to publicize their openings and meet many candidates in a matter of hours. At the same time, they offer job seekers an opportunity to learn about a variety of vacancies and establish connections with several potential employers quickly.

There are different types of job fairs. Some are held for a specific purpose—recruiting science teachers or meeting affirmative action goals, for example. Others are staged to staff whole schools, districts, consortia of districts from a given locale, or private schools. Job fairs may be held on-site at a particular district or in a conveniently located spot such as a local school gymnasium or hotel. Schools seeking excellent candidates may also "take the show on the road" by visiting local colleges to recruit.

At a job fair, you may meet real decision makers with the power to make hiring determinations, or at least with the authority to advance good candidates to the next round of interviews. At other fairs, you may encounter only scouts on a mission to accumulate resumes and create a positive image for the district. To complicate matters, you probably won't know whom you will meet until you get there.

You should treat every job fair as a legitimate opportunity to get hired. To this end, doing your homework is paramount. Bring all the materials you might need for a day filled with completing applications, filing resumes, and participating in serious interviews with prospective employers. Specifically, you should:

- Conduct some research before the job fair to determine which schools will be represented and to identify their particular needs. Sometimes, the job fair's sponsors can provide this information. (Chapter 4 provides other strategies for doing this type of research.)
- Get a good night's sleep so you can exude energy, one of the key traits a school looks for in a teacher. Maintain a high energy level so your last contact at the end of a long day is as impressive as your first.
- Dress for success. Conservative dress attire should be your rule of thumb. (See Chapter 8 for additional information.)
- Arrive early. This will give you plenty of opportunity to have a look around. More important, it allows you to meet representatives of schools while you—and they—are fresh.
- Set your priorities. If there are many recruiters at the fair, choose the ones that are most appealing or appropriate for you. Locate their booths or tables and plan the order of your visits to these sites so you can optimize the time available.
- Bring an abundant supply of resumes. We have seen candidates miss opportunities because they ran out of them.
- Make sure your portfolio is current and bring it with you. If you know something in advance about the schools attending the fair, edit the contents of your portfolio so you can use it to show how your talents meet a particular school's needs. (See Chapter 7 for more helpful tips.)
- Keep a record of the people with whom you spoke and their titles; this may be very useful in follow-up meetings. Keep a record of this information in your *Job Find File.*
- Use your conversations with school representatives as a data-gathering opportunity. Using two to three well-designed questions, try to discover as much as you can about district or school characteristics, goals, needs, programs, and working conditions. This will help you match your needs and interests with school profiles. It will also provide invaluable background information if you are invited to a follow-up interview. Record your findings soon after the fair in your *Job Find File*—don't rely on your memory!
- Don't be afraid to ask questions about the hiring process, including the timetable for reaching final decisions.
- Follow up any hot leads with a letter to the person in charge of hiring emphasizing how much you enjoyed learning about the school or district, describing how your background and skills match school needs, and expressing your interest in participating in the next level of the hiring process. See the letter on page 30 for a good example.

13 Happy Hill Road
Optimistic, California 13131
Today's Date

Dr. A. K. Demic
Headmaster
Academy Prep
Anytown, USA

Dear Dr. Demic:

It was a pleasure to meet you at the Independent School Job Fair and have the opportunity to discuss the English teacher vacancy at your school. I believe my prior experience as a tutor for private school students has prepared me to teach in Academy Prep's rigorous academic environment. While student teaching, I employed creative drama techniques to make the classics come alive in my classroom. In addition, I coached a school debate team that won first prize in a regional competition.

I look forward to the opportunity to continue our discussion of my candidacy. For your reference, I have attached a copy of my resume. Thank you for your time and consideration.

Sincerely,

Heidi Hopeful

## Networking

Networks can be an excellent source of information and leads for jobs. When looking for a teaching job, set your sights on building the most extensive network possible, and use this chain of contacts continuously. According to our survey, fourteen percent of the teachers we recently hired came to our attention as a result of successful networking. Here are a few examples from our own experiences:

- Seth hired a guidance counselor who had been employed by a local youth services organization. During her frequent contacts with the school, she impressed administrators and let it be known that she preferred a full-time, school-based job.
- Rob hired a social studies teacher recommended through the countywide principals' association.
- Another faculty member was found after she initiated a conversation on the sidelines with a teacher in Seth's school while their children were playing in a soccer tournament.

- Rob made the jump from the private sector to a public school through an acquaintance who worked in the teachers' union.

Some teacher candidates enjoy built-in networks. Their parents may be teachers, or they may have close friends who are very involved with local schools. Making connections is easier for this advantaged group. Some of their contacts may even initiate the conversation by saying, "Let me know when you begin looking for a job."

For many people, however, networks must be built from the ground up. Building an effective network takes time and effort. We offer the following guidelines to help focus your efforts:

- Socializing is the foundation on which networks are built. If you're a little shy about approaching people about teaching jobs, try role-playing with your *Job Find Friend.* Just like a salesperson, develop some opening lines that will help you break the ice and nudge the conversation toward your job search. This can be something as simple as, "I just received my teaching certification."

- Remember, too, that talking about your interest in a teaching job is perfectly acceptable in most situations, as long as you do it with a bit of finesse and sensitivity to the perceptions of others.
- Consider everyone you meet as a potential member of your job search network. People belong to many social circles. Chances are good that at least one of your acquaintances is connected to education.
- Be a good listener. In conversations that have to do with schools, try to remember important details and the names of decision makers. While you can't base your job search on hearsay, careful listening allows you to develop a general sense of school characteristics that may serve you well as you design your cover letter and resume or prepare for interviews.
- Make your mark on casual acquaintances with your enthusiasm for teaching, your maturity, and your upbeat, articulate personal style. (Again, if this type of interaction does not come naturally to you—and it doesn't for many—practice until you feel more at ease.) Use the conversation to draw attention to your accomplishments, talents, and commitment to helping children.
- Before you "name drop" during a conversation or in a cover letter, make certain you have the permission of the person whose name you are using. For example, don't call the building principal and say, "So-and-so suggested that I call," unless it's true.
- Always put your best foot forward. You never know when a person you meet will lead you to a great job.

## Become an Insider

Because there are frequently many candidates for the best teaching jobs, it helps to find some way of distinguishing yourself from your competitors. One of the best ways to do this is to become a familiar face around the school building. Nearly one in five of the teachers we've hired initially served as student teachers, substitutes, **paraprofessionals,** or volunteers in our buildings. According to our study, it has been the second most common avenue to acquire a teaching job in our schools.

How do you become an insider? At the top of the list is student teaching. Take it from us: talented student teachers get noticed, and they enjoy a competitive edge. They know the school, its culture, its programs, and its needs. They have gained on-the-job experience with the materials and curricula currently in use. They have been mentored by veteran members of the faculty who can provide sound advice about the hiring process. Similarly, they have also gained credible, easy-to-contact references and allies: their cooperating teachers.

Over the years, we've received telephone calls from education students asking permission to perform their student teaching assignments in our schools. If the school of education you're attending allows students to arrange their own field placements, you can select a desirable school and secure an advantage over the competition.

Maximize the potential of your student teaching experience. Consider your days at the school to be an opportunity to showcase your talents, not just in the classroom, but in all aspects of your daily work. Make your cooperating teacher your friend, and listen carefully to the advice he or she gives. Become acquainted with your department chairperson, team or grade level leader, union representatives, and building administrators. When you have a dynamite lesson prepared, invite the assistant principal, chairperson, team leader, or principal to observe. Attend staff training programs whenever possible and participate fully in special events at the school. Offer to help with chaperoning or afterschool activities. Come early, and stay late. Throughout your student teaching experience, demonstrate a professional manner and a strong desire to learn.

We often observe student teachers, **teacher assistants,** and **paraprofessionals** heading out the door at the end of the school day, just before faculty meetings begin. Perhaps they have busy schedules, or they do not feel they are welcome at faculty meetings. However, we encourage you to attend these important sessions, because they can provide you with an advantage over other candidates. Outside candidates are not aware of the issues under discussion nor are they able to participate in professional training offered at the meetings. If you have any doubt about whether you are welcome to attend, ask an administrator in the school.

Sometime during your student teaching experience, make an appointment with the principal to discuss possible job openings. Prepare some brief comments about how much you've enjoyed the training the school has provided and share some of the highlights of your student teaching and your education courses, using selections from your portfolio to highlight key points. Ask about the possibility of job openings and politely request consideration when vacancies occur. It's also a good idea to share your resume with the principal and ask for feedback; this will give her or him an opportunity to learn more about your accomplishments and skills, and it will help cement your relationship.

Even after your student teaching term is over, stay in touch with the school, particularly with your cooperating teacher and the principal. Remember that vacancies frequently arise when least expected, and administrators greatly appreciate someone who is ready to step in when needed.

school enrollments are rising across the country. In-house staff often decline summer work, leaving jobs available for the newest teachers. We heartily recommend this route to a regular teaching position; teachers who can demonstrate effectiveness with at-risk students attending summer programs can quickly increase their visibility to administrators.

If you take a summer school position, consider each day as an audition for a job during the school year. Spend time reviewing course materials and identify the critical understandings and skills required for students to demonstrate mastery. If your students take an exit exam of some kind, familiarize yourself with the scope and format of the test. Make sure your lesson plans exhibit your talents, and place extra emphasis on arousing interest in the material, because few summer school students come with high levels of motivation. Use your time at the school site to become familiar with school personnel and learn more about school programs and practices. Make contacts whenever you can. And, oh yes, dress

---

How do you become an insider? At the top of the list is student teaching.

---

Substitute teaching is another good way to become known and valued around a school. A substitute's life is rarely an easy one, and you can earn great admiration from teachers and administrators by serving as a reliable, skillful substitute who is an effective instructor and can handle the unexpected. If you become a substitute, try to become as much a part of the school community as possible, so that you can demonstrate your skills in the classroom and your commitment to the school. Consider the faculty and administration as part of your network, and use them as resources in your attempts to get a job. It's also important to view substitute teaching as a learning experience that gives you a better understanding of students' developmental needs, curriculum, instructional practices, and classroom management techniques. Knowledge gained in these areas will help you score points in an interview.

An increasingly common way to make a name for yourself in a school district is to teach summer school classes. Spawned by the movement to raise academic standards, summer

professionally, even if the days are long and hot, because you never know who will drop in.

If student teaching, substitute teaching, or summer school teaching is not feasible, there are other ways to establish your presence around a school. Many schools use **paraprofessionals** or **teaching assistants** in various capacities to provide additional assistance to students. In general, personnel in these job categories work with the teacher in the classroom, thereby reducing the adult-to-student ratio and/or providing support to students with special needs. Federal legislation adopted in 2002, called No Child Left Behind (NCLB), requires staff members serving in these positions to be well qualified for working with students. As a result, we expect that many schools will be looking for college-trained candidates for these jobs.

Many schools also welcome volunteers in classrooms. You can volunteer to serve as a mentor for students at risk of failure or as a tutor for pupils with reading deficits or limited English proficiency. Don't forget to check into extracurricular programs as an avenue to make a favorable impression on decision makers. Seth's school once hired a physical education teacher who had established an excellent reputation beforehand by coaching interscholastic sports.

Your goal in each of these cases is the same. First, you want to carry out your responsibilities in the very best manner to enable the school achieve its primary mission: helping students learn and grow. In addition, you want your accomplishments and skills to be noticed so that people will come to appreciate what you have to offer. Finally, you want to extend your network of job contacts so that you will have additional sources of information and assistance as you look for a position.

These approaches really work. Not only do people obtain jobs in this manner, they also learn skills that are useful in the classroom. A director of human resources once told us, "Some of the best candidates 'bubble up' from the inside. We like to hire from within."

examine school publications, or make copies, by visiting the school or district office. Public libraries often keep school district budget materials and newsletters on file, as well. Once you get copies, place them in your *Job Find File.*

## The Internet

Job openings are increasingly found on the Internet. Many state education departments advertise teacher vacancies on Web sites. Some worthwhile government-sponsored spots to visit in cyberspace are listed on page 35.

You can also take advantage of various commercial, educational, and not-for-profit Web sites that connect you to job listings. Some Web sites catalogue a myriad of vacancies supplied by school districts, while other sites allow prospective teachers to post their resumes for interested schools to see. For example, use the National Teacher Recruitment Clearinghouse at

Whether you are a student teacher, substitute teacher, **paraprofessional,** summer school teacher, or school volunteer, consider each day as an audition for a job.

## Reading the Fine Print

School publications provide a wealth of information for job hunters. Newsletters sent to the community, for instance, may explore such matters as demographic trends, school construction plans, and new curricula that have implications for the teaching force. In much the same fashion, budget brochures and related materials furnish clues about future staffing needs. A careful reading of these documents may tell you that enrollment is on the rise, a sure sign that new teachers will be hired soon. In much the same manner, an article about new computer technology purchases means that candidates with a strong background in software applications will be in demand. Initiatives in the area of inclusion should encourage applications from teachers with a special education background or serve as an incentive to learn more about this topic. Budget announcements may also include news about retirement incentives being offered to veterans on the staff; that, of course, is music to your ears. You will be able to

<www. recruitingteachers.org> to gain access to a goldmine of links devoted to openings, licensing standards, job hunting tips, and training programs. Similarly, <www.k12jobs.com> will provide you with job listings categorized according to geographic region and teaching certification. Another site, The International Educator, available at <www.tieonline.com>, posts jobs available outside the United States. Internet service providers and search engines also provide links to jobs; first try clicking on the "Education," "Employment," or "Jobs" headings on the home page. Useful sites of this type are listed on page 36 and 39. Because Web site addresses change frequently, check the authors' Web site <www. TeacherEdge.com> for regular updates.

In addition to the World Wide Web, listservs are another source of job openings. Listservs, also known as mailing lists or discussion groups, are groups of people who share a common interest and e-mail each other. E-mail sent over a listserv can be read by every group member. Specific listservs are available for elementary teachers, secondary teachers from every academic discipline (mathematics teachers, physical education teachers, etc.), private school teachers of all descriptions (e.g., Catholic schools, yeshivas, independent schools, **Waldorf** schools), teachers concerned about alternative assessment, affective education, and multiculturalism . . . the list of listservs is endless. Listservs offer job hunters a number of advantages:

- Many school officials advertise job vacancies to listserv members.
- Aspiring teachers can announce their availability over a listserv and briefly describe their training and educational views.
- Don't underestimate the power of networking over a listserv. One participant in the listserv can connect you to a colleague who may offer you a job.

The chart on page 37 lists some popular listservs. Many professional associations (a number of these are listed in Further Reading) have their own listservs. You can also refer to the following addresses that identify helpful listservs for educators:

**<http://www.liszt.com/dir>**
From the directory page, click on "Education K–12" to find a comprehensive list of topics for teachers from archaeology to zoology.

**<http://www.lsoft.com/lists/listref.html>**
Catalist calls itself "the official catalog of listservs," with over 75,000 public lists in their database. Click on "Search" and enter the term "Teacher" to generate a list.

Just as the first edition of *How to Get the Teaching Job You Want* went to press, Seth hired a teacher he recruited from a listserv. One reason the candidate was hired was because it was obvious he was computer literate.

## Canvassing the Territory

Up to this point, we've discussed strategies to help you find openings in specific schools. As a determined job seeker, however, you may be impatient with this approach, preferring instead to cover as much territory as possible so that your

resume will be available for *any* opening within a wide geographic area. Under these circumstances, you may want to try two strategies used by salespersons: bulk mailings and cold calls.

A word of caution is appropriate here. In general, we don't think these strategies are as effective as those discussed earlier. For bulk mailings, you need to develop a generic cover letter and resume, and that will limit your ability to insert information tailored to the needs of a particular school. In addition, not every district treats unsolicited resumes with great respect: There is a good chance that your mailing will be placed in the circular file, never to be seen again.

Cold calls present similar difficulties. Most school offices are busy places, and requests for information about openings are not always given much time or consideration. Often, you may just receive a curt suggestion to submit a resume; rarely will you be put through to an administrator. Nevertheless, there are four circumstances in which bulk mailings and cold calls can be useful techniques for finding openings:

- If you're considering relocating and have little information about and few contacts in the schools and districts in this area.
- If you're looking for a position during a period that is outside the usual job-hunting seasons of spring and summer.
- If you're willing to accept a part-time job or a position as a replacement for someone on temporary leave.
- If you have a license in an area of shortage and can be fairly certain that candidates in your field are hot commodities.

Should any of these cases apply to you, follow the steps below to make the most of your mailings and phone calls.

*When Writing:*

- Begin with accurate, current names and addresses, or fax numbers, of schools or districts. You can get directories from state education department Web sites and other Internet school listings—example, **<www.SchoolMatch.com>**—printed directories available from independent school associations, state education departments, regional education agencies, or the old standby, the

**STATE EDUCATION DEPARTMENT WEB SITES
LISTING JOB OPENINGS FOR TEACHERS**

| State | Web Address |
|---|---|
| Alabama | <http://www.teacher-teachers.com/alabama.cfm> |
| Alaska | <http://www.akeducationjobs.com> |
| Arizona | <http://www.arizonaeducationjobs.com> |
| Arkansas | <http://www.teacharkansas.org> |
| California | <http://www.calteach.com> |
| Colorado | <http://www.cde.state.co.us/scripts/ceeb_jobsmap.asp> |
| Connecticut | <http://www.ctreap.net> |
| Delaware | <http://www.teachdelaware.com> |
| Florida | <http://www.firn.edu/doe/menu/t3.htm> |
| Georgia | <http://www.teachgeorgia.org> |
| Hawaii | <http://www.teachhawaii.k12.hi.us/teachinginhawaii.html> |
| Idaho | <http://www.idahoeducationjobs.com> |
| Illinois | <http://www.isbe.net/teachers/Documents/vacancylist.htm> |
| Indiana | <http://ideanet.doe.state.in.us/peer/welcome.html> |
| Iowa | <http://www.iowaeducationjobs.com> |
| Kansas | <http://www.kansasteachingjobs.com> |
| Kentucky | <http://apps.kde.state.ky.us/keps/index.cfm> |
| Louisiana | <http://www.teachlouisiana.net> |
| Maine | <http://www.state.me.us/education/jobs1.htm> |
| Maryland | <http://www.msde.state.md.us/teach_md.html> |
| Massachusetts | <http://www.doe.mass.edu/mecc> |
| Michigan | <http://www.mireap.net> |
| Minnesota | The Minnesota Education Department Web site does not list vacancies for teaching positions. |
| Mississippi | <http://www.mde.k12.ms.us/mtc/vacancy.htm> |
| Missouri | <http://www.moreap.net> |
| Montana | <http://jobsforteachers.opi.state.mt.us> |
| Nebraska | <http://www.nebraskaeducationjobs.com> |
| Nevada | <http://www.state.nv.us/personnel/education.html> |
| New Hampshire | <http://www.ed.state.nh.us/about/employ.htm> |
| New Jersey | <http://www.njhire.com/DefaultNJ.cfm?CFID=91315&CFTOKEN=94383477> |
| New Mexico | <http://www.nmreap.net> |
| New York | <http://www.highered.nysed.gov/tcert/career/joblinks> |
| North Carolina | <http://www.ncpublicschools.org/Employment/employment.html> |
| North Dakota | <http://www.state.nd.us/jsnd/education/update.vac.daily.htm> |
| Ohio | <http://www.ohreap.net> |
| Oklahoma | <http://sde.state.ok.us/pro/job.html> |
| Oregon | <http://www.ode.state.or.us/supportservices/careers.htm> |
| Pennsylvania | <http://www.pareap.net> |
| Rhode Island | <http://www.ridoe.net/teachers/ed_employment.htm> |
| South Carolina | <http://www.scctr.org> |
| South Dakota | <http://www.state.sd.us/deca/jobs.htm> |
| Tennessee | <http://www.state.tn.us/education/mtjobs.htm> |
| Texas | <http://www.txreap.net> |
| Utah | <http://www.utaheducationjobs.com> |
| Vermont | <http://www.vtreap.net> |
| Virginia | <http://www.pen.k12.va.us/VDOE/JOVE/home.shtml> |
| Washington | <http://www.k12.wa.us/personnel> |
| West Virginia | <http://wvde.state.wv.us/jobs> |
| Wisconsin | <http://www.wireap.net> |
| Wyoming | <http://onestop.state.wy.us/appview/tt_home.asp> |

## MORE WEB SITES LISTING JOB
## OPENINGS FOR TEACHERS

| | |
|---|---|
| <http://www.TeacherEdge.com> | The authors' Web site is updated regularly with links to many job openings for teachers. |
| <http://www.rnt.org> | This site is sponsored by Recruiting New Teachers, Inc. (RNT), a national non-profit organization that hosts the National Teacher Recruitment Clearinghouse. The Clearinghouse provides connections for employers and job seekers. |
| <http://www.k12jobs.com> | An excellent compilation of public, private, and vocational/technical school job openings. You can search the Web site by region, by employer, and by job category (e.g., foreign language positions). |
| <http://www.odedodea.edu/pers/employment> | This page has links to teacher employment opportunities in U.S. Department of Defense schools in the United States and overseas. |
| <http://www.jobs2teach.doded.mil> | Sponsored by the Department of Defense, Troops to Teachers helps former soldiers and sailors find teaching jobs. The site advertises that it is "available to anyone," not just military personnel. |
| <http://careers.education.wisc.edu/projectConnect/MainMenu.cfm> | Project Connect's motto is: "To get the right teacher into the right classroom." |
| <http://www.teachers-teachers.com> | A Web site associated with the American Association of Colleges for Teacher Education that features free access to job postings. |
| <http://www.teachwave.com> | Another useful list of teacher vacancies. |
| <http://www.monster.com> | Extremely popular on-line site for employment opportunities and job hunting tips. |
| <http://www.altavista.com> | A Web portal: Click on the link to "Careers" first, then "Teaching." |
| <http://hireed.net> | This site, sponsored by the Association for Supervision and Curriculum Development, provides information about job openings. Fees are charged for some services if you are not an ASCD member. |
| <http://www.edweek.org/jobs> | *Education Week's* site lets you browse for jobs by title or region. |
| <http://www.careerbuilder.com> | Enter the keyword "Teacher" and the region of the United States where you would like to work. A database of jobs culled from newspaper classified advertisements appears. Many of the jobs are from companies looking for employees who have teaching skills. |

## WEB SITES LISTING INTERNATIONAL
## JOB OPENINGS FOR TEACHERS

| | |
|---|---|
| <http://www.tieonline.com> | The International Educator's Web site including international job postings and a resume bank. |
| <http://www.state.gov/m/a/os/c6776.htm> | U.S. State Department page leading candidates to American-style schools overseas |
| <http://www.edulink.com> | Contains an on-line job fair and information about teaching abroad. |
| <http://www.nafsa.org> | This association of international educators provides a job registry for candidates. Start at the home page and follow the links. |

## POPULAR LISTSERVES FOR TEACHERS

| | | |
|---|---|---|
| Art | TEACHART | <listserv@si-listserv.si.edu> |
| | UAARTED | <listserv@listserv.arizona.edu> |
| | K12ARTSED | <listserv@artsedge.kennedy.center.org> |
| Computers | EDTECH | <listserv@msu.edu> |
| | SUPERK12 | <listserv@listserv.syr.edu> |
| Early Childhood | ECEOL-L | <listserv@maine.maine.edu> |
| | ECENET-L | <listserv@postoffice.cso.uiun.edu> |
| Elementary | ELEMED | <majordomo@duke.edu> |
| Education | ELED-L | <listserv@ksuvm.bitnet> |
| English | ENGLED-L | <listserv@psuvm.psu.edu> |
| Family and Consumer Sciences | FCSED-L | <listserv@univm.uni.edu> |
| English as a Second Language | TESL-L | <listserv@cunyvm.cuny.edu> |
| Foreign Language | FLAC-L | <listserv@brownvm.brown.edu> |
| | FLTEACH | <listserv@listserv.buffalo.edu> |
| | ESPAN-L | <espan-l@listserv.tau.ac.il> |
| Gifted Education | TAG-L | <listserv@listserv.nodak.edu> |
| Library | MEDIA-L | <listserv@bingvmb.cc.binghamtom.edu> |
| | LM_NET | <listserv@listserv.syr.edu> |
| Mathematics | NCTM-L | <listproc@sci-ed.fit.edu> |
| | Math-Teach-Digest | <majordomo@forum.swarthmore.edu> |
| | MATHWEB-L | <mailserv@hcca.ohio.gov> |
| Middle School | MIDDLE-L | <listserv@postoffice.cso.uiuc.edu> |
| Music Education | MUSIC-L | <listproc@artsedge.kennedy.center.org> |
| | MUSIC-ED | <listserv@vm1.spcs.umn.edu> |
| | ASTA-L | <listserv@cmsuvmb.cmsu.edu> |
| Reading | RTEACHER | <listserv@bookmark.reading.org> |
| Science | BIOPI-L | <listserv@ksuvm.ksu.edu> |
| | CHEMED-L | <listproc@atlantis.cc.uwf.edu> |
| | PHYSHARE | <listserv@psuvm.psu.edu> |
| | NCPRSE-L | <listserv@ecuvm.cis.ecu.edu> |
| | T321-L | <listserv@mizzou1.missouri.edu> |
| Social Studies | H-HIGH-S | <listserv@msu.edu> |
| | NCSS-L | <listproc2@h-net.msu.edu> |
| | SOCSTUD-L | <mailserv@hcca.ohio.gov> |
| Special Education | SPECED-L | <listserv@uga.cc.uga.edu> |
| | SPECIAL-ED | <listproc@wcupa.edu> |

telephone book. (Libraries usually have collections of telephone books; they also can be ordered through telephone companies.)

- It's best to have a specific name and title for the addressee in your cover letter and for the address on your envelope. The resources listed above can be helpful in finding much of this information. When in doubt, direct your correspondence to the Director of Human Resources if you are writing to a school district, or to the headmaster or director of a private school. If you have the name of a specific building principal, you can also send your material to her or his attention, although procedures in some districts require that resumes be kept on file at a central office location.

- The salutation at the start of your cover letter should read, "Dear Madam or Sir," if you don't know the name of the person who will read your correspondence.

- Name the type of teaching position you are seeking in the opening sentence.

- If you are planning to relocate, or if you are willing to accept part-time or leave replacement positions, mention this in the beginning of your cover letter.

- Avoid the use of trite phrases that sound phony, as in, "I am very much aware of your district's outstanding reputation for academic excellence."
- Always use the format described for cover letters presented in Chapter 5, and attach a copy of your resume using a template from Chapter 6.

*When Calling:*

- Present a warm, poised, and mature tone. Practice what you will say, and how you will say it, in advance.
- Be specific about your purpose for calling.
- Find out the job titles and names of the people responsible for hiring teachers.
- Engage the person on the telephone in conversation. Seek to make secretaries your friends so you can call them at a later time and use them as part of your job-hunting network.
- Ask if you can send a resume and cover letter as a follow-up. Find out the name of the school official to whom these materials should be sent.
- Politely request the name and job title of the person who answered your call before you hang up the phone.
- If nothing develops, renew your acquaintance periodically with the person who handled your call.

Don't be discouraged by the lack of responses. Remember, even the best salespeople usually come up empty when they try to locate new clients. Your batting average doesn't count in this effort: The one time you connect may be the only opportunity you'll need.

## Finding a Job in Private Schools

All schools want teachers who can achieve excellence in the classroom. As a result, most of the techniques listed above apply to both the public and private sectors. However, your chances of landing a job in a private school will be enhanced if you use some specialized strategies that target the unique needs of these schools.

Private schools have existed since the early days of European settlement. Indeed, a good number of private educational institutions can trace their roots well back into U.S. history. Today, there are over 27,000 private schools in the United States, and they enroll approximately ten percent of America's school-age children. Private schools take several different forms, including parochial or religious schools, boarding schools, (where students—and frequently faculty—live on campus), international schools that follow the American style of education overseas, and day schools run by for-profit and non-profit organizations or individual proprietors. Religious schools receive their support from their sponsoring group, while the financial base for independent schools usually comes from tuition, donations, and endowment funds.

The philosophies that guide private schools are as varied as their settings. Religious schools, of course, embody the philosophies of their international, national, or local affiliations. Independent schools may follow paths similar to the one described for our fictitious Academy Prep—that is, they present a rigorous, often traditional program that prepares students for college. Other schools espouse more diverse approaches to education. One newspaper advertisement, for example, sought teachers familiar with a "child-centered, experiential philosophy," while a boarding school asked candidates to commit themselves to participation in "a caring community." Discovering the particulars for an individual school requires research.

Teachers choose to work in private schools for several reasons. Many see private settings as the ideal place to begin their careers; they anticipate receiving greater support, mentoring, and collegial and parental involvement than in public schools. Some relish the small size that characterizes most of these schools. Other teachers, however, view private school education as a calling. They endorse the central ideals of their schools, whether they are religious tenets or unique educational principles. They also relish the community atmosphere, extensive involvement in school activities, quality of students, and small class size that teaching in the private sector often brings. Remember, too, that private schools are usually not subject to the same teacher licensing requirements as their public counterparts, thereby making them very attractive to career changers, enrollees in **alternative certification** programs, and college graduates who did not complete teacher preparation programs as part of their undergraduate or graduate coursework. Although compensation is generally lower, many private school teachers would never trade places with their public school counterparts. In short, private school education may be the right match for you.

## Finding Openings in Private School Education

We recommend several strategies to discover private school vacancies. To start, we suggest you visit your local library to find books on private school education and examine directories devoted to this topic. These books include *Peterson's Private Secondary Schools 2003* (Peterson's Guides, 2003), *The Handbook of Private Schools, 2002: An Annual Descriptive Survey of Independent Education* (Porter Sargent, 2002), *Boarding School Guide* (Keegan, 2002), and *Peterson's American and Canadian Boarding Schools and Worldwide Enrichment Programs* (Peterson's Guides, 2003). Libraries usually carry collections of telephone books, and you can browse through listings to identify the schools in various areas.

Networking can provide additional information about private school opportunities in your area. Many independent and parochial schools recruit through recommendations and word-of-mouth, so spreading the word that you are interested in a teaching job may result in contacts that lead to positions. For schools associated with religions, contact the local church, parish, temple, or related organization; they can provide you with school names and addresses and the names of school administrators. Keep in mind that schools often swap resumes. As a result, sending your resume to one school may result in calls from others.

*The New York Times, Education Week,* and other newspapers carry vacancy announcements from both public and nonpublic schools, so you will want to check editions on a regular basis. The National Association of Independent Schools (NAIS) publishes *Independent Schools,* an excellent source of job listings. If international schools are part of your career goals, try *The International Educator* (NAFSA Association of International Educators), a quarterly that serves as a recruiting tool for more than 200 schools. These journals are cited in References.

Increasingly, private schools use the Internet as one of their recruitment strategies. (See the chart below for good starting points for your search.)

As noted previously, Web sites change often, so be prepared to spend some time surfing. Many individual schools also have Web sites; use the links provided in this chapter to jump from one school to another.

## WEB SITES LISTING PRIVATE SCHOOL JOBS

| | |
|---|---|
| <http://www.capenet.org/teach.html> | The Web site of the Council for American Private Education provides many links to openings in private schools, as well as information about the benefits of working in private school settings. |
| <http://www.privateschooljobs.com> | A listing of vacancies is provided and you can add your resume to a database of job seekers. |
| <http://www.aisne.org/employment/employment.asp> | Job openings in New English private schools. |
| <www.nais.org/careers/careers.cfm> | Job seekers can search the database of teaching jobs of the 1,100 member schools of the National Association of Independent Schools. Some of these schools are located overseas. |
| <www.isacs.org> | The Web site of the Independent Schools Association of the Central States. The site includes general information about private schools, facts and figures about enrollment, job benefits and salaries. Follow the links to the "Career Center" for postings about vacancies. |

## Should You Use an Agency?

Many private schools, and some public ones, use teacher employment agencies to help them fill positions. Sometimes agencies act as clearing-houses by accumulating resumes, conducting preliminary examinations of credentials, and matching job openings with resumes in their collection. At other times, agencies conduct interviews and send only one recommended candidate to a particular site. Employment agencies often develop close working relationships with private schools. The counselors at the agencies we have contacted are quite proud of their success rates, and they emphasize that they play a crucial role in connecting employers with promising candidates. Fees, which are paid either by the schools or candidates, provide agencies with their revenue.

The decision about whether to use an employment agency in your job hunt is up to you. Before you decide, we recommend that you find out what services are provided. Call several different agencies and ask about their business histories. Take a look at an application; pay close attention to the terms of the agreement you will be required to sign. Then, set up an appointment to speak with a counselor. At this conference, ask the following questions:

- How successful has the agency been in placing candidates with your profile (e.g., beginning teacher, career changer, etc.)?
- What is the ratio of candidates to successful placements?
- What specific assistance does the agency offer to help you write your resume and create your portfolio?
- Does the agency forward your resume and other credentials, "as is," or does it add materials to make your candidacy stand out from the crowd?
- Will the agency help you polish your interview skills?
- What is the specific process by which you will be informed about potential jobs?
- Does the agency specialize in certain types of teaching jobs or certain types of schools?
- Does it focus on specific geographic areas, or is its span nationwide or international?
- How well do the counselors know the schools they serve? Do they visit the sites? Do they have regular contact with administrators?

- What will happen if you find a job on your own?
- What are the fees, and who is responsible for them?
- If you are dissatisfied with the agency's service, what accommodations will be made?

Teacher employment agencies may be found by the traditional telephone book hunt or by conducting an Internet search; sites related to private school education may have direct links to these organizations. If you use the Internet to make your initial contact, follow up your e-mail with a phone call or a personal visit, so that you can make better judgments about the agency and cultivate the personal relationships so valuable in your search for the best teaching job.

## Jobs for Teachers with Alternative Certification

Some public school districts, particularly those experiencing dire shortages in certain subject areas, are now actively seeking candidates who are graduates of, or enrolled in, programs that provide a temporary teaching credential for those who did not complete a traditional, college-based course of preparation. If you fit this profile, you should maintain close contact with your program's director to ensure that you have access to the most up-to-date listings of job openings. In addition, we suggest that you conduct an Internet search to identify openings that may be of interest. Start with state education department Web sites; urban or rural school district Web pages may also contain the information you seek, as these areas frequently have difficulty recruiting teachers through traditional paths. For a state-by-state listing of alternative certification programs, visit the authors' Web site at <**www.teacheredge.com**>.

## When to Apply

When should you begin looking for a teaching position? When we began our careers as school administrators, the hiring process began in the spring, usually April or May. In today's competitive market, the hiring season starts much earlier. Schools know they have access to a better pool of candidates if they begin recruiting before their competitors in neighboring districts.

While it is difficult to gauge the exact peak of the hiring season for teaching jobs, some trends can be determined. In 2001, we tracked the number of columns of vacancy announcements appearing in the Education Job Market section of The *New York Times* Sunday edition over the course of the year. The data shown below indicate two peak periods. More teaching jobs were advertised in January than any other month. The next highest number occurs in the period from late May through June, with the exception of Memorial Day weekend.

Our advice, therefore, is to plan your job search for the coming school year to begin early in January. This means that you should complete your *Resume Reservoir, Personal Profile,* and preliminary research about schools of interest to you before the new calendar year begins. Also, because districts continue to advertise vacancies through the summer months and even into September, do not be discouraged if your initial efforts are unsuccessful. Looking for job postings on-line and in print and using your network connections should remain part of your weekly routine. Your dream job may appear anytime.

Now that you have found a job vacancy in a desirable school, it's time to do some homework to become an informed and articulate candidate. Your assignment starts in Chapter 4.

| Date | Number of Columns of Teacher Job Advertisements | Date | Number of Columns of Teacher Job Advertisements |
|---|---|---|---|
| 1/7 | 29 | 7/8 July 4th Weekend | 10 |
| 1/14 | 24 | 7/15 | 19 |
| 1/21 | 25 | 7/22 | 21 |
| 1/28 | 22 | 7/29 | 17 |
| 2/4 | 26 | 8/5 | 16 |
| 2/11 | 23 | 8/12 | 15 |
| 2/14 Presidents' Weekend | 14 | 8/19 | 15 |
| 2/25 | 17 | 8/26 | 14 |
| 3/4 | 19 | 9/2 Labor Day Weekend | 8 |
| 3/11 | 20 | 9/9 | 22 |
| 3/18 | 18 | 9/16 | 15 |
| 3/25 | 19 | 9/23 | 14 |
| 4/1 | 19 | 9/30 | 13 |
| 4/8 | 19 | 10/7 | 12 |
| 4/15 Easter Weekend | 5 | 10/14 | 13 |
| 4/22 | 24 | 10/21 | 12 |
| 4/29 | 21 | 10/28 | 13 |
| 5/6 | 23 | 11/4 | 16 |
| 5/13 Mother's Day | 17 | 11/11 | 14 |
| 5/20 | 22 | 11/16 | 11 |
| 5/27 Memorial Day Weekend | 8 | 11/26 Thanksgiving Weekend | 3 |
| 6/3 | 27 | 12/3 | 13 |
| 6/10 | 24 | 12/10 | 21 |
| 6/17 | 21 | 12/17 | 11 |
| 6/24 | 17 | 12/23 Christmas Weekend | 1 |
| 7/1 | 15 | 12/31 New Year's Weekend | 2 |

## REMINDERS

 Use all available resources to find information about job openings. Explore all options for public and private education.

 Networks work! Build your own job search network by considering everyone you meet as a potential link to a job.

 Don't be discouraged if some of your initial job search activities don't pay immediate dividends. The information you discover through the process may help you by providing the names of decision makers and information about schools and districts that will be valuable later.

 While its always good to have a specialty that is in great demand, remember that some new candidates are *always* hired, even when there is a surplus of teachers. Think positively!

# Chapter Four

# Doing Your Homework

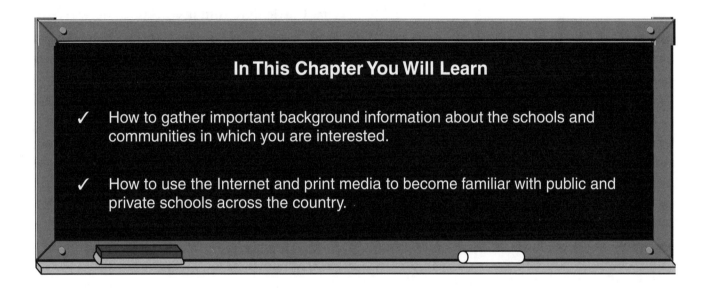

**In This Chapter You Will Learn**

✓ How to gather important background information about the schools and communities in which you are interested.

✓ How to use the Internet and print media to become familiar with public and private schools across the country.

*Elementary jobs are hard to find. Everywhere you go, there's so much competition. What really worked for me was finding information about the school. By the time I interviewed, I knew the programs that they were interested in. I was* really *prepared.*

—Elementary school teacher

*One of the things we look for in a candidate is 'fit,' how well someone matches with our programs and our general approach to teaching. The better the fit, the more we want to hire that person.*

—High school principal

I t's very logical, really: To get noticed as a candidate for the teaching job you want, you must show that you are better than your competitors. If you want to be selected, you need to demonstrate that your particular blend of achievements, talents, and skills is aligned with the needs of the school to which you are applying. The information you gather during the application process will also tell you whether the school offers a desirable opportunity uniquely suited to you. Every school has its own organizational culture, educational philosophy, community setting, and challenges. As a college placement officer once told us, "The hiring process is a two-way street. At the same time the school is learning more about the candidate, the candidate must learn more about the school."

But how do you do that? To a great extent, your success in achieving this goal depends on how much you know about your prospective employer. And to gain this knowledge, you need to do some investigating—some homework, you might say.

## What Do You Need to Know?

To make your candidacy stand out, your efforts should focus on developing answers to key questions about each school you are considering in your job search. We have provided you with a *School Profile Form* on page 45 to help you record and organize the information you find. Duplicate the form as needed, and place one form for each school in your *Job Find File.*

### What Is the Philosophy of the School or District?

Views about the nature and purposes of education often can be found in **mission statements** and **strategic plans.** In public schools, these statements usually are produced by committees composed of school and community members. In private education, mission statements and strategic plans often originate from the founder, the sponsoring organization, or the board of trustees.

Mission statements and strategic plans may be found in district and school publications and on Web sites. Careful reading can provide valuable clues about the current and future direction of your prospective employers. One Florida district, for example, proclaims that its system "is recognized as a leader in its commitment to computer-assisted instruction," a sure sign that you'd better be comfortable with instructional technology if you want a job in one of this district's schools. A district in the Northwestern United States announces that its goal is "to prepare students to positively contribute to a democratic society and world community"; here, you may find programs that are designed to build the understandings required for citizenship in a global community. Similarly, a magnet school in the Midwest announces its belief in the value of an arts-driven curriculum; one need not read too

deeply between the lines to know that this school wants teachers who know how to encourage creativity in their students. In another building, a commitment to "learning by doing" is espoused: lecturers need not apply.

When you read a mission statement or examine a strategic plan, see how well it connects with your own views on education. If you get a warm feeling when you read the words, you may be on the road to a good match. On the other hand, if you wind up shaking your head as you read, it might be better to pass on vacancies in that school.

### What Curriculum Initiatives Are Underway?

While philosophies are important in establishing a broad direction for schools, curricula will determine your day-to-day practices as a teacher. As a result, it's useful for you to find out as much as you can about what's happening in classrooms. One school district's Web site, for instance, leads you directly to a statement by the superintendent concerning the importance of educational **standards.** It's a safe bet that instruction in this system is guided by the curricula posted on the district's Web site. On the other hand, if you learn that computers are infused into all instructional programs, familiarity with commonly used applications and the Internet may be your ticket to success.

### What School or Districtwide Problems Need to Be Addressed?

"He's got lots of great ideas," said one member of an interview committee to Rob after a grueling meeting with a candidate, "but he's not right for our school. What we need in this job is someone who can work well with our **at-risk** kids, and his approach would go right over their heads." To present yourself as someone who can strengthen a school's educational program, you need to be aware of the issues that face your prospective employer. A school that is having significant problems in student discipline will be looking for candidates who can use effective classroom management skills. If reports indicate that students perform poorly on **standardized tests,** it will probably be useful to cite experience with remediation programs and express a commitment to working with students who are on the bottom rungs of the achievement ladder.

**School Profile Form**

NAME OF SCHOOL _____

What is the school's educational philosophy?




What curriculum initiatives are underway?




What school or districtwide problems need to be addressed?




What is the community like?




Who's who in the school?          Principal _____

                                 Secretary _____

                                 Curriculum Supervisor, Team Leader or Lead Teacher

                                 _____


Who's who in the school district?   Superintendent _____

                                 Curriculum Director _____

                                 Human Resources or Personnel Director

                                 _____

## What Is the Community Like?

While schools all over the country share many of the same goals, they often have a different emphasis, depending on the nature of the community that a particular school serves. Communities experiencing demographic change may be looking to address multicultural issues, and they will certainly appreciate someone who has experience working with diverse learners. Schools located in economically distressed areas, where budgets are stretched to the limit, may be looking for a candidate with the ability to construct creative, teacher-made materials. A school with a shortage of space will be happy to have art teachers who are flexible and can manage an "art on a cart" program where they must travel from room to room, while a district that prides itself on staff involvement in decision making will be most receptive to an applicant who comes across as a joiner and an effective communicator.

Seth student taught in Groton, Connecticut, where the community was dominated by a U.S. naval submarine base. Teachers in the public school system were expected to address the needs of children from transient families who were uprooted regularly as their parents were transferred from one naval base to another. In another school on the north shore of Long Island, a science candidate made a favorable impression on a search committee because she proposed testing water quality in the nearby Long Island Sound. The message: Tailor your presentation to conditions in the local community.

## Who's Who?

Knowing the names and positions of VIPs in your target school is a great advantage. An awareness of decision makers and power brokers in a school will help you to address your cover letter and resume appropriately and cultivate relationships with people who then will become part of your networking efforts. Learning this information also takes some of the stress out of interviews; in some ways, you may feel like you're surrounded by people you already know. To accomplish this goal, you will want to familiarize yourself with the names of such key players as superintendents, other ranking central office personnel, principals, and department chairs.

"I always like it when someone remembers my name at an interview, or even on the phone," confides a high school principal. "It just makes it seem like that person took the time to master the little details—and details are important to be a good teacher."

## How Do You Find the Information You Need?

Don't let the list of questions above intimidate you: finding the answers to these queries *is* possible. Let's explore the process by investigating Hypothetical School, a K–5 building located in Supertown, Growing County, New York.

## Doing Fine . . . On-line

We'll start getting acquainted with our target school without leaving the house (or the local library). Our first step is an Internet search for school achievement and other important data contained in Hypothetical's "School Report Card." This material can be accessed through the New York State Education Department's Web site, **<www.emsc.nysed.gov>**.

After accessing the site, we go to the search menu and select "School Report Card." The rest is easy; you gain access to the school or district of choice through an alphabetical listing of schools. (Note: You will need Adobe Acrobat Reader® to open individual school report cards, but this can

---

**How Can You Find Out Whether a School or District Has a Web Site?**

1. Use any Internet search engine.
2. Enter the name of the school in which you are interested.
3. Click on "search" and wait as the search engine seeks matches for your request.
4. If the search does not provide results, try a different search engine.
5. You can also try one of the directories of school Web sites listed later in this chapter, or you can click on the "Education" heading of home pages of search engines like Google or Excite. (Remember that Internet sites and search engine formats change frequently, so don't give up if some of the links are no longer "live.")

be downloaded free of charge from the New York State Education Department site.)

In a few moments, we reach the report card for Hypothetical School. It's a fantastic source of information. After reading introductory material about the purpose and design of the school report card, we soon become acquainted with recent test scores, testing history, and comparative data showing how Hypothetical's results compare with similar schools. The report card also contains demographic data and some general facts about the school district. A very useful screen provides districtwide information about students with disabilities and their placements. Congratulations! You and the Hypothetical School have just become good acquaintances!

Additional information about the school and its district can be procured through real estate-oriented tools on the World Wide Web. Let's start with the resources available through the popular Yahoo! portal. First, surf your way to <www.yahoo.com>. When the opening screen pops up, click on the link for real estate. When the screen changes, click the link called, "School Profiles." You will be presented with two choices: You can browse by address or by state. Since we do not know the exact address of Hypothetical School, we can enter the city and state in the appropriate box, and click "Submit." After the next Web page loads, we see data for all the school districts in the selected area. For example, we can determine the total enrollment in Hypothetical's district, the student-teacher ratio, the average class size in first grade, the percentage of high school seniors receiving high school diplomas, and the percentage of students who attend college after graduation.

Now we click on the link to Hypothetical's district. More information appears on your screen. We can view the average middle school class size; the grades at which foreign language, computer, band, and gifted education programs begin; as well as the number of advanced placement classes and interscholastic sports offered at Hypothetical High.

Alternatively, we try <www.msn.com>. On the opening page, we click on the link for "House and Home." At the "House and Home" page, we click on another link called, "Buying a House." From there, we click on "Neighborhoods" which takes us to a page called, "Find a Neighborhood." We enter Hypothetical's zip code, press "Enter" and watch as a comprehensive statistical profile appears on the new page. The data include a school achievement index that ranks schools on a 1–10 scale, with 10 representing the highest level. In addition, the page provides us with information about Hypothetical's spending per pupil, the ratio of students per guidance counselor and per librarian. As we are thinking of moving to the area near the school, we also consult the cost of living index shown on the page.

That's a good start, but it's not enough for us. We click on the link for "The School Report" <www.theschoolreport.com> to arrive at a new site that provides additional resources. We select Hypothetical's state and then enter more location information on the following page. We now read reports containing demographic information about the school district, and the address, phone number, and name of the principal of each school in the district. A map displaying the location of each school accompanies the data. A click on a highlighted box will enable us to receive a detailed report that includes SAT scores, school district awards and related information, but first we must complete a form inquiring about our name, address, e-mail address, and telephone number. (Note: Once you complete the form, you may receive contacts from local real estate agencies.) Another helpful location to find information in a simple, easy-to-understand format is a Web site for children sponsored by the National Center for Education Statistics <http://nces.ed.gov/nceskids/school.asp>. By now, you have already obtained a great deal of information, and you haven't even left your chair!

As you conduct your Internet searches, remember that many metropolitan newspapers have sections or continuing series devoted to profiles of local communities. Try accessing this material from the newspapers' Web sites.

Continuing our Internet tour, we find that other searches prove equally profitable. Hypothetical, as it turns out, has its own Web site. When you arrive there, you find information about school programs, special events, and grade-level curricula. Student work from various classes has been inserted into the site via a scanner, and there are links to central administration and other schools in the district. To supplement your own knowledge about innovative programs currently in place at the school, use your search engine to find sites related to such topics as early childhood education and the well-regarded **Reading Recovery** program.

**WEB SITES TO ACCESS PUBLIC SCHOOL REPORT CARDS**

| State | Web Address |
|---|---|
| Alabama | <http://www.alsde.edu/Accountability/preAccountability.asp> |
| Alaska | <http://www.eed.state.ak.us/stats/home.html> |
| Arizona | <http://www.ade.state.az.us/srcs/find_school.asp?rdoYear=2003> |
| Arkansas | <http://as-is.org> |
| California | <http://www.ed-data.k12.ca.us/> |
| Colorado | <http://www.cde.state.co.us/index_stats.htm> |
| Connecticut | <http://www.csde.state.ct.us/public/der/index.htm> |
| Delaware | <http://www.doe.state.de.us/del_schools/school_information.htm> |
| Florida | <http://www.firn.edu/doe/bin00050/flmove> |
| Georgia | <http://techservices.doe.k12.ga.us/reportcard> |
| Hawaii | <http://arch.k12.hi.us/school/ssir/default.html> |
| Idaho | <http://www.sde.state.id.us/IRI/iristats/irianalysis.asp> |
| Illinois | <http://206.166.105.128/ReportCard/rchome.asp> |
| Indiana | <http://ideanet.doe.state.in.us/htmls/education.html> |
| Iowa | <http://www.state.ia.us/educate/fis/pre/eddata/schooltestresults.html> |
| Kansas | <http://www.ksbe.state.ks.us/reportcard.html> |
| Kentucky | <http://apps.kde.state.ky.us/report_card/> |
| Louisiana | <http://www.doe.state.la.us/doe/asps/home.asp?I=REPORTD> |
| Maine | <http://www.state.me.us/education/profiles/getprofiles.htm> |
| Maryland | <http://msp.msde.state.md.us> |
| Massachusetts | <http://profiles.doe.mass.edu> |
| Michigan | <http://www.michigan.gov/mde/0,1607,7-140-5233_5978---,00.html> |
| Minnesota | <http://cflapp.state.mn.us/CLASS/selection/SelectionController?SECTION=DA> |
| Mississippi | <http://www.mde.k12.ms.us/account/ors> |
| Missouri | <http://services.dese.state.mo.us/schooldata> |
| Montana | <http://opi.state.mt.us Click on the button labeled, "Reports."> |
| Nebraska | <http://reportcard.nde.state.ne.us> |
| Nevada | Nevada does not maintain public school report cards on its state education department Web site. |
| New Hampshire | <http://www.measuredprogress.org/nhprofile> |
| New Jersey | <http://education.state.nj.us/rc> |
| New Mexico | <http://sde.state.nm.us/divisions/ais/datacollection/dcrfactsheets.html> |
| New York | <http://www.emsc.nysed.gov/irts/home.html#RecentReports> |
| North Carolina | <http://www.dpi.state.nc.us/reportstats.html> |
| North Dakota | <http://www.dpi.state.nd.us/dpi/reports/profile/index.htm> |
| Ohio | <http://www.ode.state.oh.us/reportcard> |
| Oklahoma | <http://sde.state.ok.us/home/defaultie.html> |
| Oregon | <http://www.ode.state.or.us/asmt/results/index.htm> |
| Pennsylvania | <http://www.paprofiles.org> |
| Rhode Island | <http://www.infoworks.ride.uri.edu> |
| South Carolina | <http://www.myscschools.com/reportcard> |
| South Dakota | <http://www.state.sd.us/deca/finance/Data/stats/statbook.htm> |
| Tennessee | <http://www.state.tn.us/education/mstat.htm> |
| Texas | <http://www.tea.state.tx.us/tea/data.html> |
| Utah | <http://www.usoe.k12.ut.us/eval/perf_rpt.htm> |
| Vermont | <http://maps.vcgi.org/schlrpt> |
| Virginia | <http://maps.vcgi.org/schlrpt> |
| Washington | <http://www.k12.wa.us/edprofile> |
| West Virginia | <http://wvde.state.wv.us/data/report_cards> |
| Wisconsin | <http://data.dpi.state.wi.us/data/selschool.asp> |
| Wyoming | <http://www.asme.com/wycas/TestResults/TestResults.htm> |

To learn more about the community itself, you type *Supertown + New York* in the search window of your Internet search engine, and when you click on the sites it identifies, you discover that the local chamber of commerce has a home page, as well. Using this resource, you find out about town government, note some of the area's main businesses, and link with real estate agents who supply information about home prices and attract clients by lauding the accomplishments of the school district.

Your final move in this area is to consider a SchoolMatch search. For a fee, SchoolMatch <www.schoolmatch.com> will provide you with considerable information about schools around the country. Often used by executive relocation firms, the service can help you assess the comparative status of your targeted schools.

To perform a similar search for schools in all fifty states, use the following State Web sites for School Report Cards. Check **<www.TeacherEdge. com>** periodically to review an updated list.

## Surfing the Net for a Private School Job

The Internet can be an excellent resource for positions in private schools, too. Many of these schools now have Web sites, and you can use the techniques described above to find them. You can also use the

### PRIVATE SCHOOL INFORMATION ON THE WEB

| | |
|---|---|
| **<http://www.capenet.org>** | The Web site of the Council for American Private Education contains links to Web sites of their member schools. |
| **<http://www.greatschools.net>** | A rich database that will connect you to information about public, private, and charter schools in the U.S. |
| **<www.nais.org/schools/schools.cfm>** | Directory of 1,100 member schools. You may select criteria for the school you are researching, such as school type (day or boarding school), student body (boys, girls, or coeducational), state, and country. The National Association of Independent Schools on-line directory will take you to the Web site of the particular school. |
| **<http://privateschool.miningco.com/cs/schooldirectories>** | About.com sponsors a popular directory of private school information. |
| **<http://www.aisne.org>** | The official site of the Association of Independent Schools in New England. Its directory will provide you with information about member schools and their Web links. |
| **<http://www.advis.org>** | The site of the Advancement for Delaware Valley Independent Schools. This regional association Web site will provide you with information about 129 member schools. |
| **<http://www.ezlink.com/~edu/ZZCathol.htm>** **<http://www.ezlink.com/~edu/ZZLutSch.htm>** | EZ Link provides access to Catholic and Lutheran schools with Web sites. |
| **<http://www.maven.co.il/subjects.asp?S=175>** | Provides links to Jewish schools with Web sites. |
| **<http://www.amshq.org>** | Connects you with American Montessori schools. |
| **<http://www.schools.com/directory/index.html>** | Information about individual boarding schools from the Association of Boarding Schools. |

pages sponsored by organizations of private schools, like the Council for American Private Education at <**www.capenet.org>,** or the National Association of Independent Schools at <**www.nais.org>,** to serve as a springboard for your search. *American School Directory* <**www.asd.com>**) contains links to private schools as well, although a fee is required. The National Center for Education Statistics maintains a repository of data about individual private schools at <**http://nces.ed. gov/surveys/ pss>.** For additional information, try the Web sites listed on page 49 and look for updates at <**www.TeacherEdge.com>.**

### Internet Information about Overseas Schools

If you are looking for exciting teaching opportunities overseas, the U.S. State Department and the U.S. Department of Defense host Web sites that describe schools they sponsor near embassies and military bases around the globe. Check out <**http://www.state.gov/m/a/os/c1684.htm>** (State Department) and <**http://www.odedodea.edu>** (Department of Defense). Other useful sites include:

> <**http://www.tieonline.com>**
>
> The International Educator's Web site including international job postings and a resume bank.
>
> <**http://www.edulink.com>**
>
> Contains an on-line job fair and information about teaching abroad.
>
> <**http://www.nafsa.org>**
>
> This association of international educators provides a job registry for candidates. Start at the home page and follow the links.

### Mining the Media

Local media can provide volumes of additional material. Again, let's try to find out more about Hypothetical School.

A trip to the local library in Growing County is the first order of business. After sitting down at a table in the reference section, we review several weeks of back issues of the major daily newspaper, including all weekend editions. As we hoped, there are a number of entries with significant information. We learn that Hypothetical's library has just installed several new Internet connections, a development complemented by faculty workshops devoted to using instructional technology. In much the same fashion, we discover that a bond issue for technology passed by a significant margin, an indication that the community supports its schools *and* has high expectations for educational computer applications. In another article, we learn that two classroom teachers at the school just received a grant from a local civic organization to create an artist-in-residence program for poets and children's book authors. We also encounter an article about the changing face of the community. After reading this piece, we know that so-called empty nesters have been selling their homes at a feverish pace to young families from diverse cultural backgrounds.

While you are visiting the library, ask about neighborhood newspapers. You will find that the local press contains lots of photographs and news releases from area schools, in addition to an occasional in-depth article. In our case, as we comb through editions from the past months we see striking pictures of Hypothetical's popular "Celebration of Family and Friends" and photographs of a mentoring program for at-risk pupils that involves athletes and student leaders from the local high school. A brief article describes a board of education meeting where funding was approved for a new hands-on mathematics program. In an issue published a couple of weeks later, we learn about a committee that has been formed to study expansion of the school building. Finally, a press release from the school mentions a parent education program sponsored by the PTA.

---

### Using Your Network

You can also use your job search network as an extra set of eyes and ears around your targeted community. Before soliciting information, don't forget to explain your purpose and tell your source why you selected him or her in particular, as in, "I know you volunteered to help with the school's publishing center for children's writing. What can you tell me about the program?" College career placement offices may also have good contacts with area schools. Cultivate relationships with counselors at the office, and do not hesitate to ask them for advice and information.

Next, we begin a daily routine that involves tapping into another source of information: the local cable channel. We find that the news programs offered on this channel include a regular feature entitled, "News from the Schools." Within a couple of weeks, we view a feature about a **service learning** connection between the school and a local day care center. It is now obvious that involvement with the community is an important aspect of school life at Hypothetical. On a sour note, we also watch a tape of a community meeting, where a parent representative complains that the school district's buildings are not yet fully

accessible to those with physical disabilities. As a result, we know that inclusion classes may not be fully implemented for a while.

## The Official Source

Let's remember that schools disseminate a great deal of information on a regular basis. School, school district, and PTA newsletters contain detailed descriptions of programs, accomplishments, and special events as well as general information about school operation and organization. Some districts also publish summaries of

**OFFICIAL SOURCES OF SCHOOL INFORMATION**

| Source | Tells You . . . | Available From |
|---|---|---|
| School, district, and PTA newsletters | Current information about programs, accomplishments, and special events. General information about school operations and organization. | Families of children attending the school, community residents, and faculty members; sometimes available in local library and from real estate agents, also available from school offices. |
| Annual school calendar | School policies, new initiatives, special programs, and names, addresses, and telephone numbers of school and district officials. | Same as above. |
| School Web site | Basic information about school including curriculum, special programs, mission statement, calendar, and contacts. | Available from the Internet. Start by using a search engine, but remember to insert the name of the city and state, since many schools have the same names. |
| Summaries of Board of Education meetings | School district activities and plans. | School district office or local library. |
| School public relations materials | Information about special programs and long-range plans. | Families of children attending the school, faculty members, school office, and real estate agents. |
| In-house publications—i.e., student handbook, parent handbook, teacher handbook, curriculum guides, high school student newspaper, student homework assignment books | Day-to-day policies, practices, and issues. | Same as above. |
| Annual school budget materials | New programs, staffing needs, enrollment plans, textbook adoptions, technology purchases, school construction. | Families of children attending the school and community residents; sometimes available in local library and real estate offices, also from school offices. |
| Private school brochures for student recruitment | Educational philosophy, programs, facilities, and faculty information. | Request from school office. |

board of education meetings, a rich source of material on school district activities and plans. Annual school calendars often post brief descriptions of important policies, initiatives, and special programs. You can rely on them to find addresses, telephone numbers, and the names of building and central office administrators. An examination of the programs highlighted on the monthly calendar, moreover, will give you good clues about programs that are highly valued. At Hypothetical, for example, three evening "Parents as Reading Partners" activities are scheduled for children and their parents, and the fifth grade goes on an overnight, outdoor education trip.

Schools today publish Web sites that feature comprehensive information such as curriculum guides, extracurricular activities, names of administrators, the school's mission statement, links to PTA Web sites, and much more—all just a click away on your home computer. Because of its convenience, the school Web site should be your first stop. When Rob and Seth last searched for jobs, we gleaned invaluable insights about schools from their Web sites. If a school does not have a Web site, or if the Web site is not current, you have learned something, albeit negative, about the school's commitment to technology and perhaps the availability of funds. You also impress interviewers when you mention that you checked out their Web site to introduce yourself to the school.

Schools often produce public relations materials that are quite useful in your job quest. To recruit students, private schools print glossy brochures that highlight educational philosophy, programs, and facilities, and include information about the faculty. A brochure printed by Hypothetical explains the reading program; it tells us that teachers use anthologies and sets of trade books. A district mailing on technology delineates the new five-year plan adopted by the board of education, and another set of materials describes after-school enrichment opportunities that are available twice a week.

Pay particular attention to publications issued in advance of budget votes. These materials may give you insight about school and district goals for the upcoming year, and they may enable you to learn about proposals for specific projects and programs. In this regard, budget brochures created by school districts can be excellent sources of information about enrollment, teacher hiring, textbook adoptions, technology and other instructional equipment purchases, and building and school construction. You may even learn about retirement incentives being offered to veteran staff members. All of this information may be quite helpful when it comes time to submit a cover letter and resume or participate in a job interview.

If you have contacts in the school, you may have access to in-house publications. Student, parent, and teacher handbooks can give you valuable insights into day-to-day operations and help you understand expectations for students and faculty. Similarly, the assignment books that are provided in many schools at the elementary and secondary levels frequently contain material related to the curriculum and special programs and activities. Curriculum guides and high school student newspapers offer an insider's view. The chart on the previous page lists official sources of school information.

### Take a Field Trip

If it's convenient, visit the neighborhood of the schools in which you are interested. By driving around the area, you can get a feel for the community and the school itself. Here are some specific items to look for:

- What does the surrounding community look like? How would you characterize the area in terms of population, economics, housing?

---

Although somewhat time-consuming, your search for information about schools is almost guaranteed to pay dividends:

- It will provide you with detailed knowledge that will make your cover letter and resume more appealing to readers.
- It will help you target those places where you have the best chance of getting attention because you can fill school or district needs.
- It will provide you with information that you may be able to use to your advantage during an interview.

- Are there any special clues about what's important at the school? For example, you may see a sign advertising a read-a-thon or a message board boasting about National Merit Scholars. At Hypothetical, we see a banner advertising a parent-teacher organization fund raiser for new playground equipment.
- How big is the building? What is its physical condition? Does it look well maintained? Is construction taking place? Are there ample fields for recess, athletics, and special events?
- How easy is it to get to the school? Is there parking? Is the school served by public transportation?

It's important to remember that schools are on guard against loiterers. For this reason, and to avoid seeming overly aggressive, we suggest that you conduct your observations discreetly. Unless you have an appointment, *do not* walk into the school building.

### Visiting Private Schools

Private schools may be more open to visits from prospective candidates than their public sector counterparts. The National Association of Independent Schools' Web site notes, "Most schools welcome visitors who simply want to learn more about them. You may be able to set up a visit even though a school has no current job openings."

If such a visit can be arranged, try to sample as many aspects of school life as possible. Observe classes (if they allow it); talk to faculty, administrators, and students; and learn about before- and after-school activities. Seek out supervisors who will work with you directly if you are hired and engage them in conversation—you never know when that little bit of contact may work to your advantage during the hiring process.

At the end of your visit, prepare a summary for your *Job Find File*. Record what you've learned about the school's philosophy and note whether it matches your own views on education. Jot down your impressions of the curriculum, faculty relationships, student attitudes toward the school, and supervisory expectations. Make special note of any programs or policies that you deem particularly important—for example, extensive opportunities for coaching, a strong staff development program, or innovative curricula. Don't forget to refer to the notes from your visit when writing a cover letter and resume or when preparing for an interview. Write a thank you note to the school administrator after the visit.

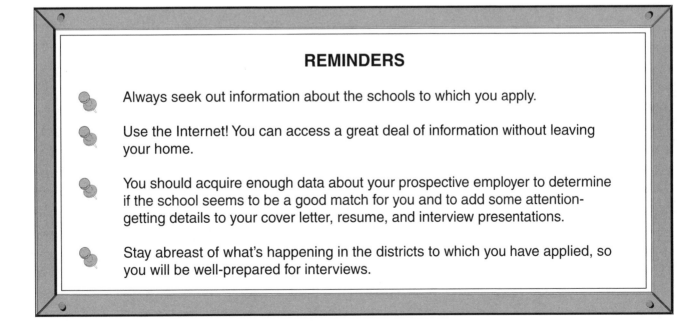

## REMINDERS

Always seek out information about the schools to which you apply.

Use the Internet! You can access a great deal of information without leaving your home.

You should acquire enough data about your prospective employer to determine if the school seems to be a good match for you and to add some attention-getting details to your cover letter, resume, and interview presentations.

Stay abreast of what's happening in the districts to which you have applied, so you will be well-prepared for interviews.

## Chapter Five

# Your Cover Letter

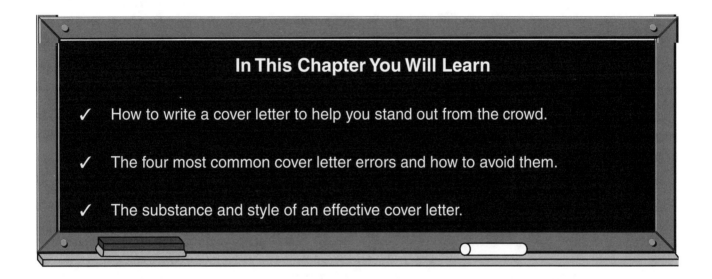

**In This Chapter You Will Learn**

✓ How to write a cover letter to help you stand out from the crowd.

✓ The four most common cover letter errors and how to avoid them.

✓ The substance and style of an effective cover letter.

*First impressions last. That's why the cover letter is so important. It serves as your first introduction to a potential employer.*

—Career counselor

*From the moment I read the cover letter, I had a feeling she was the right person for the job. The credentials she explained in the cover letter were exactly what we were looking for.*

—School principal

Think of yourself sitting in your favorite movie theater. In short order, the lights dim, the screen is revealed, and you are suddenly engrossed in a riveting, well-produced, and brief "coming attraction" that whets your appetite to see a new film.

That's what a good cover letter does: It entices the recipient to give your resume a thorough read by planting seeds of interest. Like a trailer (the technical name for the movie advertisements that precede the main feature), an effective cover letter contains the following essential elements:

• It advertises the product (you) by grabbing and holding the reader's interest.

• It's brief—only one page long.

- It maintains a crisp pace, making its points in an attention-getting manner using vivid language.
- It is well edited—every word, every sentence, and every paragraph has a distinct purpose.
- It convinces the reader to take the next essential step—reading your resume.

Remember that your cover letter, like your resume, represents you to people whom you've never met before. As a result, it plays a vital role in forming that all-important first impression.

To help you understand the principles of effective cover letter writing, it's important to understand the harried lives of school administrators who read thousands of these letters every year.

Our school day is incredibly busy, beginning in the early morning before the school doors open and often ending late in the evening after a PTA or Board of Education meeting. We rarely have time to eat a proper lunch (we normally grab a sandwich on the go), let alone read stacks of cover letters and resumes. When there are vacancies to fill, we collect the cover letters and resumes in file folders or boxes and take them home to read away from the hubbub of school. How many do we carry home? If there's a large pile, we empty a box the size of a milk crate and fill it with hundreds of cover letters and resumes. If there are only three or four dozen, we put the stack into an accordian file.

An observer would describe our reading of cover letters as efficient because it takes only a minute to skim each one and place it in either the "Consider" pile or the "Reject" pile. After reading tens of thousands of cover letters in our careers, we can readily spot the information we are seeking. As a cover letter writer, your job is to quickly sell your candidacy.

## Cover Letter Errors

Cover letters do two things: They can switch the reader's interest light on, or they can switch it off. There are four common cover letter errors that cause school administrators to dismiss job candidates. We call them *Having Nothing to Say, They All Look Alike, I Need This Job,* and *Words Speak Louder than Actions.*

### Cover Letter Error #1: *Having Nothing to Say*

What does the cover letter at the top of page 57 tell us about the candidate? If you said, "Nothing," you're right. The applicant demonstrates no personality, viewpoint, purpose, or achievements worth citing. Application procedures generally restrict a description of the candidate's qualifications to two 8 1/2- by 11-inch pieces of paper: a cover letter and a resume. *Having Nothing to Say* wastes half of the allotted space. It serves merely as a cover sheet.

### Cover Letter Error #2: *They All Look Alike*

Candidates making this type of error fail to stand out from the crowd because the cover letter only refers to commonplace qualifications. As you read the second cover letter on page 57, ask yourself whether the applicant has anything distinctive to say.

As you can see, listed items apply to countless applicants. Almost every aspiring English teacher majored in English literature, most student taught, and many worked as summer camp counselors. Even the opening sentence of the final paragraph, "I look forward to a worthwhile teaching career" is unremarkable because every candidate shares the same sentiment. After reading this letter, an administrator knows little more about a candidate than before. The letter tells

"But I don't have those qualifications," you say. While it's true that it is rare to find someone who possesses all the qualifications of the ideal candidate, we truly believe that every applicant can find some elements in her or his background that will interest the reader. In any case, every school is looking for teachers who demonstrate knowledge of their field, creativity, interest in professional growth, and a repertoire of effective teaching techniques. Examples of how you have used, or plan to use, these attributes to the best advantage are always welcome in a cover letter.

the reader *what* the candidate taught, instead of *how* the candidate worked with students. The rich details that would help the candidate come alive in the reader's imagination are nowhere to be found.

**Cover Letter Error #3:** *I Need This Job*

This cover letter asks the administrator to hire a candidate *because it will help the candidate.* Of course, the message is a little more subtle than that; we have never found an applicant so

**COVER LETTER ERROR #1: HAVING NOTHING TO SAY**

March 3, 2003

Dear Administrator:

I am very interested in applying for the social studies teaching position available in your school. I look forward to hearing from you. I have attached my resume.

Thank you for your time and consideration.

Sincerely,

The Applicant

**COVER LETTER ERROR #2: THEY ALL LOOK ALIKE**

March 3, 2003

Dear Administrator:

I am pleased to apply for the English teaching position available in your school. Highlights of my qualifications include the following:

• Completed a Bachelor's degree with a major in English literature.
• Completed all student teaching requirements.
• During student teaching, planned and implemented lessons.
• Worked as a day camp counselor for five summers.

I look forward to a worthwhile teaching career. I am available at your convenience to discuss my candidacy in further detail.

Sincerely,

The Applicant

**COVER LETTER ERROR #3: I NEED THIS JOB**

March 3, 2003

Dear Administrator:

I am most pleased to enclose my resume for the position of kindergarten teacher.

I am a very dedicated person who loves working with children. Obtaining a position in your school would enable me to realize my dream of becoming an early childhood educator.

I look forward to embarking on a career that utilizes my talents. Thank you for your consideration.

Sincerely,


The Applicant

---

self-centered and crass to actually write, "I need this job." Instead these letters mention how the job will fulfill the candidate's goals, but an administrator is interested in how the candidate will meet the school's needs. See if you can detect examples of the *I Need This Job* syndrome in the sample cover letter above.

Two sentences are illustrative of *I Need This Job*. When the candidate states, "I am a dedicated person who loves working with children," and "Obtaining a position in your school will enable me to realize my dream of becoming an early childhood educator," the administrator is being asked to put the candidate's objectives first, ahead of the needs of students.

### Cover Letter Error #4: *Words Speak Louder than Actions*

Every child knows the expression, "Actions speak louder than words," but many misguided candidates reverse the concept. Compare the two cover letters on page 59 and see if you can detect the difference.

The cover letter on the right emphasizes the job seeker's deeds, impressively citing such accomplishments as **Outward Bound** training,

knowledge of fitness technology, and starting a club for student trainers. The cover letter on the left is full of fluff, relying on self-serving adjectives such as "skillful," "creative," and "energetic" to characterize the applicant. Given the choice between these two, which one do you believe is more skillful, creative, and energetic: the one who *tells* you or the one who *shows* you?

Many candidates worry about sounding boastful during the hiring process. Raised to value modesty, they feel uncomfortable about bragging, even when they are seeking to obtain their ideal job. Whether writing a cover letter or interviewing, the way to avoid braggadocio is the same. Cite your accomplishments and let them reveal your character.

## Where Do You Begin?

Cover letters and resumes have many similarities. They serve to advertise the candidate and use many of the same writing conventions. Both draw on information from your *Personal Profile* and your *Resume Reservoir*. However, the constrained length of the cover letter requires you to be extremely selective about content. The cover letter does not simply present an abbreviated

## COVER LETTER ERROR #4: WORDS SPEAK LOUDER THAN ACTIONS

March 3, 2003

Dear Administrator:

I have enclosed a resume in application for the physical education vacancy in your school.

I am a skillful, creative, and energetic teacher. I am a very hard worker, and I know that I can help children learn and grow.

I would greatly appreciate a personal interview so that I can discuss my abilities and commitment to education at greater length.

Thank you for your time and consideration.

Sincerely,


The Applicant

---

March 3, 2003

Dear Administrator:

I have enclosed a resume in application for the physical education vacancy in your school.

For the last eight years, I have held a variety of positions to prepare me to meet the demands of physical education today. For example I attended **Outward Bound** training and applied these skills one summer with inner city children. While student teaching, all my students demonstrated improvement in the fitness segment of the school's physical education standards after I taught them to use fitness analysis software. I also initiated an extracurricular student trainers club.

I would greatly appreciate a personal interview so that I can provide you with more information about my qualifications and demonstrate my commitment to education.

Sincerely,


The Applicant

---

version of your resume. Instead, it presents an interest-generating calling card that is tailored to the needs of the reader.

To design an effective cover letter, you should work from two directions. First, start with what you know best: yourself. Review your *Personal Profile* and *Resume Reservoir* to identify your strengths and achievements. You will want to highlight these areas in your letter.

Next, reread the *School Profile Form* of the school to which you are applying. If you've done your homework well, you should be able to determine qualities the school is looking for in an ideal candidate. Your job is to find where the

school's needs and your own strengths and accomplishments dovetail.

A high school with a strong college-prep program, for instance, might be pleased to know that you taught an upper-level course as a student teacher. Similarly, a middle school would be interested in a candidate who worked on an interdisciplinary team, and an elementary school screening committee might have its curiosity aroused by a teacher who has a strong background in remediation of reading deficits.

The figure on page 6, which we call *Finding Common Ground*, shows how one candidate identified points to highlight in her cover letter. In

The cover letter does not simply present an abbreviated version of your resume. Instead, it presents an interest-generating calling card that is tailored to the needs of the reader.

**FINDING COMMON GROUND (SAMPLE)**

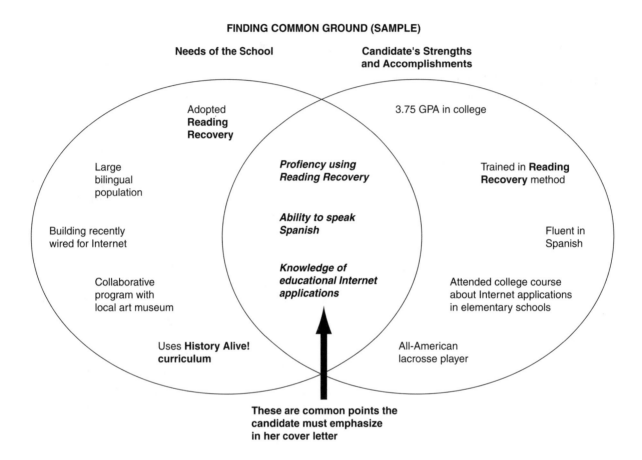

**Needs of the School**

**Candidate's Strengths and Accomplishments**

Adopted **Reading Recovery**

3.75 GPA in college

Large bilingual population

*Profiency using Reading Recovery*

Trained in **Reading Recovery** method

Building recently wired for Internet

*Ability to speak Spanish*

Fluent in Spanish

Collaborative program with local art museum

*Knowledge of educational Internet applications*

Attended college course about Internet applications in elementary schools

Uses **History Alive! curriculum**

All-American lacrosse player

**These are common points the candidate must emphasize in her cover letter**

reviewing her *Personal Profile* and *Resume Reservoir,* she recorded a few of her strengths and accomplishments, specifically her 3.75 grade point average in college, familiarity with the **Reading Recovery** method, fluency in Spanish, and Internet expertise. The *School Profile Form* revealed that the school uses Reading Recovery to raise primary literacy, features a large Latino population, developed a collaborative "Arts in Education" program with a neighborhood museum, sent teachers to a **History Alive!** workshop last summer, and was just wired with a high-speed Internet connection. Comparing the two lists, the candidate found three matching points: the school's adoption of **Reading Recovery** and her training in the same technique, the school's large bilingual population and her fluency in Spanish, and the school's interest in Internet access and her knowledge of the World Wide Web. We have provided you with a blank copy of *Finding Common Ground* on page 61.

You should complete the form before you write the first draft of your cover letter.

## Your Basic Strategy

As we noted at the beginning of the chapter, think of the cover letter as an advertisement. An effective advertisement is carefully matched to a target audience. In other words, an advertisement speaks the language of a particular audience by addressing the concerns of its members. An advertisement for you does the very same thing. In crisp fashion, it grabs the reader's attention by connecting your experience, training, and talents with the needs of the school. Obviously, your cover letter deals with some of the same items included on your resume, but only in brief. It will encourage the reader to think, "Let me find out more about that!" and then turn the page to read the accompanying resume.

**FINDING COMMON GROUND**
Duplicate as necessary

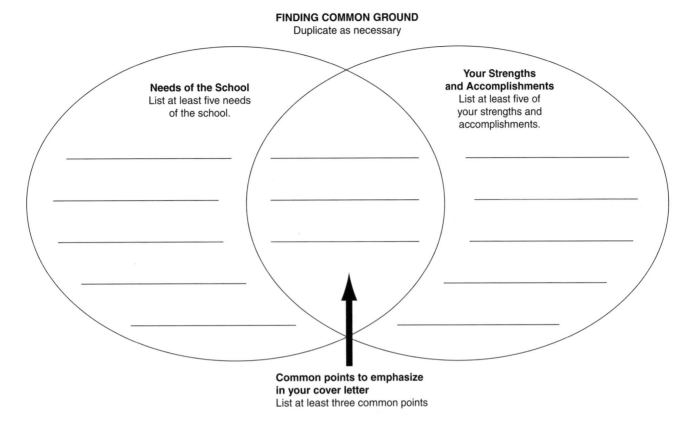

**Needs of the School**
List at least five needs
of the school.

**Your Strengths
and Accomplishments**
List at least five of
your strengths and
accomplishments.

**Common points to emphasize
in your cover letter**
List at least three common points

One final but very important note: although we suggest that you design a cover letter that follows the format we espouse, we also recognize that the letter provides an opportunity for a school administrator to glimpse your personality, that special quality that makes you who you are. To be successful, your cover letter must blend our formula with some of your own writing style and feelings to produce the genuine article. Nothing can turn a reader off more quickly than reading a mass-produced template. You have a big job ahead of you, so let's get to work.

## Cover Letter Format and Design

A cover letter is usually four paragraphs long and follows a prescribed format (see page 62 for an example).

### The Opening

Address your letter to a specific person using that person's honorific title such as Mrs., Mr., Ms., or Dr. If you are not certain whether a female administrator is married, address the letter to "Ms. So-and-so." You may be able to find the administrator's name if you search the Internet (try the directory of schools in the state education department's Web site, also listed on the author's Web site), or call the school and ask the secretary for the name of the chief administrator. If, after your best efforts, you cannot ascertain a name, we suggest you send the letter to the public school district's personnel administrator or director of human resources, the principal of a public school, or the headmaster of a private school.

### What Position Are You Seeking?

The opening paragraph is one sentence long and states the position you are seeking. After a postal worker delivers your cover letter, a secretary has to file it, along with perhaps hundreds of applications for various other vacancies received the same day. The first sentence, therefore, must state clearly the name of the position.

What if you're applying for two jobs in the same school? For example, let's say an elementary school has openings for a reading teacher and a regular classroom teacher, and you're interested in both positions. You must prepare a different cover letter and resume for each job and mail them to the

Your Street Address
Town, State, and Zip
Today's Date

} Opening (use standard business letter format)

Administrator's Name
Administrator's Title (if available)
School or District Name
Street Address
Town, State, and Zip

Dear _____: (If unknown, use "Dear Madam or Sir" not "To Whom It May Concern")

The first sentence must name the specific position for which you are applying. This is because the very first reader of your resume will probably be a secretary who needs this information to place your letter in the correct pile.

} What position are you applying for?

Begin your second paragraph with a standout sentence that accomplishes three goals: It grabs the attention of the reader, shows how you can help the school address its needs, and sets a well-written, genuine tone. Continue with a brief but effective description of your strengths and accomplishments as they relate to the needs of the school. The outline from *Finding Common Ground* is useful here. You can highlight other special skills or knowledge that sets you apart from other candidates at the end of this paragraph. If you have any special connection to the school—e.g., you are a graduate of the school or you student taught there—mention it in the first sentence of this paragraph.

} How will you meet the school's needs?

Use the third paragraph to reveal yourself more fully to the reader. You have two choices here: Candidates who are returning to the workforce after raising their families, those who are changing careers or moving from one teaching job to another, and inexperienced applicants can explain these circumstances. Alternatively, you can amplify some of your accomplishments or special talents.

} Spotlight special talents or circumstances

The fourth paragraph expresses your heartfelt commitment to teaching and to helping children. You should conclude by thanking the reader and requesting a personal interview.

Sincerely,

} Closing

Your Name

> The third paragraph of the cover letter is the place to explain special circumstances, such as inexperience, returning to teaching after a hiatus, or changing jobs.

school separately. Consequently, you can tailor the cover letters to the specific needs of each position.

## How Will You Meet the School's Needs?

In the second paragraph state your strengths and accomplishments as they relate to the needs of the school. To begin, consult the *Finding Common Ground* worksheet and identify the one overlapping feature that is most significant for the school. In other words, make your strongest point first, a strategy any salesman would endorse. Then, highlight your next one or two most relevant qualifications. Recall the common error of words speaking louder than actions. Cite accomplishments to demonstrate your most outstanding qualifications. In citing a high school course you taught, for example, tell *how* you taught the course in a superior manner, don't just list the course.

Use standout sentences written in strong, vivid language to state your best case. The sentences should command the reader's attention, show how you can connect your candidacy with the school's goals, and set a genuine, well-written tone.

If you have a noteworthy association with the school—for example, if you student taught there or you attended the school as a student—point out the connection in the first sentence of this paragraph, then follow the advice above.

Here are some powerful sentences with which to begin the second paragraph:

- My previous teaching experience in elementary classrooms, combined with reading certification, has readied me to meet the challenge of developing literacy in young children.
- Through my college's rigorous teacher preparation program, I worked with general education students and students with disabilities. As a result, I put educational theory into practice and raised the achievement of all students in the class.
- I am well prepared to contribute my knowledge of the writing process and contemporary young adult literature that I gained as an assistant editor in the children's book division of a major publishing house.

- As a student teacher in your school, I made learning relevant and created a stimulating academic environment. In my high school biology classroom, students studied human growth and development by conducting research into the causes of physical changes they saw reflected in the mirror every day.

## Spotlight Special Talents or Circumstances

You have two options in the third paragraph. On the one hand, if you have other outstanding skills or knowledge that sets you apart from other candidates, now is the time to say so. In this case, the third paragraph is really an extension of the second.

Alternatively, you can use the third paragraph to inform the reader of special circumstances. Remember, there is no such thing as the perfect candidate. Recent college graduates must overcome the hurdle posed by their lack of experience. Teachers returning to the workforce need to show they have remained current in the field. Job changers transferring to teaching from other professions must show that they are prepared for the challenges of a classroom. Teachers who are employed should explain why they are seeking new positions. Candidates graduating from **alternative certification** programs should explain their reasons for choosing a teaching career and describe their plans to achieve full licensure. Rather than ignore these real concerns, address them in the third paragraph of the cover letter.

For example, we sometimes read cover letters and resumes from promising applicants who seemingly bounced from one teaching job to the next. Without a clear explanation in the cover letter, the reader is left to imagine the cause of these puzzling circumstances. Was the teacher fired repeatedly? Laid off? Bounced from one temporary post to another? A similar problem arises when we read a resume with an unexplained gap in the candidate's career. Once again, an administrator reading the resume does not know whether the cause is parenthood, time spent finding oneself, or maybe a lengthy prison sentence!

This is an opportune time to remind you of the importance of building your resume and knowledge base. The better prepared you are, the more you have to say in your cover letter. Regardless of your special circumstances, the creditable experiences reprinted from Chapter 2 can be incorporated into a cover letter. (But not all of the experiences; remember the cover letter presents just a few highlights.)

- Take college courses
- Subscribe to professional journals
- Find a job related to education
- Volunteer at a school
- Join a professional teachers' association
- Participate in a faculty committee while you're student teaching
- Attend conferences
- Tutor in a community service agency
- Develop a job-related hobby
- Travel to interesting places
- Attend workshops offered by the school district while you student teach
- Practice with software you might use in your classroom
- Surf the Internet to find information about your field
- Take a course on the Internet
- Help sponsor an extracurricular club while student teaching
- Visit the local library to study an educational issue or a new teaching method

Administrators usually reject applicants whose cover letters don't explain special circumstances. There isn't enough time to invite all these candidates for an interview to clarify these situations, so *you* have to resolve these questions. Below we address the most common special circumstances: resuming a teaching career after a break in service, transferring from one teaching job to another, changing careers, and inexperience.

### Resuming a Teaching Career

The National Center for Education Statistics (2001) reported that twenty-three percent of newly hired teachers in a recent year consisted of former teachers returning to the classroom after a break in service. These are predominantly women resuming teaching careers after taking time off to raise their own families. We occasionally read cover letters from women who devote a lengthy paragraph to explain this and sound defensive about the whole experience. Simply say that you're resuming your teaching career in a brief and matter-of-fact sentence, because the circumstances are very commonplace.

But that is not enough. The important issue is not why the candidate took a child care leave, because most school administrators understand family concerns. The pressing question is whether a candidate returning to the workforce kept up-to-date with changes in the teaching profession. There are a number of avenues for a teacher to keep abreast of developments in the field while raising a family. You can subscribe to professional journals, attend professional development workshops or graduate-level courses, read books, or teach part-time during the school year on a paid or voluntary basis. More ideas for strengthening your background are listed in the box above. In the third paragraph of the cover letter, assuage the school administrator's concerns by describing how you kept abreast of changes in the field. A sample cover letter of a teacher returning to the workforce is included later in the chapter.

### Transferring from One Teaching Job to Another

According to the National Center for Education Statistics (2001), the largest group of newly hired teachers, thirty-two percent, moved from one public or private school to another, or from a private school to a public school, or vice versa. Teachers change jobs for a variety of reasons, some of which are explained easily and others are not. If you're relocating, say so and explain why. We recommend you do so in a simple sentence—for example:

- After getting married, I will be relocating to the Baltimore area.
- After spending the last two years in San Francisco, I plan to return home to South Florida, where I was raised.

If you accepted a series of leave replacement positions, causing you to change jobs repeatedly, explain the circumstances and remind the reader of the advantages you gained from your exposure to several schools. For example:

- From 2000 to 2002, I held a series of mathematics leave replacement positions, enabling me to learn from each school's pedagogical strengths. One school, for example, had implemented portfolio assessments, while another used a wealth of instructional technology, from graphing calculators to computer software.
- From 2000 to 2003, I held a variety of leave replacement positions in elementary classrooms. These opportunities made me a better teacher because I was exposed to the scope of the elementary curriculum from kindergarten through fourth grade.

Often there is an economic reason underlying a job change. Many teachers, for example, transfer from private schools to public schools or from low-paying public schools to ones located in more affluent districts. If you write, "I want to increase my income," you risk sounding mercenary. If you criticize your current school, you break one of the cardinal rules of the hiring process and sound like a complainer. The adage, "Discretion is the better part of valor," applies here. Most school administrators understand why you're making the move, so simply tip your cap to your current employer and say that you welcome new challenges. Here's an example: "Although I have found my tenure in my present school to be rewarding, I am ready to seek new challenges in a different school district." We recommend teachers seeking employment in another district use this line even if they are changing jobs because of philosophical differences or a problematic supervisor, assuming the teacher is not being fired.

What if you were fired from your previous teaching job or you resigned? In general, we recommend that you not mention the details. Try to turn the negative into an attribute that enhances your qualifications. For example: "As a result of the challenging experiences I encountered at the school, I developed valuable strategies for working with students who have reading and writing deficits. I am now skilled in techniques for raising literacy levels."

*Career Changers*

According to the National Center for Education Statistics (2001), eighteen percent of newly hired teachers in a recent year were changing careers. Candidates know they must explain why they are seeking a career change, but ability to transfer skills is a more critical issue. Career changers must use the cover letter to explain how their former careers will help them become better teachers. In Chapter 1, we mentioned former Grumman engineers who applied for mathematics and science teaching positions when the company's Long Island plant closed in the early 1990s. Seth hired two former accountants as mathematics teachers and a science laboratory supervisor to teach science. These comparisons are somewhat straightforward. What if you were in the military, a paint contractor, or owned a stationery store? You can use the list of creditable experiences in the box on the previous page to expand your credentials.

If you're a career changer, your task in the third paragraph is two-fold: First, briefly explain the career change. You should demonstrate that you are not a Johnny-come-lately to education; you've been considering the transition for some time. Maintain a positive tone; don't sound like a disgruntled employee because it makes a school administrator wonder whether you'll also be unhappy with your new career. Your second task in the cover letter is to demonstrate a relationship between your previous career and teaching. The point is to demonstrate that you are a well-prepared applicant and your desire to change careers is not just whimsy.

Here are some models to consider:

- As an accountant for the last decade, I noticed that my favorite part of the day occurred when I explained complicated tax law to clients in an understandable manner. If I can help people make sense of the IRS code, I realized, I should teach. I joined my agency's "Accountants in Action" program, volunteering as a mathematics tutor in a local high school during lunch breaks. My accounting background enabled me to teach mathematics applications, and I enjoyed interactions with students and parents much more than with former clients and co-workers on April 15!
- After graduating from college with a history major, I moved home and helped run a

family-owned business. Realizing that I wanted to pursue my dream of becoming a high school social studies teacher, I trained an employee to take over my role in the family business and began taking education classes at night. My experience in a family business was beneficial as I launched my teaching career because I had developed excellent listening skills in our customer-friendly store. I was able to create a simulated store in my high school economics class during student teaching. I also volunteered to share my expertise as co-sponsor of Junior Achievement.

- The military provided a wonderful training ground to prepare me for a teaching career. As an officer, my responsibilities included training recruits, preparing presentations for superior officers, and initiating an interactive Web site to keep soldiers in touch with their families.

### Recent College Graduate

If you're a recent college graduate, your classroom teaching experience may be limited to student teaching, but that doesn't mean you lack qualifications of interest to many schools. Check the list of creditable experiences on page 64. See if you can identify activities that strengthen your candidacy. And remember, you can start today to gain these experiences and enhance your background. A National Center for Education Statistics study (2001) calculated that twenty-seven percent of all newly hired teachers recently graduated from college, the second largest category of new hires.

### Alternative Certification Candidate

The primary concern of administrators considering **alternative certification** candidates is whether they are adequately prepared for the rigors of day-to-day life in the classroom. Candidates in this category must demonstrate they are knowledgeable about content areas and classroom practices, even if they did not have the benefit of student teaching or traditional coursework in pedagogy. One option is to highlight subject area expertise, or to provide a rich summary of what was learned through any field experiences. A heartwarming explanation of why the prospective teacher chose the **alternative certification** program usually adds interest to the cover letter. Finally, candidates must indicate a surefire plan

to achieve full certification in order to show administrators that they have made a long-term commitment to teaching.

### The Closing

The closing paragraph must be brief. You should have stated your most pertinent points in the second and third paragraphs. We've told you to focus on demonstrable strengths and accomplishments in your cover letter, but the closing paragraph is an exception. We advise candidates to begin the paragraph with a heartfelt statement about their dedication to teaching or their classroom goals. The final sentence of the paragraph should reiterate your desire to hear from the potential employer. Here are some effective examples:

- In summary, my experience as a teacher, my education, and my previous career have prepared me to create an enriching environment for children. I look forward to hearing from you at your earliest convenience.
- I believe that the abovementioned qualifications demonstrate my skills, achievements, and enthusiasm for teaching. Please do not hesitate to contact me so that we can discuss my candidacy at greater length.

### The Don'ts

Throughout the hiring process, we often recommend that candidates be creative and modify our system somewhat if these variations express individuality and help the candidates to stand out from the crowd. When it comes to cover letter format and design, however, certain rules cannot be broken, or your cover letter will go into the reject pile immediately.

Don't use friendly letter format. Follow proper business letter format as we demonstrate in our sample cover letters. Failure to conform to business letter conventions indicates carelessness or a substandard education, which probably will disqualify you.

Don't make any spelling or grammatical errors. Once again, a single error indicates a poor education or carelessness. Administrators reason that prospective teachers who make these mistakes in a cover letter will commit even more errors when they correspond with parents or write on a chalkboard. You can't trust your computer's spell checker because it cannot distinguish among homophones (such as they're, their, and there). One of the worst spelling errors we've seen was from the candidate who applied to Seth's school to be a school *psychiligist!* Another applicant misspelled the name of his hometown.

Do not use contractions. Remember your English teacher's advice to shun contractions in business-style letters. A cover letter is a formal correspondence between unfamiliar people, one of whom holds a position of authority. Contractions are considered inappropriately casual.

Don't exceed one page or use a font smaller than twelve points. Leave plenty of white space in each margin. Remember, the administrator reading your cover letter may not have 20/20 vision and may have to read hundreds of cover letters. A cluttered layout is unappealing.

Don't be gimmicky. Attention-getting devices usually cause the opposite of the intended effect. We've seen popular song lyrics, designs resembling greeting cards or highway billboards, self-portraits, and even a dollar bill clipped to a cover letter. These gimmicky techniques demonstrate poor taste.

Don't use colored paper. Use the same white or ivory paper that you use to print your resume. Your cover letter and resume may be photocopied repeatedly and distributed to interview committee members or to a number of school officials. Neutral colors duplicate best.

If you are e-mailing your cover letter and resume, don't send them as separate documents, as they may be separated when printed in the recipient's office. Instead, send them together in one attachment, separated by a page break.

## Standout Sentences

A cover letter must match the candidate's abilities to the school's needs, and do so convincingly. You have a maximum of one page, maybe twenty sentences, to make your point. In an effective

## 100 Power Verbs

As a rule of thumb, you should not repeat any verb in your cover letter. Choose from the list of 100 power verbs below the right word to fit each sentence. You can use the list when you write your resume, too.

| | | | |
|---|---|---|---|
| acquired | designed | gained | prepared |
| adapted | developed | generated | presented |
| advocated | devised | guided | produced |
| aided | directed | handled | promoted |
| analyzed | discovered | helped | provided |
| arranged | documented | identified | publicized |
| assessed | educated | implemented | published |
| assisted | eliminated | improved | raised |
| attained | enabled | increased | recorded |
| attended | enriched | initiated | reduced |
| authored | ensured | instilled | reinforced |
| awarded | envisioned | instituted | reorganized |
| chaired | established | instructed | reported |
| collaborated | evaluated | introduced | researched |
| compiled | examined | led | revamped |
| composed | exceeded | maintained | revitalized |
| conceived | executed | managed | solicited |
| conducted | expanded | mastered | spearheaded |
| consulted | explained | mentored | started |
| contributed | facilitated | moderated | strengthened |
| coordinated | familiarized | organized | supervised |
| counseled | formed | originated | supported |
| created | formulated | oversaw | trained |
| decreased | fostered | pioneered | tutored |
| demonstrated | founded | planned | wrote |

cover letter, every word of every sentence must be calculated to reach the target audience in a powerful, vivid manner. Consider these contrasting sentences and see if you can detect the differences:

• I student taught four ninth-grade U.S. history classes and one Advanced Placement class.
• I enjoyed the variety of challenges during student teaching, from making history come alive for freshmen to the demands of successfully preparing Advanced Placement students to earn college credit on placement examinations.

Both of these sentences say that the candidate student taught a variety of courses, but the second sets the applicant apart from the crowd through the use of more compelling language. References to "the variety of challenges," "making history come alive," and the "demands of successfully preparing students" breathe life into the language.

• In my present teaching position, I teach fourth-grade mathematics.
• In my present fourth-grade classroom, I implemented an innovative mathematics curriculum making use of re-writable CD-ROMS to help each student create electronic portfolios.

In this example, the terms "innovative" and "create" and the specific reference to "re-writable CD-ROMS" and "electronic portfolios" stimulate interest. An effective standout sentence uses verbs, adverbs, and adjectives to heighten its impact. A thesaurus is a useful tool for finding the exact word you need to describe an action or achievement. We've also supplied a list of *100 Power Verbs* (see the box on page 67) to help you. Use these verbs in the active voice only and generally use the past tense (for example, "initiated" rather than "have initiated").

Here is some parting advice before you write the first draft of your cover letter:

• Give yourself plenty of time to write. Rushing leads to poor quality; mistakes in the cover letter can lead to quick rejection.

• Do not start a sentence with the phrase, "I attempted to . . . ," because it implies that you failed to achieve the desired results. For example, instead of writing, "I attempted to implement the NCTM standards," simply say, "I implemented the NCTM standards."
• Don't start every sentence with the word, "I"; it sounds egocentric.
• As a rule of thumb, don't use more than fifteen words in any sentence. Keep your sentences and paragraphs short, readable, and to the point.
• All achievements cited in your cover letter must also appear in your resume. Administrators attempting to cross-reference these two documents become frustrated if they read, for example, about a candidate volunteering to be a Big Brother and cannot find the activity cited in the accompanying resume.
• Jargon is acceptable to demonstrate your familiarity with established curricula and pedagogical methods. (Once you get a teaching job and have to write letters to parents, avoid jargon, but a cover letter must demonstrate that you are conversant with the nomenclature of education.) Be certain that the terms you use are widely known, as in **"Title I."** Of course, don't follow this advice to the extreme and use jargon excessively, because you'll sound pretentious.
• Proofread, proofread, proofread. Walk away for a while, then proofread again for spelling, grammar, and format and to see whether the letter achieves the effect you want. Ask your *Job Find Friend* to proofread, also.
• Print the cover letter on a laser jet or an ink jet printer with the print properties set to "high quality." Use black ink only.

Feel confident as you begin this process; this will translate into a powerful letter. We've included some model cover letters on the following pages for you to study. An effective cover letter causes the reader to turn the page and scan your resume—the two together are probably the most important pieces of paper in your professional life.

**RECENT COLLEGE GRADUATE**

1 Pumpkin Lane
Cinderella, California 90019
Today's Date

Mr. M. Y. Prince
Director of Human Resources
The Castle School District
Monarchy, California 90022

Dear Mr. Prince:

I am interested in applying for the elementary teaching position that is available in your school.

In addition to completing an undergraduate degree this year, I served as a tutor in an after-school center, and devoted evenings every weekend volunteering for a crisis hotline. During student teaching, I applied my psychology degree to meet the needs of all students. I formed cooperative learning groups, organized individualized projects, created learning centers, and implemented learning style research in every lesson. Alternative assessment methods, such as portfolios, rubrics, and performance assessments, in combination with traditional tests, enabled me to evaluate children individually and comprehensively. In my tutoring position, I met regularly with teachers and parents to ensure that I was preparing students for the curriculum in their classroom.

Classroom computers presented unique opportunities to help each child achieve success. In a staff development workshop I attended called *Problem-Based Learning,* I learned to pose open-ended questions that children could research over the internet. In addition, I have studied and continue to monitor the plethora of educational software and Web sites that address the diverse abilities and interests of children.

I found the most rewarding parts of teaching derive from the nurturing relationships I forged with every child and the sense of confidence they felt as they experienced success and growth in my classroom. I look forward to meeting you to learn more about your school and to discuss how my skills can meet the needs of your students.

Sincerely,

Henry Hireme

**TEACHER CHANGING SCHOOLS**

1 Forest Drive
White Snow, California 90909
Today's Date

Dr. S. Neezy
Director of Human Resources
Prince Public Schools
27 Mirror Lane
Legend, California 90022

Dear Dr. Neezy:

I am most pleased to enclose my resume to apply for the position of social studies teacher at Legend High School.

My work during the past four years at Visionary Academy, an independent school, has enabled me to develop teaching skills and strategies needed to implement the state's new standards-based curriculum successfully. For example, I designed several curriculum units that integrated English language arts, music, and art to raise levels of student motivation and produce lasting learning. Under my direction, students also created digital portfolios that documented their progress toward standards and used the latest advances in instructional technology. In addition, my proposal for establishing the school's first history magazine received a mini-grant from the Visionary Foundation.

As a lifelong learner, I have continued to seek professional growth at every opportunity. In this regard, I established a very successful tutoring program for children with special needs at my local community center. Similarly, I recently completed graduate coursework designed to enrich my background in reading in the content area. I also devoted the past summer to building a collection of primary source materials that can be used in high school classes.

I am thoroughly convinced that teachers shape the future. My commitment to my students is evident in the long hours I devote to helping them and the outstanding work they produce. Thank you for your time and consideration. I look forward to discussing my candidacy at greater length in a personal interview.

Sincerely,

Drew Pey

**RETURN TO TEACHING**

1 Schoolhouse Street
Learning, Louisiana 00001
Today's Date


Dr. Marty Gras
Director of Personnel
Delta Public Schools
14 Cajun Circle
New Bayou, Virginia 00002

Dear Dr. Gras:

In response to your advertisement for a teacher with combined special education and remedial reading responsibilities, I have submitted a copy of my resume and teaching license.

For ten years, I used my dual degrees in reading and special education in elementary through high school classrooms. I designed an emerging literacy program still used in the Dick and Jane School District, and taught reading across the curriculum strategies to the faculty of the middle school and high school. Supervisors reported that I raised test scores and promoted a love of reading. Years before inclusion became a buzzword, I informally placed special needs children in mainstream classes and provided general education teachers with a variety of supports through co-teaching, consulting, and adapting materials.

When I left the classroom to be a full-time parent, I understood that the field of special education changes constantly. I prepared to resume my career by returning to college as a non-matriculated student and by writing software reviews for a professional journal. I also started a program for disabled learners in a religious school.

As the enclosed resume attests, I have much to offer your school, including extensive experience and an impressive set of accomplishments. Above all, I am dedicated to teaching and totally committed to the success of every student in my class. I look forward to discussing how my unique and diverse background can advance your school's educational goals.

Sincerely,


Paige Meenow

**CAREER CHANGER**

47 New Clear Drive
Brookhaven, New York 10101
Today's Date


Dr. Ian Stein
Science Department Chairman
Relativity High School
22 Proton Way
Iona, New York 01010

Dear Dr. Stein:

In response to your advertisement in *The New York Times* for a physics teacher, I am submitting a copy of my resume for your consideration.

I believe that I have much to offer the students at Relativity High School. A graduate of Oppenheimer University, I am certified to teach physics, chemistry, and biology. As a student teacher at Quantum High School, I was indeed fortunate to work with the advisor to the Science Research Program. During the course of the year, I developed a rubric for scoring research presentations and participated in a faculty committee that created a new core curriculum for students preparing to enter the "Science Scholar" competition. In addition, I designed numerous hands-on laboratory experiences that addressed such topics as ionization, acceleration due to gravity, and the scientific method. I also volunteered to serve as assistant coach of the junior varsity field hockey team.

I owned a store in my "former life," but I found the work unexciting compared to teaching. Through my retail sales and management experience, I understand the importance of motivation and possess excellent listening skills, two characteristics that earned me "Manager of the Year" recognition from the regional office of the national chain. I participated in my company's "Seeds of Learning" program, volunteering each week as a teacher's assistant in a local public school. I was assigned to provide remedial instruction in the computer laboratory to students who could not afford a computer at home.

From my first day of student teaching, I realized that I had made the right career move. I am confident that my skills will help students at Relativity High School reach high levels of achievement while nurturing them at a critical stage of their lives. I would be happy to meet with you to discuss my qualifications in greater detail.

Sincerely,


Molly Cule

## REMINDERS

Think of the cover letter as a promotional advertisement for your candidacy. The goal of the cover letter is to lead the reader seamlessly, almost effortlessly, to your resume.

Most cover letters get only a minute or two of consideration, so you must make sure that you grab the reader's interest immediately. Make your points quickly and clearly.

The best cover letters show how your qualifications match the needs of the school.

To the maximum extent possible, focus attention on your achievements, not your personal characteristics.

Appearances count! Pay attention to format! Proofread! Then proofread again!

# Chapter Six

# Your Resume

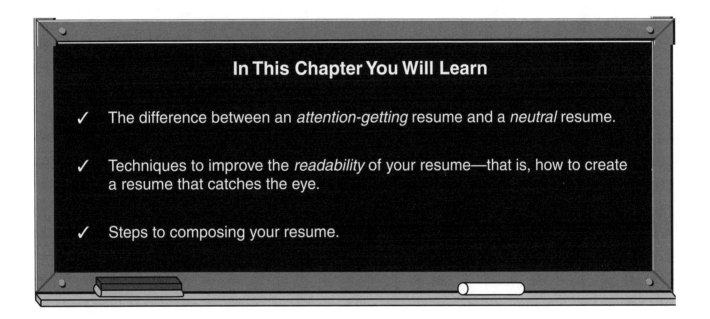

**In This Chapter You Will Learn**

✓   The difference between an *attention-getting* resume and a *neutral* resume.

✓   Techniques to improve the *readability* of your resume—that is, how to create a resume that catches the eye.

✓   Steps to composing your resume.

*The resume sells the candidate. You can't get an interview unless you have a good resume.*

—School principal

At this point, you've studied the particular needs of the school to which you are applying, and you've identified the education, work experiences, and achievements you have to offer. Your cover letter has highlighted your most outstanding qualifications for the position and emphasized that you are ideally suited to meet the school's needs.

An *attention-getting* resume will convince an administrator to invite you to the next step in the hiring process . . . the all-important interview. Evaluating the effectiveness of your resume is simple. If you receive a call to arrange an interview, then you provided information that whetted the school's appetite.

In preparing your resume, you must continue to follow the four basic principles of this book.

## Doing Your Homework

Your resume must address the distinctive circumstances of each school. Having used the research methods recommended in Chapter 4, you understand the unique needs of each school and revise your resume accordingly. Remember that the reader does not know you, so judgments about your professional abilities will be made solely on the basis of how well you prepared your resume.

## Build Your Resume and Knowledge Base

Your resume is a work in progress. As you build your knowledge base and gain teaching-related experience, revise your resume to reflect your new and improved qualifications.

## Be Yourself

Other candidates may have enrolled in similar college courses, student taught in similar settings for an equivalent length of time, and have work experiences not unlike your own. The challenge of a resume is to communicate the reason why you are a special candidate, within the standard editorial constraints explained below. Competition for the best teaching jobs is intense. If your resume is similar to your competition's, it's more likely to be rejected. The ten successful candidates who are granted interviews will have submitted resumes that make them stand out from the crowd.

## Target Your Strengths to the School's Needs

An attention-getting resume must reflect what you've learned about the school and make the administrator think, "This is exactly the candidate I've been looking for!" Let's examine how this works. Suppose you're applying for a middle school social studies position. Your research unearths facts about the school itemized on the left side of the chart below, the school's profile. Next, the right-hand side shows how you can address this information in your resume.

Read and compare Anita Job's and Wanda Work's resumes on page 77. Which do you prefer? Why?

Both resumes have similarities—the same margins, font size, headings, and other format features. The two candidates have identical educational backgrounds and work experience. We've shown these sample resumes to workshop participants, and the audiences are always unanimous in agreeing that Anita Job's resume is better. *Yet, most resumes we receive are more like Wanda's than Anita's.*

| School Profile | How These Points Can Be Addressed in a Resume |
|---|---|
| Census data demonstrate that this is a multicultural community in which diverse ethnic groups are represented. | Identify courses you have taken or lessons you have planned that promote multicultural understanding. You can learn more at the library or on the Internet. |
| The average reading level of students in this school, according to state education department data, is below grade level. | Refer to your knowledge of strategies for reading across the curriculum. You can also cite interdisciplinary lessons you planned during student teaching that required students to read historical novels. |
| The existence of teams and an advisory program implies that the school expounds a middle school philosophy. | Emphasize how your classroom would respond to the unique cognitive, emotional, social, and physical needs of young adolescents. |
| A new statewide proficiency test requires students to answer **document-based questions.** | Demonstrate how you have prepared students to interpret original source material or cite courses you have taken that provide training in this area. |

# WANDA WORK
12 Urban Avenue
High Rise, Virginia 10101
(098)765-4321

**EDUCATION**
Mortarboard and Robes College
Bachelor of Arts, 2003
Psychology Major, Education Minor
G.P.A. 3.86

Elementary Teacher Certification, Virginia Dept.
of Education

**TEACHING EXPERIENCE**
Student Teacher, Feb–May 2003
Warm N. Fuzzy School; Gleeful Glen, Virginia
*Taught grades 1 and 5. Planned lessons.*
*Prepared bulletin board displays.*

Camp Counselor, NASA Space Camp,
Liftoff, Texas
Summers 2000–2002
*Assigned to 12-year-olds' division*

Remedial Tutor, 2001–2003
Adam Upp Middle School; Sunnyville, Virginia
*Assisted 13-year-old students in mathematics.*

**RELATED EXPERIENCE**
J.V. Lacrosse Assistant Coach, April–June, 2001
Reed N. Rite High School, Virginia

HelpLine Counselor, 1999–2001
Crescent County Suicide Prevention

**INTERESTS**
Varsity Lacrosse 2000–2003

# ANITA JOB
11 Suburban Street
Happy Homes, Virginia 01010
(123)456-7890

**EDUCATION**
Mortarboard and Robes College
Bachelor of Arts, 2003
Psychology Major, Education Minor
G.P.A. 3.86

Elementary Teacher Certification, Virginia Dept.
of Education

**TEACHING EXPERIENCE**
Student Teacher, Feb–May, 2003
Warm N. Fuzzy School; Gleeful Glen, Virginia;
Grades 1 and 5.
*Emphasized hands-on, discovery learning in all*
*curriculum areas, Created classroom computer*
*center, Used rubrics and portfolios to assess*
*language arts progress.*

Camp Counselor, Summers 2000–2002
NASA Space Camp; Liftoff, Texas
*Helped students design experiments to be*
*considered for inclusion on actual Space Shuttle*
*missions. Supervised lunar module lab. Head*
*counselor for 12-year-old girls.*

Math Tutor, Part-time 2001–2003
Adam Upp Middle School; Sunnyville, Virginia
*Volunteered weekly in after-school program*
*designed to sustain girls' interest in*
*mathematics.*

**RELATED EXPERIENCE**
Assistant Coach, J.V. Lacrosse,
April–June, 2001
Reed N. Rite High School, Virginia
*Began Volunteer coaching during student*
*teaching and continued until season ended.*

HelpLine Counselor, Part-time 1999–2001
Crescent County Suicide prevention
*Undertook two-week training course. Assumed*
*weekend shifts on alternating weekends.*

**INTERESTS**
Varsity Lacrosse 2000–2003

We call Wanda's version a *neutral resume,* while Anita's is an *attention-getting resume.* The neutral resume fails to make the candidate stand out from the crowd. For example, Wanda says that she "prepared lesson plans" when she student taught. But all teachers write lesson plans, so this doesn't say anything unique about her. She also listed courses she instructed while student teaching, but every student teacher in the state probably taught similar ones because the curriculum is prescribed by the education department.

Why would an administrator want to hire Wanda? Her resume doesn't supply any extraordinary reason, while Anita's resume cites numerous superior qualifications. As you write your resume, heed our warning to avoid the dreaded neutral resume.

## Appearances Count

*Readable* should be the key word to describe how your resume looks. Remember, your resume will be placed on a pile with perhaps hundreds of resumes written by similarly qualified candidates. According to career placement studies, the average resume receives just sixty to ninety seconds of attention before going into a "yes" or "no" pile. A readable resume allows the administrator to ascertain the main points at a glance.

*Consistency* is another important attribute of a visually appealing resume. A resume reflects the candidate, and few resume flaws make you look more unprofessional than changing the format midstream. All design features, including section headings, font style and size, boldface, italics, and margins, should be standardized. Your *Job Find Friend* can help you detect inconsistencies.

On the following pages, we recommend rules for designing your resume. Bear in mind that for every rule a career counselor can state, valid exceptions are permissible. For example, Seth hired an art teacher who masterfully violated the prohibition against using borders, clip art, and scanned images. A tasteful Etruscan border and thumbnail images of student artwork demonstrated amazing graphic design expertise that seemed ideally suited to the school's emphasis on computer skills. So the rule is . . . you *can* break the rules once in a while as long as it serves a worthwhile purpose.

### Word Processor or Typewriter?

Resumes typed with a word processor demonstrate that the candidate is computer literate and has the potential to create lessons using the latest educational technology in the classroom. For this reason, we automatically reject the rare candidates who submit typewritten resumes.

### Paper Color

The traditional white and ivory are the only acceptable colors. Other colors are often considered gaudy and do not duplicate well.

### White Space

In the desktop publishing field, white space refers to unused, blank space on a page. White space enhances the readability of a document in two ways. First, it relieves eyestrain by providing a visual break from the text. Second, white space tends to highlight the text that it surrounds. But white space is like rain in springtime . . . you don't want to have too little . . . or too much. Excessive white space, caused by large margins and hanging indents, indicates that you don't have much to say.

### Margins

The standard rule is to maintain one-inch margins on the top, bottom, and sides. However, you can "sneak" smaller margins if it enables you to keep your resume to one page. A half-inch bottom margin or a 3/4-inch right-hand margin is barely noticeable. No one carries a ruler while reading resumes, so you can take liberties with margin sizes as long as the page doesn't look cluttered. To save space, every line in your resume must be left or full justified.

### Font Selection

The font should be 12 points and easy to read, like Times New Roman. Three exceptions are permissible to the 12-point font rule:

- For emphasis, your name can be printed in a larger font size up to a maximum of 24 points.
- You can increase font size to highlight section headings, up to 18 points.

- Detailed descriptions of each job you held can be written with a smaller font, but no smaller than 10 points, if you need to conserve space. Note that 12 points is still preferable for these job descriptions, and there must be plenty of white space elsewhere on the page to avoid an overcrowded look.

Boldface type can be used to emphasize your name, section headings, job titles, and other features. Be consistent. If one job title is typed in boldface, then the same style must be applied to all job titles. Underlining is considered too old-fashioned since the advent of word processors. Italics are acceptable if applied consistently. For desktop publishing experts, recommended fonts are generally serif type, characterized by small strokes at the ends of each letter.

Avoid fonts that are decorative, pompous, or difficult to read. The box below contains some examples.

## Length

Resume writing is more an art than a science. Just as some art critics prefer Andy Warhol to Botticelli, the authors of this book disagree about resume length. Rob feels that a two-page resume is acceptable when you have many relevant achievements and skills to list. Seth maintains that the space limitations of a one-page resume require the candidate to edit more carefully and, consequently, write a more powerful resume. We'll leave this decision to you and your *Job Find Friend*.

## Bulleted Lists

Bulleted lists allow you to present detailed information and increase white space at the same time. The bullets themselves should be dignified diamonds, squares, or other geometric shapes. Checkmarks, pointing hands, and other symbols are too informal and showy. Sometimes candidates can type a bulleted list in two columns to conserve space. For example, you can list your collegiate extracurricular activities as shown below.

## Other Design Don'ts

Unless you have an extraordinarily good reason, such as the art teacher mentioned previously, don't use graphics such as clip art, scanned images, or borders. These features are considered frivolous and distract the reader from the

---

Times New Roman is the most popular font style for resumes.

Century Schoolbook is another highly readable, crisp-looking font.

Book Antiqua is another distinguished-looking and popular font.

---

*Cursive fonts, such as Brush Script, are difficult to read.*

**A resume is no place to make a fashion statement using decorative fonts, such as Britannic Bold.**

`Since Courier appears to have been printed using an old manual typewriter, it implies you are not computer literate.`

---

- Choral Society 1997–2001
- College Newspaper 1999–2001
- Dorm Advisor 2001

- Varsity Soccer 1999–2001
- Captain, Varsity Soccer 2000
- All-American Soccer 2001

---

**Space Savers**

Your resume is one page long . . . *plus* two lines. Here are some ways to eliminate a few lines and keep your resume to one page.

- Inconspicuously reduce margins to less than one inch.
- Although commonplace in a business resume, teachers can eliminate a job objective section because the purpose is obvious in the education profession.
- A list of references is premature on a resume unless it is requested. Instead, prepare a one-page directory of your references and hand it to the employer at the conclusion of the interview. The statement, "References available upon request" is also unnecessary.
- Two-column format is permissible when listing certain brief items such as workshops attended or honors earned.
- Learn to use your word processor's line spacing tool to condense the length of your resume. Spacing between section headings can be reduced to 1.5 lines and still separate different sections.
- Wordy descriptions waste space.
- Abbreviations, another space saver, are acceptable if not overused. Contractions are never acceptable.
- Eliminate hanging indents.

---

candidate's serious qualifications. Never attach a photograph of yourself.

## Your Resume Step by Step

### Your Name

Center your name along the top margin, highlight it with boldface type, and use a font size up to 24 points. Do not use Mr., Ms., Mrs., or Miss immediately before your name or academic titles such as B.A. or M.A. immediately after it. If you have a doctorate, you can use the title Dr., Ed.D., or Ph.D. It is acceptable to write your entire name in capital letters. Use the formal version of your name. (Robert or Elizabeth is preferable to Bob or Liz). Women should use the legal version of their name in any form (Smith, Smith-Jones, and Smith Jones are all acceptable). The appropriate occasion to introduce your nickname is at the beginning of an interview. One exception: If you commonly use an Americanized nickname, the interviewer will be able to address you without hesitation if you place a nickname you prefer in parentheses, for example, Sung (Susan) Kim.

### Where You Can Be Contacted

Revert to 12-point type when writing your street address, telephone number, and e-mail address. Be certain to note your permanent address if you plan to move shortly. Include your e-mail address to demonstrate that you are computer literate and write your fax number if you have one. The

address and phone number should be centered below your name. Include your cell phone only if it is your primary phone. Abbreviations of such common terms as street and apartment and the names of the fifty states are permissible.

### Job Objective

Books about business resumes recommend that you include a section in which you state your job objective. In education, this section is unnecessary and wastes valuable space. Why? Job objectives are helpful if you're applying to a company that has an array of jobs for which you might be suited. Teacher candidates are generally qualified to hold only one job in a school, and the cover letter already states the specific job for which you are applying. We consider this section a waste of space and recommend that you eliminate it. If a job counselor insists that you write a Job Objective, cite one based on the needs of the particular school as determined by your research. (For example, "To secure a position as an elementary school reading specialist using **Reading Recovery** and other techniques.") The objective must refer to the school's needs, not your own.

### Education

The Education section tells the reader how your education has prepared you for a teaching position. The section must list the names of colleges or universities from which you earned degrees, the year in which each degree was conferred, and

---

**Basic Format for Education Section**
(Notice the use of two columns as a space-saving device.)
**EDUCATION**
**Teachers University,** New York, NY                    Master of Arts, 2003
Major: Curriculum and Teaching                          GPA: 3.66

**Lerner College,** Chalktown, CT                        Bachelor of Arts, 1998
Major: Biology                                          Dean's List all semesters

---

**Enhanced Format for Education Section**
(Notice the inclusion of Extracurricular Activities and Relevant Courses.)
**EDUCATION**
**Lerner College,** Chalktown, CT                        Bachelor of Arts, 2003
Major: Chemistry                                        Minor: Biology
National Honor Society                                  Nouveau Rochelle Scholarship Recipient

Relevant Courses:
*Using the Internet in the Foreign Language Classroom*
*Interdisciplinary Studies in Secondary Classrooms*
*Including Special Education Children in the Mainstream Classroom*
*Study abroad at La Sorbonne for one year*

Extracurricular Activities:
*Chord'n Blues (College Choir)*                          *Captain, Girls' Varsity Lacrosse Team*

---

your major field of study. The section can also list such academic honors as GPA (if it exceeds 3.5) and Dean's List. Citations should be listed in reverse chronological order, with the most recently attended school on top.

If you have limited experience, you can use the opportunity presented in the Education section either to list courses that are applicable to the school's needs or to cite exceptional extracurricular activities. You may list such extracurricular activities in this section as clubs, music, or sports, especially if you played a leadership role. If the extracurricular activity involves teaching or counseling, save it for the Teaching Experience or Professional Experience section.

Some mature candidates omit the year they graduated from college. We've encountered this many times and consider it to be counterproductive. Withholding information normally included in a resume makes a candidate appear to be dishonest.

### Certification

Unique to teacher resumes, the certification section documents that you meet eligibility requirements. We recommend that you cite your certifications even if you are applying for a private school job. Two alternatives to the standard format are noteworthy. First, if you have completed requirements for certification and submitted the paperwork to your state education department, write "pending" next to the title of the certificate. Second, you can conserve space by omitting the certification section entirely if the advertisement for the position asks you to attach a copy of your certificate.

### Teaching Experience

This section, also called Professional Experience, is the heart of your resume. It lets the reader know that your pedagogical experiences and ideas will meet the school's needs. Your objective is to let the administrators know that you have

---

**Fourth Grade Teacher,** Truman School, Independence, MO, Sept. 1999–June 2002

**Resource Room Teacher,** Quark High School, San Diego, CA, April 2000–May 2003

---

the expertise they're seeking. The goals of the school will be your guide as you compose descriptions of the jobs you've held. In writing descriptions of each experience, you need to make editorial decisions about which skills and accomplishments should be included, and which must be omitted because of space limitations. If your research about the school has been unproductive, then use the descriptions you write to showcase your greatest strengths.

As above, begin by detailing the following information: title of each position you held (for example, Fourth Grade Teacher, Resource Room Teacher); name of the employer; city and state where employer was located; and years of service with the employer. You can get this information from your *Resume Reservoir*.

Next, each paragraph must summarize your responsibilities and main accomplishments in sufficient detail to highlight your credentials. Writing that you "planned lessons" is nothing to brag about because it does not differentiate you from other teachers, and does not indicate the *quality* of the lessons you planned. "Planned interdisciplinary lessons" is also not specific enough to demonstrate your talent. "Planned an interdisciplinary unit on immigration culminating with a field trip to Ellis Island" is an impressive achievement worthy of mention on a resume.

Your accomplishments must also be significant. Candidates occasionally boast that they "created artistic bulletin boards," a common teacher responsibility but not worthy of citation in a resume.

Teaching experiences generally are listed in reverse chronological order, with the most recent job first. If you just completed student teaching, title it "Student Teaching" and place the entry first in the section.

## Related Experiences

In addition to teaching experience, it is useful to include other information in your resume if it will help your candidacy. Military service, employment or volunteer work for a social service agency, business experiences involving skills that may be transferable to a classroom (for example, an accounting background for an aspiring mathematics teacher), or frequent contact with the public may enhance your appeal. Like all other resume sections, begin the citation with the job title, city and state, and dates of employment. Follow this information with a brief job description that demonstrates how the skills you used in the job better equipped you to teach (see below).

For any experience you have working with children, specify the connections to teaching. In the following description of a swim instructor, for example, notice how *instructor* becomes the operative term. The bulleted list details achievements in an efficient and visually appealing fashion.

---

**Accountant,** Hoil, Toil, and Trubble Accountants (*Big Five accounting firm*)
New York, NY, July 1993–August 1999

• Managed major accounts
• Responsible for training accountant trainees in work group

---

**Swim Instructor,** YMCA Camp, York, PA, July–August 2003

• Planned sequential group lessons for pre-K through sixth-grade children
• Individualized instruction to accommodate diverse abilities
• Developed rubric to assess progress

> **HOBBIES**
> Actor in Kalamazoo Community Players, 1998–2001
> Concert pianist
>
> **TRAVEL**
> Extensive travel in South Pacific, Summers 1997 and 1999

## Hobbies, Travel, Foreign Languages Spoken

These items may be referenced with supporting detail if they relate to the teaching position or if they are truly exceptional. Examples include extensive travel to unusual places, or speaking a foreign language fluently, especially if you found in researching the school that a sizable population of students also speaks that language. Hobbies, such as playing a musical instrument at an advanced level or performing regularly in community theater, may also be noted (see above).

To get to know a candidate better, interviewers like to ask questions about hobbies, travel, and languages cited in this section. If you list an item, such as travel to a far corner of the world, be ready for questions such as, "Why did you (travel there, acquire this hobby, or learn that language)?" and, "How will it help you be a better teacher?"

## References

As noted earlier, citing references on your resume is premature because school administrators probably will not begin checking references until after the interview. Therefore, the common tag line, "References available upon request," serves no useful purpose because school administrators know you will supply the information when asked. References are discussed in Chapter 10.

## Frequently Asked Questions

- *Should I cite parenthood on my resume if I left a career to raise my family?* No, but explain the circumstances in your cover letter as suggested in the previous chapter.
- *Should I cite a job unrelated to teaching?* We recommend that you cite an unrelated career only if the preparation required a college education or you were a supervisor. Refer to these unrelated jobs in a section called Other Work Experience. If a job was unrelated to teaching and did not require a college education, such as working for Burger World, omit it from your resume; but if you were the manager of Burger World, then you can mention it.
- *Can I mention my status as a minority candidate?* Many schools seek a diverse teaching staff to meet affirmative action goals. If you choose to identify yourself as a member of a minority in your resume, we think the best way to communicate this fact is by noting an extracurricular activity or work experience associated with the minority group. For example, you might note "Secretary, African-American Student Congress," or "Sunday School Teacher, Korean Methodist Church" at the appropriate point in your resume.

---

### Better Left Unsaid

A resume is not the place to reveal certain personal information.

- Age
- Marital status
- Height
- Weight
- Children's names and ages
- Religion
- Race
- Ethnicity
- Political party
- Sexual orientation
- Never attach a photograph of yourself

# Resume Language

## Sentence Fragments

Short descriptions of your accomplishments on each job should be written using sentence fragments, not complete sentences. Resumes omit the subject part of a sentence and use only powerful, predicate phrases. Personal pronouns, such as *I* and *we,* should never appear.

## Verbs

Since resumes refer to experience in your past, use the past tense form of verbs. Use the active verb form, rather than helping or being verbs. Refer to the list of *100 Power Verbs* in Chapter 5 to find precisely the right verb for each line in your resume.

## Jargon

Educators have a reputation for writing incomprehensible jargon that only fellow educators can understand. Yet, because resumes must demonstrate specialized knowledge of the education field, using some buzzwords is appropriate. An English teacher's resume, for example, might contain such terms as **writing process, balanced literacy,** and **portfolio assessment** to emphasize knowledge of up-to-date instructional practices.

## Emphasize Accomplishments and Results

An effective resume refers to your actual accomplishments, not your personality. How do the resume entries below differ?

In citing two examples, teaching reading skills applicable to social studies and presentation of **document-based questions,** the fictitious social studies teacher demonstrates his pedagogical expertise. The teacher also evidences personal concern for students by citing extracurricular positions he held as yearbook advisor and intramural coach. The second social studies teacher asserts that he is a masterful teacher who maintained excellent relationships with students, but he does not prove this with supporting details. The second candidate sounds boastful because he applauds himself instead of identifying his real accomplishments.

| | |
|---|---|
| *Right* | Founded football league for town recreation center. Composed rubric to assess cooperative learning groups. |
| *Wrong* | I founded a football league for town recreation center. I wrote a rubric to assess cooperative learning groups. |

| | |
|---|---|
| *Right* | Planned interdisciplinary unit on theme of immigration. |
| *Wrong* | Plan interdisciplinary unit on theme of immigration. |
| *Wrong* | Was responsible for planning interdisciplinary unit on theme of immigration. |
| *Wrong* | Had planned interdisciplinary unit on theme of immigration. |

| | |
|---|---|
| *Right* | **Social Studies Teacher,** Parkside High School, Spokane, WA Sept. 1999–June 2003 <br>• Taught content area reading skills to facilitate students' comprehension of the textbook. <br>• Used document-based weekly questions. <br>• Yearbook advisor and intramural sports coach every season. |
| *Wrong* | **Social Studies Teacher,** Parkside High School, Spokane, WA Sept. 1999–June 2003 <br>• Masterful teacher. <br>• Maintained excellent rapport with students. |

### Adjectives and Adverbs

Adjectives and adverbs indicate the quality of your deeds and skills. Properly used, adjectives and adverbs add spice to otherwise mundane lines. We often find the following adjectives in attention-getting resumes: challenging, creative, demanding, effective, original, stimulating, successful.

## Editing Your Resume

**Rubrics** have become an increasingly popular assessment tool used by teachers to provide detailed feedback. The *Resume Rubric* on the next page will help you determine the quality of your resume. Show your resume to your *Job Find Friend* and to a person who is knowledgeable about grammar. Never rely on your word processor's spell checker because it cannot distinguish between homophones. A single grammatical or spelling error in your resume may cause your candidacy to be rejected.

## Sample Resumes

Sample resumes are provided on the following pages. They are designed to help aspiring teachers from a variety of backgrounds, including recent college graduates, returnees, and career changers. These resumes may be used as models as you create your own.

You have now completed your cover letter and resume, two traditional application instruments. Next we turn to the newest tool you must prepare to assist your job hunt—the portfolio.

### RESUME RUBRIC

|  | Out of the Running | Neutral Resume | Getting Better | Attention-Getting Resume |
|---|---|---|---|---|
| **Content** | The candidate's qualifications for the position are not apparent from the resume. | The resume lists schools attended and job titles without qualitative descriptions of these experiences. Alternatively, job descriptions cite commonplace tasks such as, "Wrote lesson plans." | Descriptions of jobs and volunteer work are related to teaching skill. Significant accomplishments achieved in each position are noted. | The descriptions are targeted to the needs of each school as determined by the candidate's research. |
| **Appearance** | The resume format is disorganized, inconsistent, and difficult to read. | While it is orderly and consistent, the format is also unattractive and bland. | Typeface, font size, white space, and other design elements create a logical and consistent order that is inviting to read. | The format attracts the reader to qualifications of the candidate that are related to the needs of the school. |
| **Language** | The resume violates standards of written English and other basic resume conventions, such as prohibitions against the use of personal pronouns and complete sentences. | The resume demonstrates proper English, uses predicate phrases rather than complete sentences, and avoids personal pronouns. | The choice of adjectives and verbs are pedestrian, failing to make the candidate stand out from the crowd. | Powerful predicate phrases portray the candidate's extraordinary abilities in an interesting manner. |

## RECENT COLLEGE GRADUATE

# Henry Hireme
**2 Resume Road   •   Hopewell, NJ 21212**
**212-121-2121   hehe@e-mail.com**

**EDUCATION**

**Olive University,** Valentine, Nebraska          Bachelor of Arts, 2002
Psychology Major                                          Dean's List all semesters

**New Jersey Teacher Certification,** grades N–6

**TEACHING EXPERIENCE**

**Fifth Grade Student Teacher,** Ida Know Elementary School, Wayne, NJ, Feb.–April 2002
*Initiated literature-based language arts program featuring reader's workshop, response journals, and trade book literature circles. Integrated computer software into math curriculum. Used portfolio assessment to assess student achievement of national science standards.*

**Tutor,** Curtain Climbers Community Center, Bountiful, NJ, June 2000–present
*Developed individualized curriculum, consulted with public school teachers, and conferred with parents. Led recreational, art, and leadership training programs to enhance children's self-esteem and social development.*

**Swim Instructor,** Passaic River Swim Club, Wayne, NY, July–Aug. 1998 and 1999
*Planned instruction for weekly group lessons for 6- to12-year-old children. Designed rubric to evaluate skills in accordance with Red Cross benchmarks.*

**Homework Hotline Volunteer,** Learn M. Good Public Schools, Jan. 1998–June 2000
*Volunteered to tutor elementary students through innovative homework hotline.*

**COUNSELING EXPERIENCE**

**Crisis Hotline Counselor,** Phone-A-Friend Hotline, Knice County, NJ, May 1998–Feb. 2002
*Participated in training for suicide prevention hotline.*

**Big Brother,** Juvenile Court Probation Dept., Clenare, NJ, Jan. 1998–June 2000
*Counselor to adolescent on probation.*

**Camp Counselor,** Camp Runamuck, Hackensack, NJ, Summers 1997–1999

**INTERESTS**
College Varsity Basketball, 1999–2001

## EXPERIENCED TEACHER

# Ima T. Cher
**1 Schoolhouse Street   •   Learning, Louisiana 00001**
**212-121-2121        tchr@schl.edu**

**EDUCATION**
**Teacher's University**                 MA, 1998. Postgraduate courses 1998–present
Major: Special Education         Recipient of community service award

Postgraduate Courses 1998–2000: *Trends in Special Education, Making the Reading/Writing Connection, Authentic Assessment, The Bilingual and Multicultural Student*

***Scholastic College***                 Bachelor of Arts, 1985
Major: English                     Honors: Dean's List all semesters

**Reading and Special Education Certification,** Louisiana

**TEACHING EXPERIENCE**
**Reading Teacher,** Grades 1–10, Dick and Jane School District, 1985–1995
*Designed emerging literacy program; taught reading across curriculum workshops for secondary teachers; organized Title I Reading Lab, including assessment and intervention services.*

**Software Reviewer,** *Special Educator Magazine,* 1995–present
*Wrote monthly reviews of software and Web sites for professional journal.*

**Religion Teacher,** Episcopal Church, 1997–present
*Initiated special education inclusion program for Sunday school. Led workshops to sensitize lay faculty to needs of special education children.*

**RELATED EXPERIENCE**
**Computer Camp Counselor,** Camp Hard Drive; Summers 1991–1995
*Created curriculum and purchased educational games for new camp.*

**Dorm Counselor,** Al B. Seeyan University, 1981–1995
Selected by dean of students to supervise dormitory. Responsibilities included freshman orientation and crisis referrals.

**ORGANIZATIONS**
Founding Member, Special Education PTA
Trustee, Louisiana Child Advocacy Center

**CAREER CHANGER**

# Molly Cule
11 New Clear Drive   •   Centrifuge, OH 10101
101-010-1010      mollycule@mynet.com

**EDUCATION**
**Oppenheimer University**                                    Bachelor of Arts, 2002
Chemistry Major, Biology Minor                         G.P.A., 3.41
Coursework included senior honors project and internship with independent testing lab.

**Countem College**                                              Associate in Arts, 1992
Concentration: Business and Accounting            G.P.A., 3.14

**Chemistry, Physics, and Biology Certification,** Ohio

**TEACHING EXPERIENCE**
**Student Teacher,** Chemistry and Physics, February–May, 2002
Quantum High School, Helium, OH, Grades 10 and 12
*Emphasized hands-on experiments and use of scientific method for problem-solving. Assisted with Science Research Program to prepare students for national competitions. Developed rubric for assessing research presentations. Conducted tutorials for at-risk students.*

**Computer Volunteer,** Hans Ohn Middle School, Greenery, OH, 1997–1999
*Teacher's assistant in computer laboratory one afternoon per week. Designed hands-on, individualized lessons for students lacking computers at home. Created scavenger hunts to teach Internet research skills. Organized pen pal e-mail exchange with school in Switzerland.*

**RELATED EXPERIENCE**
**Assistant Coach,** J.V. field hockey, 2001–2002
Jock High School, Helium, OH
*Taught fundamentals of field hockey to new team members. Supervised practices. Helped students win "Scholar-Athlete" recognition.*

**Sunday School Teacher,** 1997–1999
Greenery, OH

**OTHER WORK EXPERIENCE**
**Manager,** Sprouts Flower Shop, Greenery, OH, 1995–99
*Managed high-volume retail store for national chain. Directed work of twenty-three full- and part-time employees. Designed orientation program for new employees. Received "Manager of the Year" award from regional office for outstanding customer relations.*

# ALTERNATIVE CERTIFICATION

# May Kabuk

**1 Strives Row  •  Ledger, Louisiana 12345**
**999-999-9998      commission@sales.com**

### EDUCATION
**Horatio Alger University**               M.B.A., 1995
Concentration: Marketing                  G.P.A., 3.26

**Loman College**                          Bachelor of Arts, 1990
Major: Accounting                          G.P.A., 3.41
Minor: Mathematics

**Currently enrolled in Alternative Teacher Certification Program at Dewey College.**
Program includes intensive coursework in pedagogy and field placements supported by
weekly seminar.

### TEACHING EXPERIENCE
**New Employee Instructor,** New Age Computers, Monitor, LA, 1998–2002
*As marketing associate for technology company, responsibilities included directing
orientation program for new employees. Trained new employees to use specialized software.*

**Sunday School Teacher,** Grades 5–7, All Faiths Congregation, Lordstown, LA 1997–2002
*Taught comparative religion. Facilitated students planning community service projects. Led
youth group. Chaperoned dances and field trips.*

### RELATED EXPERIENCE
**Marketing Associate,** New Age Computers, Monitor, LA, 1990–2002
*Created multimedia presentations to explain complex computer applications to prospective
clients. Demonstrated software to end users. Prepared monthly statistical sales reports.*

**Girl Scout Assistant Troop Leader,** Ledger, LA, 2001–2002
*In inner-city neighborhood, initiated small business merit badge program to teach
entrepreneurship skills and economic principles.*

### INTERESTS
Fluent Spanish speaker. Highly proficient in graphics, spreadsheet, and database
applications. Hardware troubleshooter.

# REMINDERS

Use your resume to illustrate how your abilities meet the needs of the school. These needs are determined by your research (see Chapter 4).

An effective resume details your unique achievements and makes you stand out from the crowd.

In terms of appearance, an effective resume must be readable and consistent. Readability refers to such factors as font size, white space, and margin width which help draw the reader's eyes to important information. Use these elements consistently.

Use your job descriptions to highlight achievements and results. Instead of saying what kind of teacher you are, prove your point by demonstrating what you did.

Use vivid and powerful language throughout your resume.

# Chapter Seven

# Portfolios with Punch

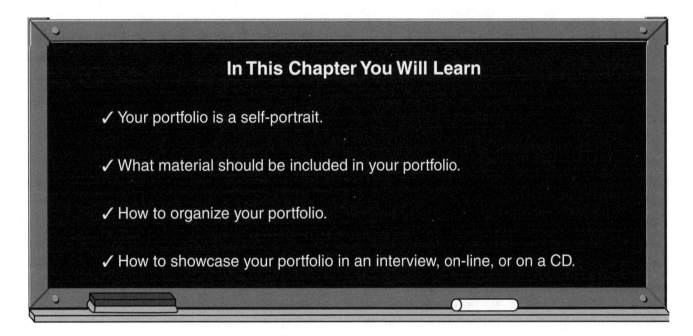

**In This Chapter You Will Learn**

✓ Your portfolio is a self-portrait.

✓ What material should be included in your portfolio.

✓ How to organize your portfolio.

✓ How to showcase your portfolio in an interview, on-line, or on a CD.

*A professional portfolio can be a "useful tool for an effective job search" because it is "a very personal job advertisement."*

—Cook and Kessler, 1993

*Since the portfolio provides support and documentation, candidates can respond to questions without self-promotion.*

—Hurst, Wilson, and Cramer, 1998

## What Is a Portfolio?

Not long ago, **portfolios** were the sole province of art teachers. They would bring large leather cases into interviews to display pieces of art they created. During the 1990s the "portfolio" became an increasingly popular form of **alternative assessment,** part of a movement that recognized the limits of traditional paper and pencil tests and tried to find more genuine, performance-based means of evaluation. In classrooms across America, students collected samples of their best work in folders to demonstrate what they learned. Schools of education began requiring aspiring teachers to accumulate lesson plans, position papers, and photographs from field placements as a way of experiencing portfolio assessment themselves. According to Hurst, Wilson, and

Cramer (1998), students began taking these portfolios to job interviews. They tell the story of a student who was hired, according to an administrator, because her portfolio made her stand out from the other applicants. Today, an estimated sixty percent of the prospective teachers Rob and Seth interview tote portfolios, one of the most significant recent changes in the job search process.

The portfolio serves three purposes. First, your portfolio showcases your accomplishments for prospective employers. New teachers can overcome the burden of inexperience if they show real-life photographs of how they implement what they have learned in teacher education programs. Second, portfolios advance the principle of targeting your strengths to a school's particular needs. A well-designed portfolio demonstrates that you understand the school's priorities and can fulfill them. Third, the portfolio models your ability to present information in a literate, organized, and creative manner. Selectivity distinguishes a portfolio from a filing system. You must choose representative samples of your work carefully to illustrate your achievements. There will be limited time to show your portfolio during the interview, so the adage *less is more* applies when deciding which exemplars to incorporate.

Traditional teaching portfolios can be maintained in three-ring binders or leather artists' portfolios, generally one to two inches thick. Today, portfolios can also be produced digitally, and then either posted on the Internet or burned on a CD-Rom or DVD.

## What Materials Should Be Included in a Portfolio?

Like your cover letter and resume, a portfolio is a highly personalized document. The following sections itemize materials that many candidates include in their portfolios. The items marked with an asterisk are considered optional; the others are mandatory.

### Table of Contents

The table of contents allows the reader to see how your portfolio is organized. Since the portfolio always changes, you don't need to number the pages.

### Resume

Put two copies of your resume in your portfolio. This will achieve two purposes: First, if you compare the portfolio to a book, the resume serves as an introduction. Second, an extra copy of your resume may come in handy if one is requested during an interview.

### Statement of Philosophy*

A Statement of Philosophy is a reflective piece, generally one to two pages long, that summarizes your core educational beliefs. The statement may explain why you chose teaching as a career or describe essential goals that you hope to accomplish in your classroom. Your *Personal Profile* (Chapter 2) can stimulate ideas to help you compose your Statement of Philosophy. Consider the following questions as you draft your essay:

- Why is teaching an important profession?
- Was there an influential person, perhaps a revered teacher, in your life who shaped your career goals and your views about teaching?
- Was there a theorist, a researcher, or a book about education that inspired your teaching philosophy? How?
- What is your teaching style, and why do you feel it is effective?
- What is the ideal relationship between teachers and learners in the classroom?
- How do you view yourself as a learner?
- How do you want students to remember you?

Since the Statement of Philosophy also serves as a writing sample, it must demonstrate mastery of spelling, grammar, and other rules of written English. We strongly recommend that you ask a respected English teacher or your college career counselor to review the content and style. Don't rely on your computer's spell or grammar checker. The essay should be double-spaced and a maximum of two pages long.

### Lesson Plans

Plans from successful lessons you have taught show your style as a teacher and address the specific needs of the school as identified in your research. You should compile a bank of successful

---

**Sample Lesson Plan Outline**
(Adapted from Hunter, 1982)

    I    Anticipatory Set
    II   Objective
    III  Purpose
    IV   Input
    V    Check for Understanding
    VI   Modeling
    VII  Guided Practice
    VIII Closure
    IX   Independent Practice

---

and original lesson plans from student teaching or previous teaching jobs. Then select the three you consider to be most relevant as you prepare your portfolio for each interview. These plans should follow the standard lesson plan format you learned in your teacher education program or the outline you use in your present teaching position. If your program was steeped in the **Madeline Hunter Method,** for example, follow the style in the box above.

## Photographs of Classes

There is no better advertisement than a photograph showing happy students engaged in a creative lesson designed by the candidate. The old adage, "A picture is worth a thousand words," is true. Photographs enable administrators to get a glimpse of the kind of teacher you aspire to be. Carefully selected, candid photographs succinctly demonstrate what you believe is important about teaching. Photographs should include action shots of students learning, group pictures showing you interacting with children, and vivid depictions of learning centers and bulletin board displays that exhibit student work. Typed, explanatory captions, one or two sentences long, should accompany each photograph.

- A music teacher's portfolio displayed photographs of student ensembles composing a musical piece in the classroom and performing it on stage. Captions placed beneath each photograph provided explanation. A copy of the score itself, artfully presented,

appeared in the background behind the photographs. A headline across the top of the page quoted the National Art Education Standard that advocates student creativity and self-expression.
- A science teacher included photographs of student laboratory groups participating in a hands-on experiment. Each photograph showed students performing a different step of the scientific process. The photographs were organized in chronological order from left to right across facing pages, each with an explanatory caption. A headline read, "Learning the Scientific Process."

## Materials from Lessons You Have Taught

Along with photographs and lesson plans, this section ranks among the most informative. Materials may be homemade teacher or student products, but never commercial educational supplies. Examples of teacher-constructed materials are **manipulatives, rubrics,** games, or worksheets that apply higher levels of **Bloom's taxonomy.** Samples of student work, such as essays, reports, posters, and artwork are also beneficial and convincing to a prospective employer. If something is too large to place in your portfolio, use a photograph.

- A social studies teacher showed student archeologists attempting to determine the location of a civilization on the basis of cultural artifacts that the teacher presented. The portfolio displayed photographs of the artifacts and students working in cooperative groups, captions for each item, and the lesson plan. The headline read, "Teaching Higher-Level Thinking Skills."
- A science teacher built a planetarium from lawn trash bags and flashlights. Pinholes in the trash bags represented planets and constellations. Photographs of students participating in the astronomy lesson with explanatory captions and lesson plans were most impressive.
- An English teacher incorporated haiku verses composed by students and artwork they created to illustrate each poem.
- Some candidates include sample **rubrics** used to assess student performance.

## Lists of Accomplishments*

Lists of accomplishments are impressive because they demonstrate extensive achievements in a concise format. If a school prioritizes hands-on mathematics instruction, for example, a mathematics applicant might list the **manipulatives** she feels qualified to use. A list of software you've used in your lessons highlights your educational technology skills.

## Student Evaluations*

Farewell letters written by students at the conclusion of student teaching add a warm touch to your portfolio. At the secondary level, candidates may include copies of evaluation forms that students completed to provide the teacher with feedback after a lesson or unit. Three student evaluations should be sufficient to make your point.

### SAMPLE LIST OF ACCOMPLISHMENTS

**Pete Thagoras**

**Mathematics Manipulatives**

I used these manipulatives while student teaching, tutoring, and studying mathematics pedagogy:

Abacus
Algebra Balance
Alge-tiles™
Attribute Blocks
Base Ten Blocks
Cuisenaire® Rods
Dial Clocks
Dice
Dominoes
Fraction Blocks
Geoboard
Money
Pattern Blocks
Pentominoes
Polydron Frameworks™
Snap™ Cubes
Tangrams
Unifix® Cubes

## Reflections, Inspirational Quotations, or Poetry*

Inspirational quotations or poems, illustrated with photographs taken of your classroom, may provide additional insights about you. These items may also be used as headlines to summarize central themes of your portfolio. The quotations must be attributed and quoted accurately.

- An elementary teacher quoted Henry James, "A teacher affects eternity," to headline pages containing good-bye letters from fifth grade students in which they poignantly expressed how much they learned.
- A mathematics teacher used John Dewey's maxim, "Learning by Doing" as the title of a page showing photographs of students involved in a statistical research project and the graphs they created to show the number of hours in a week they watched television.

## Autobiography*

If your background is unique, you may choose to include a one- or two-page autobiography. If you changed careers, for example, you can explain the reasons. Peace Corps volunteer service or teaching jobs in extraordinary locations such as the Bering Strait may also contribute punch to a portfolio. The problem with an autobiography, and the reason why we recommend most candidates omit one, is because an autobiography can cause unwanted trouble. An interesting lifetime spent sailing the seven seas and experiencing other cultures can seem exotic to some people, but unfocused and frivolous to others. Information listed in the box *Better Left Unsaid,* in Chapter 6, should not be disclosed.

## Evaluation Forms Completed by Student Teacher Supervisors

These forms usually consist of checklists and anecdotal comments. If you are a recent graduate, include the most outstanding evaluation or two from your cooperating teacher and/or college supervisor.

## List of References

Include in your portfolio a list of references who can vouch for your personality, your talents, and your job performance. References are usually supervisors and co-workers from your current and previous jobs and college professors. Insert an extra copy of your reference list in your portfolio, so you have one available for a prospective employer. More detailed information about how to select your references is provided in Chapter 10.

## Letters of Recommendation

Letters of recommendation may be written by school administrators, cooperating teachers, college education department professors, former students and their parents, and employers. These letters must commend your teaching skills and work habits, and describe relationships you established with students and colleagues.

As a rule of thumb, you should include a maximum of three letters in your portfolio. They should be organized in order of their effectiveness, with the best one placed on top. Remember our basic principle—you must match your strengths to the needs of the particular school. If the school is looking for a computer-literate candidate, a letter from the director of the summer computer camp or the manager of the computer store where you worked helps your cause. Letters of reference can also highlight your connections with noted people or institutions.

Many administrators view letters of recommendation with a grain of salt, knowing that candidates never include negative references in their portfolios. For this reason, we believe letters of recommendation should be the second-to-last section of the portfolio. However, if you have a truly extraordinary letter, you may break this rule of thumb.

## Official Documents

The following documents demonstrate proof of your eligibility for employment: student copy of college transcripts (an official copy mailed directly from the college registrar's office must be supplied at a later stage), teacher certificates from the state education department, and PRAXIS and other certification test scores. You want the administrator to review other sections first that characterize your teaching abilities, so place this section last.

# How Do You Organize Your Portfolio?

There are two ways to organize your portfolio, or you can use a combination of these organizational styles.

## Thematic

This organizing system, our favorite, can have dramatic results. Themes are individualized according to the message that the candidate wants to convey. The selection of themes must relate to the school's needs, the candidate's strengths, and the subject matter.

- An art teacher candidate devoted a section of her portfolio to units she had taught across many grade levels. Sections were titled

---

**But I Don't Have a Copy of My Certification Yet . . .**

Relax. Administrators certainly understand this common problem. If you completed your state's requirements for certification recently, there will be a bureaucratic delay before you receive the official document in the mail. Until it arrives, a letter from your teacher education program director affirming that you have completed the requirements satisfactorily and that the application has been submitted to the state education department is sufficient. A copy of this letter can be included in your portfolio or attached to your resume, if requested by the school.

To use your portfolio effectively, you must be able to flip to the page you need immediately. To do so, you must know your resume like the back of your hand. We've seen candidates waste precious interview time thumbing through their portfolios, saying, "I know the page I'm looking for is here somewhere."

"Painting," "Graphic design," "Computer-generated Art," and "Pointillism."

- Two tenets of a social studies teacher's philosophy were teaching children to understand American citizenship and to appreciate cultural diversity. The statement, "Teaching Children to Understand and Cherish American Citizenship," was the headline across the top of one section of the teacher's portfolio, followed by lesson plans and photographs of a class trip to City Hall. Another section was titled, "Teaching Appreciation of Cultural Diversity," and featured related lesson plans and photographs.

The remaining sections of the portfolio, such as the resume, official documents, and letters of reference, follow the thematic chapters.

### Genre

This is the most common method, but not necessarily the best. Create one section for each of the headings listed in this chapter (for example, "Official Documents," "Autobiography"). We recommend placing each section in the order in which we cite them.

## Strategies for Introducing Your Portfolio

Portfolios are such a recent phenomenon that many administrators have not yet learned to incorporate them into the interview process. More often than not, an administrator doesn't even ask to review the portfolio. All your work preparing the portfolio and the powerful case it makes to support your candidacy could go by the wayside.

Even if an administrator asks, "Would you like to share your portfolio?" you still face the difficulty of presenting it effectively. If a committee conducts the interview, it is impossible for members to ask

their questions and examine the portfolio carefully within the time allotted for the session. Furthermore, when the portfolio is circulated around a table, your destiny is to be determined by luck. Since they cannot read the entire portfolio, committee members will flip through the pages quickly. Impressions may be determined by the page they see first. In addition, the most influential committee member may not have enough time to study the portfolio if he or she happens to be the last to see it.

Don't leave your future to chance. Use these strategies to introduce your portfolio strategically during the interview.

### Use Your Portfolio to Document Points during the Interview

To use your portfolio effectively, you must be able to flip to the page you need immediately. To do so, you must know your resume like the back of your hand. We've seen candidates waste precious interview time thumbing through their portfolios, saying, "I know the right page is here somewhere."

Suppose you are a middle school mathematics teacher and the committee asks you about age-appropriate teaching strategies. After explaining your belief in using manipulatives, point out relevant documents in your portfolio that support your response, including photographs of classes in session, lesson plans, and positive evaluations written by your cooperating teacher.

### Introduce the Portfolio Yourself

Before you pass around your portfolio, explain its contents so you exercise control over how the document is viewed. Emphasize the components of the portfolio that are targeted to the school's particular needs. If you organize your portfolio around themes, highlight the major sections to the committee.

### Adapt to the Interview Committee Size

If the committee is large, turn your portfolio so it is facing the group, and display material the committee members can see easily, such as dramatic photographs. Alternatively, if you are being interviewed by one or two administrators, you can spend more time pointing out significant details.

### The Second-Round Interview

Once you reach the second-round interview, we recommend that you offer to leave your portfolio with the interviewers so they can review it more thoroughly. If they are agreeable, arrange to retrieve it in a few days. This strategy has several benefits: First, it ensures that everyone has the time to read it. Second, having to return to the school to pick up your portfolio provides you with an additional chance to see the school in action. Developing a digital portfolio as described below is very helpful at this point. You can make any number of copies on CDs and edit the contents to suit each vacancy.

### Electronic Portfolios

Digital portfolios burned on a CD-Rom or DVD or posted on the Internet are becoming increasingly common. Electronic portfolios offer two advantages over the traditional paper variety: (1) The candidate's computer literacy, a desirable qualification, is apparent when the prospective teacher cites a personal Web site in a cover letter or leaves a CD or DVD portfolio at the conclusion of an interview. (2) An electronic portfolio contains much more information than its print ancestor. A digital portfolio, for example, can contain mutlimedia video and sound clips that are more telling than a simple photograph and impossible to display on paper.

What should a candidate include in a digital portfolio? Effective electronic portfolios may contain all the materials found in a print portfolio, enhanced by the following:

- Images, such as digital photographs of lessons taking place during student teaching experiences or samples of student work.

- Multimedia presentations that show lessons in action and clips of student presentations or performances. Using a digital camcorder, for example, one teacher recorded a clay animation project produced by students. Another teacher attached a PowerPoint slide show she had created to illustrate a lesson.
- Copies of Web pages generated by the teacher candidate. Some teachers seeking to change jobs incorporate Web pages used in classes they teach.

Campbell, Cignetti, Melenyzer, Nettles, and Wyman (1997) recommend that teacher portfolios demonstrate knowledge of subject matter, human development, and principles of learning, and depict classroom management, instructional planning and assessment skills. In addition to these characteristics, Kilbane and McNergney (2003) suggest that a digital portfolio shows the candidate's dedication to teaching and provides evidence of efforts to communicate with parents and the community.

On-line portfolios are generally organized like a Web site. A set of hyperlinks on the side or the bottom of each page serves as a table of contents, directing the reader to each component. Hyperlinks might include: statement of philosophy; the names of two or three units taught; PowerPoint presentations; resume; letters of recommendation and/or feedback from students, colleagues, parents, and administrators; samples of student work; examples of how professional development experiences influenced teaching; and other topics that mirror a paper portfolio. Internet-based portfolios can also include hyperlinks to direct readers to related research, school Web sites or resources from professional organizations.

CD or DVD portfolios must be organized through a logical file system. Individual folders contain the different sections of the portfolio.

On the next page you will find a sample introductory page (or home page) for a fictitious social studies candidate.

The box on page 99 lists Web sites that illustrate electronic teacher portfolios. Since these Web sites are frequently outdated, we have listed current teacher portfolios available on-line on our own Web site, <**www.teacheredge.com**>.

My Resume

Philosophy of Teaching

8th Grade Civil War Unit

Student Inventions from Age of Industrialization Unit

Interdisciplinary Immigration Unit

Rubric for Student Bill of Rights

Meet Your Teacher Night PowerPoint

Homework on the Web

Student and Parent Feedback

Letters of Recommendation

Contact Me

# Dewey Truman

Welcome to my digital portfolio! I am a middle school social studies teacher with two years of experience. In my classroom, we bring the past to life through reenactments, journal writing, students  projects, and lively discussions. My students learn, as Eugene O'Neill said, "The past is the present . . . it's the future too."

My portfolio will demonstrate my experiential teaching style. You will find samples of student work from interdisciplinary projects I have planned with colleagues and other exciting, hands-on lessons. In addition, this portfolio contains a rubric created to assess student progress in a unit about the Constitution. Don't forget to read reviews from students, parents, and supervisors.

I firmly believe that technology is a uniquely powerful teaching tool. Students love using the toys, but computers also enable students to conduct research and access resources from around the world. Parents also appreciate the ability to check homework assignments on my class Web site.

If you would like to reach me, my e-mail address is **dewey@tribune.net**.

<http://depts.washington.edu/ncate/exhibitroom/worksamples/studentwork.html>
University of Washington College of Education Web site containing sample teacher portfolios
<http:www2.ncsu.edu/unity/lockers/project/portfolios/nbcfile1.html>
Sample teacher portfolios demonstrating compliance with standards for National Board Certification
<http://www.csuchico.edu/educ/estport.htm>
Sample contents of electronic teacher portfolio from the California State University's Chico branch. You may also reach this Web site by entering the keywords "Chico State teacher portfolio" in the Google search engine.

A word of caution is appropriate here: Digital portfolios must be designed and assembled with the same care as the traditional paper variety. We have encountered some CD or DVD portfolios that contain overly fancy fonts, distracting color schemes and sound clips, and simply too much information. Good editing and design skills are essential, as well as competence with word processing, desktop publishing, scanning graphic images, and, in the case of portfolios posted on the Internet, Web authoring software. Advanced computer users may also wish to demonstrate proficiencies in digitizing sound and video. The work of Helen C. Barrett, an expert in teacher training and staff development, provides an excellent guide for candidates interested in digital portfolios. Her work can be accessed at <**www.electronicportfolios.com**>.

Since digital portfolios are not yet commonplace, having one really will set you apart from the crowd! Be sure to mention your on-line portfolio and its Web address in your cover letter.

Now you've prepared all the material you need—a cover letter, resume, and portfolio—to secure an interview and to show off your talents. The interview is the first step of the hiring process that requires you to think on your feet, but that doesn't mean you can't prepare for it. In Chapter 8 you learn how to get ready for an interview.

## REMINDERS

- The portfolio is a reflection of you. It must demonstrate your achievements and be organized thoughtfully and meticulously.

- Be selective when compiling your portfolio and produce a new version for each interview that documents your ability to meet the school's instructional needs.

- When it comes to portfolios, often *less is more*, because the committee's time to review your portfolio is limited.

- Take an active role in using your portfolio during the interview. Consider it your responsibility to introduce its contents before passing it to the committee or the administrator. Refer to the portfolio when answering questions.

- If you have the computer skills, you can really stand out from the crowd by creating a digital version of your portfolio on a CD, DVD, or your personal Web site.

# Chapter Eight

# Getting Ready
# for the Interview

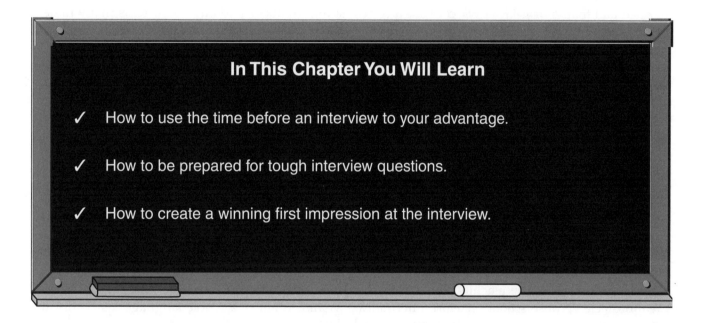

**In This Chapter You Will Learn**

✓ How to use the time before an interview to your advantage.

✓ How to be prepared for tough interview questions.

✓ How to create a winning first impression at the interview.

*It seemed like an eternity. I sat in the office, waiting to be called in, and I kept getting more and more nervous. I didn't even want to shake hands with anyone—I thought no one would hire anybody whose palms were so sweaty.*
—Guidance counselor candidate

You've done it! After crafting a great resume, you've landed an interview! Excitement courses through your body as you contemplate the job that lies ahead. But wait! Anxiety quickly mounts as question after question suddenly comes into your head: Whom will I see? What will I be asked? What is the competition like? How should I dress? What if I can't think of anything to say? All of a sudden, the prospect of an interview seems almost as terrifying as not getting any calls at all.

Hold on a second. We can provide you with strategies that will let you take charge of the interview situation and score points with your future employers. Let's take things one step at a time.

## Preparation Starts as Soon as You Send Out Your Resume

Rob remembers an interview nightmare of his own when he applied for a job. One day he answered the phone, and the person on the other end began to talk about coming for an interview. He knew the name of the person "rang a bell," but he just couldn't place it. When the lady on the phone asked if he could come in the next day, Rob became absolutely panic-stricken: He couldn't recall the position, where the school was, or anything about the place.

It's true—your phone can ring any time after you start looking for a teaching job, so you need to anticipate getting a call from the moment you drop your cover letter and resume in the mailbox. First, make certain that your *Job Find File* contains a copy of the cover letter and resume you sent to each school, the *School Profile Form* with notes you accumulated from your research, and the *Finding Common Ground* worksheet from Chapter 5 delineating similarities between your talents and the school's needs. If you responded to a newspaper advertisement, a copy of the ad should be in your *Job Find File*. If you learned of the job through a networking source, write down who referred you and what the person's connection is to the school in question. Keep the file handy so you can retrieve it easily when those calls start coming in.

When taking the call, use the *Interview Informer* on page 103 to record vital information.

We still encounter candidates who do not have telephone answering machines or voice mail, a real obstacle because school secretaries normally call to arrange interviews during the workday. We have also called candidates and heard bizarre messages. Keep your message short and businesslike.

Sometimes a school secretary calls and gives you a choice of interview times. Candidates ask us whether there is an advantage to going first, last, or in between. Our first answer is that an outstanding presentation is always recognized, regardless of the order. However, if interviews go on all day, our advice is to opt for the morning, when everyone is fresh.

## Doing Your Homework—Revisited

After the appointment has been set, your preparations must begin in earnest. There are two reasons to do your homework in advance of an interview. First, following the theme of our book, you want to target your strengths to the specific needs of the school you'll be visiting. Second, doing your homework enables you to anticipate questions you may be asked about key issues of concern to the school. After you've identified potential questions, you can begin rehearsing your responses.

As a first step, take another look at all the information you've assembled about the school. This includes the location of the school, demographic information, educational issues currently under discussion, the school's standardized test profile, special programs, initiatives that are being considered for future implementation, budget data, awards received, comparisons with similar schools, and any other items that will help you match your abilities and accomplishments to the school's needs.

If you don't have a complete profile of the school yet, now is the time to fill in the missing pieces. Use the resources and techniques described in Chapter 4 to get the information. Of course, your information should be as up-to-date as possible, so carefully check Web sites, review newly printed materials, and talk to your network contacts to find out if more recent test scores have been published or if the school budget will fund new programs. "If you're going to quote some data, be sure it's current," urges an elementary school administrator. "One recent applicant told us how much she supported our total commitment to whole language. Actually, we haven't been a whole language district for the past several years."

Private schools require some specialized research. Many such schools are organized around a religious doctrine or a core set of beliefs that permeate the organization. Some schools, for example, follow a traditional curriculum, while others emphasize innovation. Some private schools are linked to national or international associations, like the **Montessori** movement or the **Waldorf** schools. **International schools** often boast that they offer an "American-style education," although the specific meaning of that phrase may vary from school to school. Some private schools insist that all their instructors have teaching credentials, but others care only that their teachers have content knowledge in specific areas of the curriculum.

# INTERVIEW INFORMER

| | |
|---|---|
| Name of school | |
| Date of appointment | |
| What time is the interview scheduled to begin and end? | |
| Who will be present (e.g., principal or headmaster, panel, curriculum coordinator)? | |
| Is there anything I need to bring in addition to my portfolio? | |
| Is a writing sample required? | |
| Is this a brief interview for screening purposes or an in-depth interview? (Ask these detailed questions only if the secretary seems patient and knowledgeable.) | |
| How do I get there? | |
| What is the school's telephone number? | |

Every interview includes at least a couple of difficult questions. If you're prepared for these moments, you won't feel so ill at ease when they arise. As a general rule, address difficult questions by refocusing attention on your strengths; don't try to apologize for any perceived deficiencies.

Newcomers to the educational stage, **charter schools** also require a good deal of research. Charter schools are funded with public money, but they are exempt from many of the rules and regulations that regular public schools must follow. Most charter schools offer a distinct view of the educational process, which may run the gamut from highly experimental to archly conservative. As with private schools, you need to identify the key beliefs that guide the charter school's operations to determine the best approach to advancing your candidacy (and to determine whether you fit in the school's unique environment).

Once you can create a fairly detailed picture of the school in your mind's eye, take the next opportunity to develop an even more substantive image of how you can address the school's needs.

- Take a careful, thoughtful look at the resume and cover letter you sent to your potential employer, and use a highlighter to identify their key points.
- Review your *Finding Common Ground* worksheet for the particular school. Next, look back at your *Personal Profile,* your *Resume Reservoir,* and the *School Profile.* Identify elements that can strengthen your candidacy that you did not itemize in *Finding Common Ground.* For example, you might decide to include volunteer experiences working with special needs children if you know that the school is embarking on an **inclusion** program. Similarly, you might seek out more information about the latest educational software if you find out that the school is opening a new computer lab. Consider the testimony of these two successful candidates:

I knew that computer technology was a "hot issue" in the district [said Brenda, an elementary school teacher who recently completed a master's program in instructional technology], so I knew I had to stress how I would integrate computers into the daily curriculum.

[Diana, a teacher in a parochial school, recalled,] I really think that my ability to speak Spanish gave me an edge over other candidates. The population in the area had changed a lot, and when I reminded them that I had a good working knowledge of Spanish, I saw the principal nod her head, as if she were saying, "That's exactly what we need."

- Look through your portfolio to make sure it is up-to-date. You want to become so familiar with its contents that you can turn to any entry in a matter of seconds. Candidates who can illustrate their points quickly through their portfolios are guaranteed to impress an audience looking for the best candidate.
- Based on the preceding steps, create a list of possible questions that you may be asked. *Always* be prepared to answer questions about your general background and education, because queries of this type usually are asked in those very important first minutes of the interview. Career changers and former teachers returning to the profession must prepare for questions about life changes they have made that resulted in their decision to teach. Develop answers that highlight your strengths and accomplishments and address the talking points you have identified as critical to your presentation (see the box on Talking Points on p. 105.). See Chapter 9 to review a list of *Top 100 Interview Questions.*
- Practice answering the anticipated questions aloud, preferably in front of your *Job Find Friend,* so you can get meaningful feedback. If no one is available, use a tape recorder. This kind of practice helps build your confidence, because you'll know half of the interview script—that, is, what *you* are going to say. The answers will roll off your tongue, even though you may feel nervous. This is why performers from baseball players to ballet dancers practice . . . and then practice some more. You can transform the interview experience from a firing line to another opportunity to advertise yourself. "I like when candidates show confidence when answering questions," commented a parent

---

**Talking Points**

Public relations specialists and politicians (is there a difference?) use "talking points." Talking points remind speakers of items that should be covered in their presentations. For teacher candidates, talking points should include items that might be covered in an interview:

- Describe your educational background and work experiences (often the first question).
- What questions do you have (often the last question)?
- A list of your strengths that have a direct connection to the needs of the school.
- Notes containing key phrases to help you recall a brief concluding statement (three or four sentences) that you can say at the end of the interview to summarize your strengths and provide the interviewers with a reason to consider your candidacy above all others.
- Anything else that you do not want to overlook during the interview—e.g., community resident, special talents, interest in coaching.

   Jot these important notes on a pad of paper or a 3 1/2- by 5-inch lined index card. When the interview begins, take out your *Talking Points*, place it discreetly on the table in front of you, and refer to the information when needed. By the end of the interview, you should have woven all of your talking points into the conversation.

   See Chapter 10 for more detailed information about interview strategies and techniques.

---

who served on an interview committee. "It tells me that they know their field when they don't have to fumble for answers."

- Practice your summary statement until you commit it to memory. Here's an example: "I would like to thank you for providing me with this time to speak with you. I am sure that my strong background in teaching mathematics to primary-level students will result in students who understand the concepts behind working with numbers and can solve problems. As you saw in my portfolio, my students enjoy math, and they can demonstrate their knowledge in many ways."

## Planning for Potholes

Now for the more uncomfortable part. You need to consider possible sources of difficulty.

   Start by reviewing your resume once again. This time, look for areas that may need additional explanation. For example, if there are time gaps in your education or employment records, some-

one might ask, "What did you do from 2001 to 2003?" Similarly, if you have little experience in the lower grades and you're applying for a first-grade position, you need to demonstrate your understanding of effective practices in reading instruction. Remember, though, there is really no such thing as a perfect candidate . . . or a perfect interview. Be confident that you know a lot about your craft: Poise and confidence are a winning combination in any interview situation.

## Get Ready, Get Set . . .

Your preparation should cease by the night before your interview. You'll need a good night's sleep to look, feel, and act your best at the interview, and "cramming" is never an effective method for attaining the best state of readiness. Moreover, you don't want to be so rehearsed that your answers seem overly practiced and insincere.

   Everyone has a different recommendation for combating sleeplessness. Remember that caffeine makes it more difficult to relax, and alcohol

---

One of your most important steps is to put together an "interview kit." This collection of items should include your portfolio, a copy of the cover letter you sent to the school district, extra copies of your resume, a good pen, and a small notebook in which you have recorded your "talking points" and the questions you'd like to ask your interviewers. If you're a poor speller and a writing sample is required (writing samples are discussed later in this chapter), include a small pocket dictionary or electronic spell checker in your interview kit.

may prevent you from having the deep, restful kind of sleep you need most. Moderate exercise can promote a good night's rest, but not right before bed. Whatever your approach, try to keep to your regular nighttime pattern.

**Dress for Success**

Whether or not you realize it, you make a fashion statement when you walk into an interview room. We have witnessed the demise of candidates who failed to make a good impression in front of interview committees and potential supervisors because they wore clothing and accessories that detracted from their presentations. You need to give considerable thought to your outfit for the interview.

The first thing to remember about your wardrobe is that you're dressing for an audience. Your appearance is the first thing that interviewers note about you, and many judgments are formed during the opening minutes of your meeting. (Actually, the judgments start the moment you enter the office. Secretaries "size up" candidates immediately, and may report these impressions to decision makers.) It's impossible to know what type of clothing the interviewers prefer, so your best bet is to create a look that is mature, conservative, and totally professional. We can sum up this look in one word: *classic.*

As you know, quality clothing is not cheap. However, this investment will pay handsome (pardon the pun) dividends by creating a positive first impression, so we advise you to invest some money in finely tailored outfits. (We stress the plural, "outfits," because you shouldn't wear the same clothing twice if you have more than one interview for a school.) For men, this means a suit of a medium to dark color and a matching shirt and tie. The tie should be knotted neatly and pulled right up to your collar. Make sure your face is neatly shaved; if you have a beard or mustache, it must be trimmed carefully.

Women can't go wrong with suits, as well. As an alternative, you may consider a conservatively designed dress or a jacket with a well-matched skirt. Your choice of a blouse is also important; again, classic, quality material is essential. We've heard interview panels discussing women's necklines after the candidates left, so put modesty at the top of your fashion priorities. Accessories should be selected with care.

Although they can add considerably to the impact of an outfit, you don't want to overwhelm anyone. To demonstrate this last point, listen to an elementary principal describe how an interview was derailed by, of all things, a pocketbook.

> One of the candidates for a position was an articulate woman who wore a very stylish, very expensive-looking, very large pocketbook. It was very, very deep, and when she reached in it to get a tissue, her entire hand seemed to disappear, much like when a magician reaches into a top hat. I think she saw everyone gawking at her, and I'm not sure anyone really heard her answer to the next question.

Some considerations apply to both sexes. For example, shoes are critical pieces of your personal fashion statement and should not be overlooked. Footwear now takes many forms, with casual styles often leading the pack. However, your choice for an interview must be formal—by this we mean standard dress shoes for men and women. In all cases, shoes should be free of scuff marks and dirt.

Similarly, take steps to make sure that all of your interview outfits are clean and pressed: Wrinkles and spots neutralize the positives of an interview presentation very quickly. Go lightly on colognes; scents can be nice, but they can also be overpowering in a small room. Then again, you never know who might be allergic to what you're wearing. And let's not forget that you'll probably use your hands at various points during your meeting: unkempt nails are a faux pas. Finally, pay attention to your hair to make sure that it, too, conveys the professional impression you want to create.

In interviews, as in many other parts of life, the details count!

## Planning Your Arrival

Whenever possible, make a practice run before the interview. Try to schedule your test drive at the same time of day as your interview appointment. Determine how long it will take you to arrive at the school, park, and walk to the location of your interview. On the day before the interview, make sure your car is ready, because "I ran out of gas" will lead to a dead end. If you're taking public transportation to the interview, review the timetables, route numbers, transfer points, and station or street names that are involved in the trip. If you plan to take a cab, call for a reservation if possible, because being late to an interview is simply not acceptable.

Plan to arrive at least thirty minutes early. This will give you spare time in case you hit an unexpected delay. It also will allow you to relax a few minutes before the interview begins.

## Using Check-In Time to Your Advantage

Try to check your appearance before you enter the interview room; a few moments of straightening up are usually needed after your trip. Next, put the name of your interviewer on the tip of your tongue (that is, "I have an appointment with Mrs. So-and-so"), so that you sound professional when you announce your arrival.

The walk to the interview office may be one of the most nerve-racking parts of your day. In all likelihood, you may feel accompanied by hundreds of butterflies, and it may be hard to maintain your composure. Keep in mind that these are natural feelings. Our advice: tell yourself that you have lots to offer and focus your attention on the task at hand. Then walk in and calmly, confidently present yourself for the interview.

Remember that your interview really begins immediately. If you're early or, as is often the case, if the previous interview is running late, you'll probably be shown to a seat. Believe it or not, this waiting time is actually a favor to you because it gives you a chance to prepare for the next stage of the process.

Think of the waiting period as a time to hunt for hidden treasures—that is, little nuggets of information that may be valuable in the interview. Scan the room to see if you can find within easy reach:

- Publications that provide you with information about the school and the district. A school calendar, for instance, usually has lots of information about programs, important people, and policies.
- Bulletin boards that feature samples of student work. These can provide you with insights about curricula and materials used.
- Announcements that provide school news and highlight special activities.
- School newsletters that offer insights into the "personality" of the school and give you a sense of what the community considers valuable and newsworthy.
- Flyers describing initiatives related to budget and programs that could affect teaching jobs.
- Information about how the school is using technology, both for administrative purposes and for instruction.
- Clues about the tone of the office. Is it bright and cheerful or very functional and businesslike? Does it seem warm and friendly or very formal? Is it decorated in a style that students would appreciate? How do people address each other? Are employees smiling?
- Evidence of building maintenance. Although there are no guarantees, a well-maintained office might indicate a school in which cleanliness and upkeep are high priorities.

---

**Give Yourself a Break!**

If the door isn't open yet, and you've done your scanning and participated in some chit-chat, you still have a chance to put this extra time to good use. Engage in some relaxation, even under these anxiety-provoking circumstances. Impossible, you say? Try this:

1. Sit in an upright but not stiff position.
2. Fall into a regular breathing pattern.
3. Avoid trying to listen to what's going on in the interview room—this can only be a distraction.
4. Focus your attention on relaxing muscle groups from your toes to your head, literally.
5. Use mental imagery to give yourself a break. Picture in your mind's eye a reassuring, restful scene, for example, waves breaking gently on a shore or a beautiful sunset. Add some "mental" sounds to make the vision more appealing.
6. Find a good position for your hands. If it feels comfortable, put them at your sides. If it seems more natural, clasp them together and rest them on your thighs.

Want to know even more about what's going on at the school? Engage the secretary in some light conversation—upcoming holidays, school activities, pictures of children, even the weather will do. Frequently, secretaries find ways to present their assessments of candidates to interviewers, so don't miss out on this opportunity to solidify your standing. Then, if you get the job, you'll already have a relationship with one or more of the key players in any school. (Of course, don't press; if the secretary seems busy or unwilling to chat, drop it—fast.)

In addition to verbal communication skills, which will be assessed during the interview, teachers must demonstrate exemplary written communication ability when they write on the chalkboard, correspond with parents, and file various reports. School officials understand that candidates may have received a great deal of assistance composing their cover letters and resumes; these materials may not paint a true picture of a candidate's writing ability. For this reason, a school may require you to report to the interview session early to complete a writing sample. The school secretary will supply you with paper, perhaps a clipboard, or maybe even a computer, and an essay question (make sure you have a pen!). Sometimes the candidate is escorted to a quiet setting to work; other times the applicant must contend with distractions and noise in the main office. If you're a poor speller, we recommend you place a pocket dictionary or an electronic spell checker in your pocketbook or suit pocket just in case. The question you will be assigned to write about probably appears among the *Top 100 Interview Questions* listed in Chapter 9.

Sometimes a creative school thinks up other exercises before the interview begins. For example, in Seth's school, science candidates are given copies of actual student lab notebook entries and asked to grade them. His school has provided prospective reading teachers with folders containing student test scores and **running records,** and asked candidates to prescribe remediation strategies. Rob's district requires teachers to write a critique of a lesson that they have presented.

Remember that you have already accomplished a good part of your goal just by landing an interview—very few of your competitors have made it this far. Consider each interview a significant step on the road to the teaching job you really want.

The door is opening: it's time for the interview to begin. Stand up, reach deep for some extra confidence, and stride into the interview room with a smile, and a drive to succeed!

## REMINDERS

- Review your resume, cover letter, portfolio, and *Job Find File* to identify areas that will be valued by the school. Develop a brief list of *Talking Points*.

- Practice interview questions and answers aloud with a partner. Don't shy away from developing responses to difficult questions.

- Dress in a conservative, tailored style to create a professional image.

- While waiting for the interview to begin, use the time to check your appearance, gather information about the school, and make a positive impression on the secretary.

- Anxiety is normal, and moderate levels even invigorate performance. You can use the relaxation techniques mentioned in the chapter to control your nerves.

# Chapter Nine

# The All-Important Interview

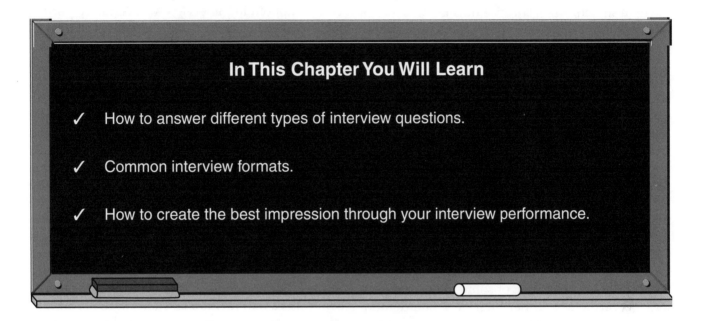

## In This Chapter You Will Learn

✓ How to answer different types of interview questions.

✓ Common interview formats.

✓ How to create the best impression through your interview performance.

*Successful interviewing is a skill just like hitting a baseball or playing the violin. You need to learn a technique, and then you have to practice.*
—Career counselor

*I've done a lot in my life. I've been all around the world, and I've taught in overseas schools in countries where I didn't even speak the native language. But nothing was as intimidating as walking into the room for the interview. My knees were shaking when I came in, and it wasn't much better when I left.*
—Sixth-grade teacher

*My writing skills are pretty good, and I think my resume can get noticed. But I'm really worried about the interview. You never know what they're going to ask you, and I'm afraid I'll say the wrong thing and then lose my chance for a job.*
—Recent college graduate

An effective cover letter entices a school administrator to turn the page and read your resume. A well-written resume persuades an administrator to pick up the phone and arrange for an interview. However, the first time an administrator thinks, "We should definitely hire this candidate," is during the interview.

Sometimes administrators formulate preconceived notions about a candidate on the basis of a cover letter and resume, but these perceptions can change quickly during the interview itself. If the hiring process were a horse race; the interview is the final stretch, when surprise finishes often occur. Front-runners fall behind, and dark horses may come out ahead. Committee members at one of our schools still talk about the atrocious insensitivity of a promising guidance counselor candidate who had all the right credentials on paper. The interviews were held after school and one member, a science teacher, felt tired because he had already worked a nonstop, 12-hour day. When he inadvertently muffled a yawn during the interview, the candidate rudely snapped, "Am I boring you?" The committee asked one or two courteous questions and then dismissed the candidate—forever.

On the other hand, many times a dark horse candidate wins the race. For example, an excellent social studies teacher hired by Seth lacked the experience, on paper, of some of her competitors. Nevertheless, in her interview, she demonstrated intelligence and an understanding of innovative, active instruction, and she smiled wholeheartedly when she described her affinity for teenagers. By the end of the session, she was the committee's unanimous choice.

Interviews are the most time-consuming step in the hiring process. We have as many as ten teachers, parents, and administrators in our schools, all leading busy lives, who must spend the better part of a day interviewing candidates for a single position. We sometimes hear aspiring teachers ask whether a hiring committee "has its mind made up already." Our answer is no, because considering the time commitment involved, a committee would not bother to interview a candidate who was not under serious consideration. If you make it to the all-important interview round, you have a realistic chance of being hired.

Another concern we hear comes from internal candidates—that is, candidates who student taught, volunteered, or served as **paraprofessionals** or leave replacements in a school. They ask whether a bad interview will negate all their hard work. To these candidates, we reply that administrators recognize the difficulties of showing one's real talents under the pressure of an interview situation. After months of commendable service, administrators usually discount a subpar performance during an interview. This is one reason why it is advantageous to identify the school where you want to teach and work there on a paid or voluntary basis. One disappointing interview will certainly put the kibosh on an external candidate, but this is not necessarily true if the aspiring teacher is an insider.

The opening scene of *Blackboard Jungle,* a 1955 movie about an English teacher's efforts to rehabilitate a high school gang, shows how interview procedures have changed over the years. Glenn Ford, playing the heroic new teacher, Mr. Dadier, sits with other applicants outside the principal's office on the opening day of school. When he is called in for his appointment, he convinces the principal in five minutes of his high moral character and his knowledge of classic English literature.

Longtime administrators contrast today's procedures to the "good old days" depicted in *Blackboard Jungle.* Today the process requires up to three separate interviews and involves search committees that include teachers, parents, administrators, and sometimes even students. Discussion during an interview has many focal points: content knowledge, pedagogy, instructional technology, and educational philosophy, to name but a few. No longer can you walk in with your resume and walk out with a job.

## Making an Entrance

As the saying goes, "You never get a second chance to make a first impression." Rob and Seth attended a conference of ranking school and district administrators recently in which the facilitator asked how long it takes them to decide on a candidate after he or she walks in the room. The consensus of the group was three to five minutes!

People have different feelings about walking into the interview room. For some, each step seems like a mile traveled in a gravity suit. Others step briskly into the room, propelled by a shot of adrenaline. As interviewers, we have also seen a variety of expressions on the faces of candidates, ranging from the anxiety that often accompanies a trip to the dentist to a confident smile.

As mentioned in Chapter 8, the first moments of any interview call for a friendly (but not exaggerated) smile and a steady gait into the room. Remember, these details count! Putting your best foot forward when you enter the interview room is the first of several things every candidate has to do. Here are some helpful hints that address important concerns:

• Can I move the chair? Many candidates are disadvantaged because their chair happens to be located in an awkward position and they don't feel comfortable moving it. If you're shown to a table, bring the chair close enough to rest your elbows comfortably on the tabletop. In this way, you will be able to clasp your hands in front of you or refer to your portfolio without awkwardness. In our experience, candidates who sit too far from the table seem remote. If there is no table,

make sure your chair position allows you to face your interviewers directly.

• What posture should I assume? You should strive to create a feeling of relaxed alertness. On the one hand, looking as if you are watching television in your living room won't impress the committee. On the other hand, if you place your body in a stressful position, you'll feel nothing but tension. Sit straight, but not rigidly. *Do not* cross your legs or sit on the edge of your chair. If seated at a table, place both hands in front of you in a gentle clasp. If there is no table in front of you, clasp your hands gently in your lap.

• Should I shake hands? In one-to-one interviews or settings where the interviewers are not sitting behind a table, this question is answered for you, but as a general rule, you should try to shake hands with those who are presented to you. If the interviewers provide their names when introducing themselves, repeat their names when returning the greeting. For example:

**Interviewer:** "Hi. My name is Barbara."
**Candidate:** "Hello, Barbara. Nice to meet you."

---

### Interviewing with Style

It is very important for you to appear at ease and in control at your interview. Take note of the following recommendations:

• Avoid nervous habits, such as pen tapping, nail biting, hair twirling, or repeatedly saying, "okay," "you know," and the like.

• Be an active listener—nodding your head occasionally as others speak to you, making eye contact, and paraphrasing others' concerns helps your interviewers feel "connected" to you.

• Keep in mind that everything about you is on display during an interview, including the manner in which you speak. Avoid colloquialisms and slang, and make sure you pronounce words carefully, so that every idea is communicated clearly. Observe rules of grammar and usage.

• Use a normal, conversational pace in your answers and strike a balance in vocal strength that enables you to project your words to everyone present without having to raise your voice.

• Make sure you understand the question before you begin to formulate an answer. If you are unsure about its meaning, ask—many candidates do not seek clarification beforehand, so they give the right answer to the wrong question.

• It is certainly acceptable to pause to think before giving your ideas; no one expects you to have all the answers at your fingertips. Short pauses can also be used to give phrases extra emphasis.

• Once you give the answer, let go of it in your mind so you can focus on the next query.

• Don't try to analyze the motivation behind every question. Instead, base your responses on your strengths, your awareness of the school's needs, and your own values and beliefs.

• Be genuine! If you make a mistake, say so (more about this later). If you're not familiar with something, ask for additional information. If something is funny, smile.

Shaking hands with members of large groups seated around a table is very cumbersome, however. Unless others offer their hands, it's best to take your designated seat and acknowledge everyone by smiling, nodding, and saying a quick "hello."

- If a glass of water is provided, is it acceptable to drink? Yes, of course, and you may find that it improves your performance.

## Interview Formats

Interviews are staged in different ways and serve a variety of purposes.

> I walked into the principal's office, and sat down in front of her desk. It seemed so quiet for a few moments—I felt a little awkward. We talked for about twenty minutes, and it was really kind of pleasant. Nothing really difficult, just questions about my background and interests [Darren, a middle school guidance counselor].

Darren just described a *screening* or *snapshot interview*. In this format, an administrator, sometimes accompanied by one or two colleagues, will conduct a brief question-and-answer session. Purposes include verifying the material on your resume, determining whether your general approach to educational issues is consistent with school philosophy and/or needs, and assessing your verbal skills and general demeanor.

The Gallup Organization, the same company famous for its election polls, has developed three standardized interviews for screening the potential of teachers, called the *Teacher Perceiver Interview*, the *Urban Teacher Perceiver Interview*, and the *Automated Teacher Screener*. In an effort to give the hiring process more scientific validity, Gallup interviewed master teachers about their craft, then trained thousands of school district personnel around the country to administer a similar survey to teacher candidates. Responses evidencing attitudes, feelings, and behaviors consistent with master teachers earn candidates access to the next round. The Teacher Perceiver and the Urban Teacher Perceiver Interviews are administered in a one-on-one conference involving a school administrator and a candidate in the administrator's office and last between twenty and forty-five minutes. The Automated Teacher Screener requires candidates to dial a toll-free number and respond to questions using the telephone keypad. Applicants can take the Automated Teacher Screener, approximately a ten-minute process, by calling from the comfort of their own homes. Copyright laws prevent public disclosure of Gallup survey questions.

> Darren continues, "The next time I came for an interview, the principal, a chairperson, and a teacher were sitting at the conference table in the office. It was much, much more intense. We talked about my experience with kids, the way I would approach certain situations, my counseling techniques, and the expectations they had for the job. I was there for at least forty-five minutes, maybe longer."

Darren's second round consisted of an *in-depth interview*. This form of interview, as the name suggests, provides an opportunity for prospective employers to explore your qualifications—and for you to make your case—in a more extensive manner. You can expect at least one in-depth interview during the pre-employment process. Some schools use a traditional one-on-one format. During this time, you may meet with a department chairperson, the principal, or a representative of the district's central office. Frequently, however, interviews are conducted by a panel. Composition of these panels varies, but expect to meet building administrators and supervisors, teachers, parents, and, depending on the school, representatives of the shared decision-making team. High school panels may include students as well.

> At my interview, I was asked to do some role-playing. I played the teacher, of course, and one of the interviewers played a student. We did a **writer's workshop** conference together—they even had a sample piece of writing for me to evaluate [Elana, a third-grade teacher].

Elana describes a *performance interview*. This type of interview offers candidates a chance to show how they would deal with situations they might encounter on the job. Elana was asked to conduct a lesson with an individual student, but many other tasks are possible. For example, a candidate might be asked to develop and explain a unit plan. Another activity might require simulating a parent-teacher conference about a student who is performing poorly in your classroom. Other examples include evaluating a student's art

---

**Leaving "The Gang" Behind**

It's not easy to be interviewed along with several of your competitors. To be effective, remember these pointers:

- Don't be intimidated by your perceptions of the other candidates. If you've followed our system, you'll be better prepared than any of them.
- Listen carefully to instructions and questions. Others may misinterpret the panel, but you won't.
- Remember, your goal is to impress the panel, *not* the other candidates. Frame all of your responses with the panelists in mind, and look at them as you speak.

---

project or critiquing instructional materials. Performance interviews may take place before a single interviewer or a panel.

> I have to say it was very strange. I was sitting in a room with three other candidates. We were all asked the same question about how we would teach research skills to fifth graders. Everyone got to hear everyone else's answers, and you didn't know whether to feel sorry for someone who was having difficulty or be happy that the competition wasn't doing so well [Angela, an elementary school teacher].

Angela's experience is not unique: the *gang* or *group* interview uses a format very different from the traditional model. In a gang interview, candidates appear before a panel with their competitors. Each is called on to perform the same task, perhaps discuss a "hot topic" like **authentic assessment, inclusion,** or effective classroom practices in reading.

## "Tell Us about Yourself . . ."

In all likelihood, the first question you will be asked is: "Tell us about yourself." The question is designed to provide a general introduction to the candidate and to relax her or him because it's relatively straightforward. If you follow our protocol, you will have outlined your answer among your *Talking Points,* so you can glance at these notes, if necessary, as you reply.

"Tell us about yourself" offers you an immediate opportunity to spotlight your strengths and overcome weaker aspects of your candidacy. Everyone has relative weaknesses—there is no such thing as the perfect candidate. You can turn some of these potential difficulties into strengths by accentuating the positive. Let's look at some of the possibilities.

### Case #1: Recent College Graduate

Relax; your interviewers already know this just by looking at your resume. The fact that you have been invited to an interview means that they see your potential. In your response, highlight your expert training, your accomplishments during student teaching, your high energy level, your comfort with technology, your willingness to contribute to co-curricular activities, and your understanding of youth culture.

Although they may not yet realize it, young teachers possess some natural advantages over veterans. First, they've grown up with computers and feel at ease with new forms of instructional technology. It is also likely that novices just out of college learned about such cutting-edge teaching methods as **cooperative learning** and **portfolio assessment** in their preparation programs. By virtue of growing up during a time of demographic change, many young teachers can make a case that they are uniquely positioned to be sensitive to students from diverse backgrounds; they also may be more aware of how to address students with disabilities. Experience shows that young teachers possess an openness to change that may be more difficult to find in veteran candidates.

There is one other benefit schools see in new teachers: employing them probably will cost a good deal less than someone with experience. "We're not the richest district," said one middle school principal. "So we go after new teachers more than those with lots of experience. And it's paid off for us: we've hired some excellent, dynamic people who really make things happen."

## Case #2: Teacher Changing Schools

Veteran teachers can cite results to sell their candidacy and show why they should be considered ahead of the competition. Our advice for experienced teachers is to use interview questions as opportunities to showcase proven classroom skills and training. A rich portfolio can assist this approach greatly, because it can provide examples that demonstrate real accomplishments. "If we're given the choice between someone who has little or no experience, and someone who has a strong track record, we like to go with the teacher who has more experience. We feel we're getting someone who can make an impact right away, rather than someone who needs time to grow into the job," said a suburban school district personnel director.

Experience is a definite advantage when confronted with an unanticipated question later in the interview. Having faced a range of classroom situations, a veteran teacher is better able to formulate a knowledgeable response.

Veteran teachers, however, can fall into "the experience trap." In answering interview questions, they have a tendency to describe methods practiced in their current school. Asked, for example, "How do you teach reading?" an experienced candidate might reply: "In my school, we stress phonics." While this answer seems appropriate, more often than not the administrator meant to ask, "How *would you* teach reading in our school?" The difference in wording is significant. Does the interviewer intend to ask about practices in the candidate's current school, or does the administator want to know methods that the candidate prefers? We suggest you ask the interviewer to clarify any ambiguity in the question.

A science candidate from a school with few resources may have limited capacity to conduct hands-on experiments in a classroom. The school to which he or she applies, in contrast, may have stocks of modern laboratory equipment and may believe students learn science best by discovery. During an interview, it would be a mistake for a candidate accustomed to limited resources to spend much time describing a program that has little relevance; we suggest that you instead make a transition to discuss "best practices" in science education, one of the *Fabulous Four* response strategies discussed in this chapter. Conversely, a candidate applying for a science position in a school that cannot afford expensive laboratory materials should explain how to get the most bang from a buck by citing an anecdote in which everyday household items were used in a motivating laboratory experiment.

As we have previously stated, if you are changing jobs because you are relocating, or if you filled a leave replacement position and are now seeking a permanent job, say so succinctly. Often there is an economic motive underlying a job change. Many teachers transfer from private schools to public schools or from low-paying public schools to districts with a significantly higher salary scale. In most cases, the interviewers already understand the reason why the candidate is seeking a new position and no justification is needed. If asked, briefly tip your cap to your current employer and express your desire to meet new challenges.

Suppose you are changing jobs because you disagree with your present school's educational tenets, or you do not see eye to eye with a superior? We recommend that you simply state, "Although I have found my tenure in my current school to be rewarding, I am ready to seek new challenges in another school district." Pressed for details, focus on what your new school would have to offer.

## Case #3: Returning to Teaching

Many candidates have gaps in their work histories. Frequently, this can be ascribed to child-rearing responsibilities, but some teachers leave the profession for a while to pursue other options, either by choice or as a result of layoffs, relocation, family needs, and so on.

Candidates in this category must show how experience gained away from the classroom has become an asset. They should prepare for questions about this phase of their lives by taking a good look at their *Personal Profile* and *Resume Reservoir*. Raising children, demonstrating responsibility over a period of years to an employer, and assuming leadership positions in the community have, in fact, prepared them to meet the challenges of the teaching profession. The statements below are provided as examples—use them to develop ideas and create your own responses.

---

**Honesty *Is* the Best Policy**

You can count on some tough questions if you've been out of teaching for a while. While your responses have to be tailored to your own situation, one rule applies to everyone: *never lie.* If you left teaching to take a higher-paying job only to discover that you missed working in a classroom, explain that to your prospective employer. If you relocated and then found that you didn't like your new surroundings, be honest about that, too. While there may be a moment or two of awkwardness, being honest rarely backfires or disqualifies you for a job. Instead, you may improve your chances by impressing the interviewer with your sincerity and commitment to education.

---

- "I really gained a great deal of awareness about child development while raising my own children, and now I realize that each child is different and requires instruction that addresses her or his own needs."
- "The time I served as a school literacy volunteer enabled me to become familiar with wonderful children's books that I would use in my own classroom."
- "My job at [name of company] involved training others; some were just out of high school. A teacher can adapt some of these techniques to the regular classroom. For example, . . ."
- "Even though I was out of the field for a while, I stayed current with the latest developments. I joined ASCD [Association for Supervision and Curriculum Development, a professional organization for educators], kept up with my professional reading, and attended conferences, like . . ."

As you plan for your interview, remember that the interviewer must be convinced that you are determined to return to teaching. Make sure that this commitment comes through loud and clear in your responses *and* in your body language and facial expression.

### Case #4: Career Changers

If you are in this category, take comfort in the fact that you're not alone. According to the U.S. Education Department, eighteen percent of new teachers were career changers in a recent year (National Center for Education Statistics, 2001). Many of the comments we made about teachers returning to the classroom also apply to career changers. Much like former teachers returning to the profession, career changers can score points by emphasizing life experiences. Their proven accomplishments as employees or entrepreneurs, community leaders, and parents are impressive. The trick is to demonstrate how their skills are transferable to classrooms. A second advantage of career changers is the passion they exhibit for teaching. Career changers have the courage to disrupt their lives, leave a profession, take the requisite teacher preparation courses, and start on the bottom rung of a new career ladder. They have surmounted daunting obstacles and are among the most highly motivated teachers.

Career changers must be prepared to explain the circumstances involved in the decision to teach. The best answers show that they are committed to teaching, not running away from an unsuccessful career. Consider the examples below:

- "I loved chemistry, but I felt stifled as a pharmacist. Then I realized what I liked most about pharmacy was consulting with customers about how their medications worked. One day my wife suggested that I consider teaching. I never looked back."
- "After working in advertising for several years, the money no longer interested me as much. The best part of my day was coming home to my preschool children. I loved watching them on the playground—learning to socialize with other children, asking questions about where sand comes from, and building public works projects on their own scale. The more I watched, the more fascinated I became. I took an adult education course in child psychology, and then I was hooked."
- "My mother, father, and older brother are teachers, so, naturally, for a long time I resisted the impulse to teach. I was always secretly interested, but first I had to try something different. But my work never

seemed as meaningful as the discussions around the dining room table about teaching. Finally I gave in to genetics and enrolled in a teacher education program. I really can't wait to have my own class."

After establishing their motivation to teach, career changers must show how their experiences and abilities make them stand out from the crowd. These important qualifications should be noted in the candidate's *Talking Points.* Here are some examples of career changers explaining the relationship between their past and their future:

- "Any pharmacist knows science. But a pharmacist you trust can explain complicated chemistry in simple terms and show that he or she cares about you as an individual. I can bring this to my teaching."
- "A big part of advertising is arousing interest. You have to make the consumer want to learn more about your product. In my teacher preparation courses, nobody had to convince me of the importance of motivating students. As a matter of fact, it is one of my greatest strengths."
- "Education has always been central to my family. I know the issues. I have learned how accomplished teachers plan lessons and deal with crises. I also know that good teachers are up late at night designing lessons, marking papers, and talking to parents. I know good teaching is hard work."

### Case #5: Fired

There is no doubt that this set of circumstances presents some challenging problems. However, the situation is not totally bleak. In fact, we have met successful teachers who overcame this hurdle and enjoyed productive careers.

In this case the key to succeeding in an interview is to emphasize the notion of change. Most educators have a deep respect for the ability of humans to change, adapt, and improve; if they didn't, they probably would have selected another profession. To reach their goals, job seekers who left a teaching job under inauspicious circumstances must show how they have addressed past deficiencies and now possess a very desirable package of skills and understandings about teaching and learning.

If you have been asked (or required) to leave a teaching position, you must assume that interviewers will ask about the reasons for your departure. (Even if the question doesn't arise at the interview, there's a good chance it will come up when you're asked for references or when you complete an official application for employment.) Therefore, you must be ready with some credible responses that advance your candidacy. Use the following statements as food for thought as you consider the best course for your own circumstances.

- "It was a challenging experience, but it did make me grow personally and professionally. I learned that not everyone is cut out to be a kindergarten teacher. As you can see from the student teaching evaluations in my portfolio, I thrived when I worked with the upper grades."
- "I was just out of college and, frankly, I was not ready for the demands of the job. I've learned a great deal since then, and I can't wait to get back into the classroom and apply all that I know now."
- "I have really worked at becoming a more effective teacher since that time. I've always loved working with kids, and now I've taken courses, participated in workshops, and substituted. I know that I am a much better teacher than I was before."
- "I realized that the public school system just wasn't suited to my style. I really appreciate the feeling of community in private schools."

There is one issue that we cannot decide for you: how open you should be about personal difficulties that might have led you to perform unsatisfactorily in a previous teaching assignment. Unfortunate developments in one's personal life can have great impact on job performance, and few would suggest that sickness, death in the family, divorce, or other traumas can be ignored while on the job. If a personal problem affected your work and contributed to your leaving a teaching job, the decision about how much information to share should be determined well in advance of an interview. Should you decide to share personal information of this type, you should also take the time to state that the difficuilties have passed. Remember, there is no

---

**Practice, Practice, Practice**

If you need to explain why you left or were asked to leave a job, we cannot overemphasize the importance of practicing your answers to specific questions about your experience. There will be some concerns based on your record, so you must take measures to ensure that you don't raise more questions during your interview. Everything about you, from your dress to the way you speak, must communicate integrity, professionalism, and a deep commitment to teaching. Anticipate difficult questions, develop sound replies, and remember that your most important objective is to demonstrate that you have remedied deficits and now stand as the candidate who can best address the school's needs. Whatever path you choose, *never* blame your previous employer, your former students, their parents, or the community for the difficulties encountered on the job.

---

requirement that you explain *anything;* after all, your life outside of school is private. On the other hand, comments about why your work was less than stellar may resolve questions that may be associated with your candidacy.

## The *Fabulous Four* Responses

We have participated in enough interviews (on both sides of the table) to understand that each situation presents its own unique challenges; there's always a chance that a totally unanticipated question will be asked, and the candidate will have just a few seconds to develop an answer. Nevertheless, we agree with the advice given in the renowned career handbook, *What Color Is Your Parachute?* (Bolles, 2000), that almost any question presented in an interview can be answered effectively in a response that ranges from *twenty seconds as a minimum to two minutes as a maximum.* Of course, candidates don't often bring stopwatches to their interviews. For this reason, we advise you to time your responses in practice sessions to develop an accurate, internal clock that can keep your answers within the optimal time frame.

"Know your audience" applies here, as well. You need to maximize the impact of your answers by presenting a balance between technical terms—that is, the language of education (see the *Glossary* for some of these)—and everyday conversational speech. In this way, you show that you are knowledgeable about current programs and practices without sounding overrehearsed or affected. "Jargon," said a superintendent we know, "is fine for educators. But if you have parents on the panel, jargon will turn them off quicker than you can say, 'Don't call us, we'll call you.'"

Successful candidates for teaching jobs know how to make their points succinctly and emphatically. Whenever possible, use one of these *Fabulous Four* strategies to create powerful responses to questions:

- Tell an anecdote.
- Refer to your portfolio or list of accomplishments.
- Cite a Web site, "best practices" used by master teachers, or research from a college course, journal, or book.
- State your philosophical belief, then substantiate it by showing how you translate that position into successful work in the classroom.

Let's take a look at how these strategies can be used to answer the general question, "How would you teach math in your elementary classroom?"

### Tell an Anecdote

"I feel that **manipulatives** must be incorporated into math lessons because they really help students grasp difficult and abstract concepts. When I was student teaching the fourth grade, I noticed that Sam, one of my students, was having a lot of difficulty with all of our work with fractions. One day, I brought manipulatives to the classroom and . . ."

### Refer to Your Portfolio or List of Accomplishments

Recall our observation in Chapter 7 that administrators may not ask to see your portfolio. You can take a proactive approach and introduce it into the conversation yourself as follows: "I would like to show you photographs of a unit that I taught on fractions. You can see that . . ."

---

**Think Time**

Classroom research advises teachers to use wait time—that is a three- to five-second delay—before they call on a student to answer a question. The pause allows the students time to think through an answer before speaking. We advise candidates to take a few seconds to compose answers to difficult questions, as well.

Rob was once offered a job, he was told afterward, because he appeared to be more reflective than the other candidates. At the interview, he was the only one who paused to ponder complex issues. Seth once served on an interview panel in which one member remarked about a candidate, "He hesitated so long before answering questions, at first I thought he had lost his train of thought. Then he came out with the most insightful, brilliant answers." The exceptional candidate was hired.

---

*Alternatively:*

"On this page of my portfolio you can see the slogans children created for our celebration of the hundredth day of school."

*Alternatively:*

"In my list of accomplishments, you can see the many manipulative aides that I used with much success during my student teaching."

### Cite a Web Site, "Best Practices," or Research

"If you look at the NCTM [National Council of Teachers of Mathematics] Web site, you can find references and links to many really good ideas about using manipulatives. I've adapted many of these ideas to my classroom, as when I . . ."

*Alternatively:*

"I was just so fortunate to work with a master teacher during my student teaching experience. She always introduced a new math unit by providing manipulatives for the students to explore. In the unit on fractions, for example . . ."

*Alternatively:*

"Piaget stressed that elementary school children are not developmentally ready to understand complex abstractions. Manipulatives, however, can help them master concepts in math, as when I . . ."

### State Your Philosophical Belief, Then Substantiate It

"I believe that elementary students must experience success to develop confidence in math and sustain motivation for learning. Math manipulatives enable me to achieve this goal because they provide a way for students to experience first-hand the abstract concepts that serve as the foundation of mathematics. Probability can be very confusing for students, for instance, but when you relate it to something real, like a deck of cards . . ."

One additional note: an effective interviewee varies answers among the *Fabulous Four* strategies. For example, if you always cite research, it will make you seem one-dimensional. Exclusively stating your philosophy will make you appear egocentric and unfamiliar with the body of educational research. The best result is achieved with a blend of the four approaches.

## Situational Questions

Many interviews feature questions that focus attention on specific incidents in your teaching career or ask how you would handle situations that teachers frequently encounter. An interviewer might ask, "Tell me about a time when you had to deal with a difficult parent." Similarly, a member of an interview panel could ask, "How would you deal with an eighth grader who refused to do work in your classroom and became angry when you asked him to complete his assignment?"

In both cases, remember that there are no perfect answers to these difficult circumstances; we're all still looking for good ways to address these issues. Therefore, the purpose of these types of questions is to gauge your poise, gain insight into your general views about teaching, and sample your problem-solving abilities.

When confronted with questions about problematic situations, we recommend the following approach:

- Use *Think Time* before beginning your answer. Determine what issue is at the base of the question and which of your experiences best matches the given situation.
- Always assume that the actors described in the situation are operating from the purest of motives. Don't, for instance, use the question as an opportunity to assault other people's parenting skills or express cynicism about today's youth.
- Use anecdotes wherever possible to respond to these types of questions. If you are just entering the profession and have no experience in the area under discussion, use a philosophical statement or a "best practice" to frame your answer.
- Demonstrate in your answer that you will put the needs of your students first. Let's try responding to several situational questions.

**Q:** How do you deal with a difficult parent?

**A:** I know that dealing with parents sometimes can be quite challenging. But in my view, parents are partners in the education of their children. I once had a parent who called me all the time to find out how well her child was doing—it got to the point where I couldn't go a day without having a long conversation with her about what the child did or didn't do. After a while, I realized that my usual methods for reporting student progress just weren't doing the trick. So I worked with the student to develop a daily self-reflection sheet about what went on in class, and I had the parent sign the form every day. Once the form was in place, I was able to use an end-of-the-week phone call to touch base with the parent, and she could not have been more pleased. As an added benefit, I liked the reflection sheet so much that I've now made it part of my classroom routine.

**Q:** How would you deal with an eighth-grade student who refused to do work in your class and became angry when you asked him to complete his assignment?

**A:** Middle school students are wonderful, but all the stresses and strains of adolescence can sometimes make them very challenging. I would address this situation in a few ways. Rule number one is that I would not get into an argument with the student: both of us would lose if that happened. Instead, I would project a calm, reasonable image to the child and to the rest of the class. I would say something like, "You are choosing not to work, and that is not acceptable in this classroom. You need to see me after class to work on this." After that, I would turn my attention to the rest of the group, and I would make certain that the class was focused on the work. That's my short-term plan. From my student teaching experience, I have also learned that teachers on your team and guidance counselors can provide many insights and suggestions about student behavior, so I would consult with them to work out a long-term strategy to prevent this type of situation from arising in the future.

Note that the answers presented here do not find fault with the parent or the student, and they address the questions in a clear and succinct manner. In addition, both responses stake out strong philosophical positions that demonstrate professionalism. In the first case, the candidate asserts, "Parents are partners in the education of their children," a statement guaranteed to find support among the members of an interview panel. The second response cites an important rule of thumb that every skilled teacher recognizes: never get into a tug-of-war with any student. Similarly, both examples provide useful strategies for addressing the problems presented in the questions.

## Controversial Questions

Controversial questions can cause candidates to lose their poise, break out in a cold sweat, and pray that a fire drill interrupts the interview. Controversial topics raise anxiety levels because they have no correct answers.

Take the question of **tracking**—that is, placing students in separate classes solely according to their achievement or aptitude levels. According to Paul George (1988), a nationally recognized professor at the University of Florida, eighty-five percent of educational research finds serious fault with tracking, yet eighty-five percent of all school districts track students nevertheless. Thus, if your personal beliefs lead you to oppose tracking, the chances are good that some of the people who interview you will hold the opposite opinion. On the other hand, if you support tracking, you may encounter interviewers who are adamantly against it. So, what do you do if you are asked, "What is your position on tracking?"

Many candidates freeze when they hear a question like this because they feel pulled in different directions at the same time. They worry that if they tell their interviewers what they really think, they may forfeit their chances of getting the job. However, if they respond with what they believe the questioners want to hear, they're not being true to themselves. A third possibility exists, as well: Candidates may not have yet reached their own verdicts on this complex, multifaceted topic.

Before offering our suggestions, let's examine two major reasons why interviewers ask questions about controversial issues in the first place. In some cases, the question is truly designed as a litmus test, to determine the candidate's potential fit with a school that has a strong philosophical foundation or mission. The second reason why controversial questions are asked is that interviewers want to observe how a candidate thinks on her or his feet, much like the situational questions described in the previous section. By asking difficult questions for which there is no correct answer, interviewers can make some predictions about how new teachers will handle pressure-filled situations that may occur in a classroom at a moment's notice.

The foremost rule in addressing a controversial issue is: *answer the question.* Some candidates try to avoid controversy by changing the topic, hoping the interviewers won't notice. Be forewarned: they do notice, and they will hold your failure to answer the question against you. It is similarly unwise to skirt the issue as in, "Well, I think it can be effective sometimes, and not so useful at other times." An answer like this tells interviewers very little about you.

If you're truly unsure about the topic, say, "My thinking about this issue is still evolving. I

can see that it is an important question for the school. If I got the job, I would spend a good deal of time talking to teachers and administrators and doing a lot of reading about it. My current thoughts are . . ."

What if your own views clash with the positions perceived to be held by your interviewers? In such cases, remember one of our guiding principles: Be yourself. A response that challenges a school's practices or opinions will not disqualify you automatically from most jobs. In fact, administrators are sometimes looking for teachers who can bring fresh insights and an impetus for change to their schools. We have never heard of any school where everyone was always in agreement; instead, creative work environments are enhanced by staff members who hold diverse opinions on everything from the philosophy of education to how to arrange the desks in a classroom. As a candidate, you can offer your opinions, as long as you observe two essential requirements: be respectful of the views of others, and state your unequivocal willingness to follow the policies of the school.

Should you take a job in a school where policies and practices clash with your own deeply held values and beliefs about education? This decision must remain an individual choice. We know of several instances in which new teachers helped bring about significant changes in their schools. On the other hand, we also remember cases in which new teachers felt alienated and isolated because their views conflicted with those held by their peers and supervisors.

With all of this said, let's return to the issue of tracking and see how it can be handled effectively by using two of the *Fabulous Four* strategies cited earlier. Each model begins with a brief summary of each side of the controversy. Let's consider a couple of sample responses addressing the tracking issue.

### Refer to Your Portfolio

Tracking is one of those very difficult and complex issues that educators confront. I know that there is a considerable body of research that shows tracking does not seem to help either poor students or high-achieving students. On the other hand, tracking is one way that schools try to address the varied learning styles and

---

**Interview Etiquette**

Our approach stresses the positive—that is, what you *should* do in an interview. Nevertheless, there are a few things you should most definitely avoid.

- As we've stated before, never lie or try to pretend that you know something when, in fact, you don't.
- Don't evaluate the interviewers. Don't say, "That's a good question," or "I really like that question."
- Avoid mention of other interviews, as in, "When I interviewed at the Riverview School, they also asked me about my experiences with inclusion."
- Don't ask for feedback at the end of the interview. Most interviewers are not ready to make informed judgments without giving themselves time for reflection.
- Never, never, never criticize a previous employer. Interviewers sometimes ask why you're leaving another job, or ask your opinion about another school. If you're pressed to state an unfavorable point of view, graciously respond, "They had a different way of doing things. If given a choice, here is what I would do . . ." Always take the high road; otherwise, you create the impression of being hypercritical, not a desirable trait in a teacher.
- Turn off cell phones and pagers *before* you enter the school.

---

achievement levels that students bring to the classroom, and teachers really do need to provide different types of instruction for different learners. I worked in a tracked school as part of my student teaching experience. I discovered there really is no such thing as a homogenous group because even students in tracked classes have very diverse needs. *As you can see from this page in my portfolio,* my solution to this problem was to develop math assignments that addressed the topic of angles differently. Students who didn't understand the concept very well could work on this basic assignment with manipulative aides, while those who were ready to move ahead got the second assignment sheet, which required them to solve math riddles by applying their understanding of the properties of different kinds of angles. The kids had a lot of fun, and they all felt proud of their accomplishments at the end, as you can see by the smiling faces in this photo. Of course, if a school doesn't track students in math, I would use this kind of approach with a mixed group. I know I can teach in either type of classroom.

### Cite Research

According to educational researcher Jeannie Oakes, most of the current research advocates detracking. Tracking has been shown to have a number of negative effects, including lowering the expectations of teachers for students assigned to the bottom groups and creating self-fulfilling prophecies that actually promote failure among students. On the other hand, tracking is one way that schools try to address the very diverse learning styles and achievement levels that students

bring to the classroom, and teachers really do need to provide different types of instruction for different learners. Personally, I believe that heterogeneous classroom environments are better for students. I think that they provide much more stimulation for most kids. I read an article in *Educational Leadership* that cited a number of strategies for teaching in heterogeneous classrooms, including **cooperative learning,** flexible grouping, and enrichment activities. I think these methods have great potential to improve the performance of all students. Of course, if the school has a tracking system in place, I would do my best to individualize work for each student, and knowing what I do about the research, I would be careful to maintain high academic expectations for all my students. I know I can teach in either type of classroom.

## High-Pressure Interview

A variation on the controversial question format, and one that we personally deplore, is the high-pressure interview. To determine how a candidate functions under stress, some interviewers deliberately seek to arouse anxiety by continually challenging everything the interviewee says. One form of this strategy occurs when the interviewer plays the devil's advocate role to the hilt; this method of examining all sides of an issue can bring even the most confident candidate to the point of meltdown by making it impossible to say anything without feeling attacked. Instead of disguising their technique, other high-pressure interviewers take direct

---

**What If I Don't Know the Answer?**

Our first response to this question is to say these words of comfort: it happens. If you find that you don't know the answer to a particular question, don't try to fake it. Instead, turn this awkward moment into a chance to demonstrate your professionalism by stating how you would get the answer, as in, "I really don't know much about **problem-based learning,** but I'll look it up on the Internet as soon as I get home."

---

aim at the candidate by arguing or even by commenting about the candidate's personal style, speech patterns, philosophy, or interests.

High-pressure interviewers may be misguided, but they think that their strategy provides them with valuable information about a candidate's potential to handle troubled students, disgruntled parents, and burned-out colleagues. They think it is much better to determine the fortitude of a candidate in the safety of the interview room than to send into the fray someone who is untested.

Here's our advice for dealing with high-pressure interviews:

- Maintain a smile and a sense of humor.
- Use the concept of "think time." As noted earlier, it is perfectly acceptable to wait three to five seconds before responding. Use that time to frame a measured, well-designed answer. Think time also demonstrates to your interviewer that you don't become unglued in stressful situations. The technique has the effect of slowing down the pace of the interview, thereby reducing the emotional temperature of the discussion and providing you with time to gather some strength.
- Stick to your guns. Remember that the interviewer is trying to see if you can hold fast to your positions, even under strong pressure. Remain focused and support your views by using one of our *Fabulous Four* approaches. (Of course, if the interviewer exposes an error in your thinking, admit your mistake or misunderstanding and move on.)

After leaving a high-pressure interview, you may want to contact the members of your job search network to find out whether the drama you just survived was an act—a way of learning more about you as a person—or is a

consistent part of the school's managerial style. If your network warns you, or if subsequent interviews are also conducted in a high-pressure atmosphere, consider whether you want to work in an environment where such conditions are a way of life.

## What If I Make a Mistake?

Speaking of pressure, what do you do if you are halfway through a question when you realize:
. . . you completely lost your train of thought?
. . . you phrased your answer poorly?
. . . you misunderstood the question?
. . . you just thought of a better answer to a previous question?

The first thing to know about these difficult and sometimes frightening situations is that they occur relatively frequently. Look, interviews are stressful. Many people say and do things during these times that they might not have said or done if they were not so nervous, and administrators adjust their expectations accordingly. A second point: we have never observed a perfect interview. You don't need to give a flawless performance to land a job.

If you find yourself in one of the situations described above, resist the urge to panic. Instead, put your emotional energy behind maintaining a sense of humor. Seth hired a guidance counselor who completely flubbed a question during a final interview in which the superintendent of schools and the assistant superintendent were present. Nonplussed, the interviewee smiled at the mistake and said, "I'll take a mulligan on that one." (In golf terms, a mulligan is a do-over.) It worked! As a matter of fact, everyone was impressed with his poise and sense of humor!

As you can see, an honest statement, accompanied by a genuine smile, often resolves a difficult situation. Statements such as these can also help:

"I'm sorry. Would you please repeat the question?"

"I'm sorry. I thought of a better answer to that question. I'd rather respond in this way . . ."

"Before we move on, I would like to add an important point to the question about . . ." If you choose this route, update your response, but be brief so the interview can move ahead.

We offer one last hint on this topic. If you're prone to forgetfulness when you become stressed, you can jot down a key word or two on your *Talking Points* pad or index card as questions are asked.

## Illegal Questions

In earlier generations, interviewers had a great deal of leeway in asking personal questions. Over time, however, laws and regulations have been adopted that protect people from questions that violate their civil rights. Employers are not allowed to discriminate on the basis of sex, race, color, national origin, religion, age, or disability. In general, questions must be related to an individual's ability to perform the essential elements and tasks of the job. The following questions, therefore, are *not* appropriate:

- When were you born?
- Are you married?
- Do you attend church regularly?
- What illnesses kept you out of work last year?
- It's obvious that you are pregnant. Why do you want this job now?
- How long have you had that disability?
- Where did your family originate?
- Have you ever declared bankruptcy?
- When are you planning to start raising a family?
- What political party do you belong to?
- What is your religion?

### Responding to Illegal Questions

Unfortunately, illegal questions do arise from time to time, frequently from interviewers with good intentions but a limited understanding of the law. Illegal questions can place applicants for teaching jobs in the throes of a dilemma: answering the question may violate their civil rights, but

refusing to respond may jeopardize their chances of securing a position.

The determination of how to respond to this type of question must rest with applicant. We offer three possible strategies for your consideration.

### Answer the Question

Remember, there are penalties for employers who make these inquiries, not for candidates who choose to reply to them directly:

- I am forty-eight years old.
- My disability is permanent.

### Address the Issue, Not the Question

First, try to address the concern that prompted the question. Then create a response to demonstrate one of your strengths or your commitment to teaching. For example:

- I was born without fingers on one hand. On the first day of class, I do a handstand in front of the children to show that it is not a handicap for me. (Seth once hired a physical education teacher who made this remark at the very beginning of an interview, putting the interview panel at ease.)
- Of course, I look forward to having a family, but my career is important to me now. I look forward to contributing as a teacher for many years.

### Just Say No

You can politely and respectfully decline to answer the question: "I'm sorry, but I feel uncomfortable with that question because it doesn't relate to how well I can perform the job. Perhaps I misinterpreted it."

If you choose this route and do not get the job, it may help ease your mind to realize that a school where interviewers ask illegal questions is probably not the place where you will feel most valued and content as a teacher.

## "Do You Have Any Questions for Us?"

In many cases, candidates are offered the chance to ask questions of their own in the last phase of an interview. Some candidates put this time to good use, but many pass on the opportunity, probably

**Not Yet**

In Chapter 10, we discuss the differences between first-round interviews and second- or third-round interviews in greater detail. In the first round, don't ask about salary, benefits, vacation schedules, and other compensation issues. In addition, it's not appropriate to ask about how you can get your contract renewed. You'll have an opportunity to ask these questions further down the road.

because they can only think about how much better they'll feel once they escape from the room.

It is very important to ask questions of the interviewer or the panel if provided the opportunity to do so. Well-designed questions can elicit valuable information about the needs of the school, the culture of the workplace, and the personalities of the people who will be your colleagues and supervisors if you get the job. The hiring process is a two-way street; this is your chance to interview your potential employer so that you can make an informed decision should you be offered a job. Don't abuse the privilege, however. Rob and Seth have both experienced interviews in which candidates literally talked themselves out of consideration because they asked questions ad nauseam. Limit your questions to no more than three and write them down beforehand in your *Talking Points*.

Many candidates ask about the general nature of the school. Consider the following possibilities:

- I would like to know more about the school. Would you please describe the student body in more detail?
- Where are the students drawn from? (This is a particularly important consideration for private schools and **magnet schools.**)
- How would you describe parent expectations for students? For teachers?
- Are parents active in the school?
- What major issues will the school address in the coming year? (A question about teaching and learning always impresses interviewers.)
- You mentioned the _____ [a curriculum initiative] in one of the questions. Could you tell me a little more about this?
- I'm very interested in building my skills as a teacher. What staff development opportunities are offered?
- How is the reading program (or any other curriculum area) organized?

- What new programs or activities are being considered for the coming year?
- What computer or other technological resources are available?
- What support services are provided to students? (These questions are appropriate if you're applying for a special education job or if you're interviewing for a position in an alternative school or other setting that works with special populations.)
- Is the curriculum aligned with particular standards?
- Do teachers work in teams? How are the teams organized? (This is a great question for middle school interviews.)

Another question may explore extracurricular activities. Try to use your question to alert your potential employer to your special strengths and interests.

- Are there any responsibilities outside the classroom that are expected of teachers? (This is often the case in private schools, especially boarding schools.)
- I enjoy working with students after the regular day is over. What extracurricular programs are offered?
- I would love to share my interest in _____ (name of hobby). Are there opportunities to work with students in clubs or special activities?
- Coaching is one of my passions. Are there openings for coaches in the coming year?
- As I mentioned, I have a lot of training in piano. Is there a school play? Would it be possible for me to help with the music?
- I think parent involvement is so important. Is there an opportunity to work with parents on special activities or projects?
- (If you are applying to a parochial school, try this one.) How is religion incorporated into

---

**Don't Ask!**

Do not ask a question if the answer is readily available on the school's Web site. Such questions make the administrator wonder why you did not prepare adequately for the interview by familiarizing yourself with the school beforehand. If you seem lazy getting ready for your all-important interview, administrators will wonder whether you will work hard enough if given the job. Undoubtedly some candidates competing for the teaching job *you want* did check out the Web site. It is impressive to ask, "After surfing your Web site, I have a question about . . ."

---

the school's extracurricular programs? How can I become involved?

It is also acceptable to ask a question about job security:

- Looking ahead, do you see this position as a stable one?
- Is this a probationary position leading to tenure?

## "Is There Anything Else You'd Like to Share?"

Candidates are sometimes given the opportunity to summarize their strengths and explain why they should be considered above the other applicants. If this offer is tendered, first check your *Talking Points* where you should have recorded key phrases to help you craft your response. Seize the chance to put the "icing on the cake" by combining a sincere thank you with a reminder of your ability to enable the school to meet its needs. One of the most effective examples of this type came from a candidate for a third-grade position who had just finished student teaching.

> I just want to say thanks for giving me this interview and tell you that I am really looking forward to working here. I know you are looking for someone who can help your students improve their reading. I truly believe that I am that person. I love kids, and I love books, and I know that there is a book out there that can grab even the ones who say they hate to read. If I get the chance, I can make this happen in my classroom.

P.S. That person got the job.

Ready for more? Take some time with your *Job Find Friend* and try answering questions from our *Top 100 Interview Questions*.

## Top 100 Interview Questions

### General

1. Tell us about yourself. (This is the most common opening question.)
2. What is your educational preparation?
3. Describe your experiences working with children.
4. Why did you decide to become a teacher?
5. Why do you want to leave your present position?
6. Why should we hire you?
7. What special skills or talents can you bring to this school?
8. What is your philosophy of education?
9. Name a book, concept, experience, teacher, or person who has influenced your professional development. How?
10. If you were the successful candidate, how would you prepare for your new job?
11. What do you like best about teaching? What do you like least?
12. What three adjectives would your (students/cooperating teacher/colleagues/supervisors) use to describe you?
13. What three adjectives would you use to describe yourself?
14. What have you learned from (student) teaching?
15. What are your career goals five years from now? Ten years from now?
16. What professional development goals do you have for your own improvement?
17. How have you improved your professional skills recently?
18. What professional associations do you belong to?
19. What professional journals do you subscribe to?
20. What are your strengths as a teacher?

21. What extracurricular activities would you like to be involved in?
22. Teaching requires time management and organization skills. How do you address these challenges?
23. How do you cope with stress?
24. What hobbies, recreational activities, and/or interests do you enjoy?
25. What book greatly influenced your personal development?
26. What is the last book you read about teaching? Discuss the book.
27. How will you develop a productive relationship with your supervisor?
28. What questions have I not asked you that you wish I had raised?
29. What questions do you have for us? (This is the most common final question.)

## Student-Centered

30. What academic, affective, and social goals would you have for students at this age level?
31. How is a fourth-grade student different from a fifth-grade student? (Pick any two adjacent grades.) Alternately: How is a middle school student different from a high school or elementary school student? (Mix and match any combination, as appropriate for the position.)
32. Describe your goals for the first few days of school and how you would achieve them.
33. How would you maintain student discipline?
34. How would you involve students in the development of classroom rules?
35. How would you address **affective education** goals in your classroom?
36. What measures would you take if a child failed a test?
37. How would you accommodate the learning and emotional needs of students with disabilities? **LEP (Limited English Proficiency) learners? Gifted and talented** students?
38. A student tells you confidentially that she is using drugs. What would you do with the information? (You can substitute any other situation in which you are told something in confidence—e.g., divorce, pregnancy, child abuse, or neglect.)
39. How do you develop rapport with students?

40. How would you handle a student who is a consistent behavior problem in your class?
41. What have you found to be the toughest aspect of discipline?
42. A child has been talking incessantly in your class. What would you do? How would you follow up if your first measure proved ineffective?
43. You tell a student to do something and she refuses. She seems determined not to follow your instructions. What would you do?
44. A child repeatedly fails to complete homework assignments. How would you respond?
42. Describe your background working with computers and other forms of **instructional technology.**
43. What opportunities would you take to provide students with extra help?
44. What is the role of a teacher in the classroom? Outside the classroom?
45. What characteristics make a master teacher?

## Curriculum, Instruction, and Assessment

46. Describe the physical appearance of your classroom.
47. If I walked into your classroom on a typical day, what would I see taking place?
48. How would you describe your teaching style?
49. Describe your approach to teaching this subject (or grade level).
50. Why is your field important for a student to study?
51. What are the most important concepts and/or skills that students should master in this subject?
52. What are some of the best practices for teaching (in this field, at this grade level)?
53. What are **standards**? How do you align your curriculum and units of study with our state standards?
54. What are the key standards for this subject area?
55. How do you communicate to students your expectations for an assignment?
56. How do you teach study and organizational skills to your students?
57. Describe how you would modify a lesson to meet the needs of a student with disabilities, an **LEP** student, or **gifted and talented** student.

58. What techniques do you use to check for understanding during a lesson? What techniques do you use with students who don't "get it" the first time?
59. Describe the format you would use to develop a lesson.
60. Describe a successful lesson you have taught. What were the objectives and the format of the lesson, and how did you assess whether the objectives were achieved?
61. How would you use **differentiated instruction** to meet the needs of all students?
62. What principles do you use to motivate students to learn?
63. Describe curriculum trends in your field of study. Which is most interesting or exciting to you?
64. How would you plan differently for a **homogeneous** or **heterogeneous** classroom?
65. Think of a lesson that was less than successful. Describe what you learned from it.
66. How would you address the needs of students in your classroom who come from diverse cultural backgrounds?
67. How would you take into account the local economy (e.g., a fishing village or a large local employer) in the lessons you plan?
68. What is your grading philosophy? How do you decide what grade to assign to a student?
69. How would you assess student work?
70. How do you design a unit of instruction?
71. How would you use **alternative assessments** (or **portfolios** or **rubrics**)?
72. How do you use **standardized test** results?
73. Describe independent projects that you might assign.
74. Choose a topic and tell us how you would teach it and assess student learning.
75. What is your philosophy regarding homework? Describe some types of homework assignments that you would require from your students.
76. What is **constructivism**? How would you use this approach in your classroom?
77. How would you use **cooperative learning** techniques in your classroom?
78. In a **cooperative learning** lesson, how would you ensure that every group member actively participates?

79. Describe how you would develop **interdisciplinary** connections in the lessons you present to students.
80. How would you use computers as a tool for teaching and learning?
81. How would you use the Internet in your classroom?
82. How would you incorporate **(career education, character education, problem-based learning, service learning)** into the curriculum?
83. How would you teach reading or writing across the curriculum (an elementary school question)? How would you teach reading or writing in your content area (a secondary school question)?
84. What units would you include in teaching _____ (name of course)?
85. How would you deal with controversial subjects in the classroom?
86. What curriculum materials have you developed?
87. When you try something new in the classroom, how do you know if it works?
88. Would you group students in the classroom? If so, on what basis?
89. Explain how you would stimulate higher-level thinking among your students.
90. How would you incorporate Gardner's theories of **multiple intelligences**?
91. What criteria would you use to evaluate textbooks for possible adoption?
92. How would you use the resources of the school library?

**Parents and Community**

93. How would you involve parents in the learning process?
94. How do you communicate pupil progress to parents?
95. A parent calls to question a student's grade, performance in class, or homework assignment. How would you address the parent's concerns?
96. Role-play a call to a parent to seek a solution to a classroom problem.
97. Describe how you would prepare for a parent-teacher conference.
98. How would you involve parents in homework assignments? How would you try to

ensure that they are not overly involved in their child's homework assignments?

99. How will you learn about our community?
100. How would you use community resources to facilitate learning?

Breathe a sigh of relief. Your interview is over. You've cleared a major hurdle, but your work isn't done. Catch your breath and then turn to Chapter 10 to learn about the final steps in your search for the teaching job you want.

---

## REMINDERS

- Your interview starts the moment you walk into the room. Present yourself as a mature, dedicated professional at all times.

- Become familiar with the various interview types. Be ready for any format and for difficult questions about teaching or your background.

- Focus attention on your strengths and always try to show how you can address the needs of the school.

- Use the *Fabulous Four* strategies for answering questions. Remember: answers should not go beyond two minutes. Refer to your portfolio to support your points.

- Stay cool—even if pressed or if you make a mistake. Interviewers need to know that you can maintain your poise and think clearly during stressful moments.

- Use an invitation to ask your own questions as an opportunity to learn more about the school.

# Chapter Ten

# After the Interview

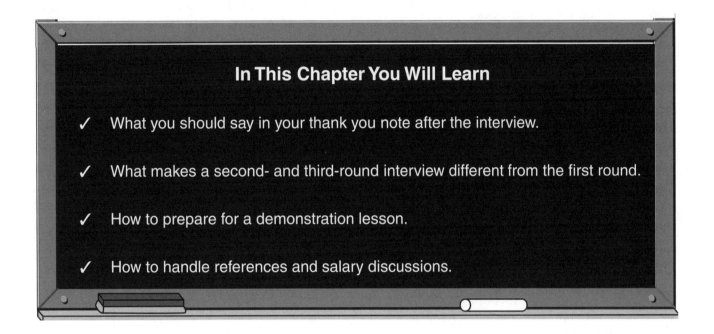

**In This Chapter You Will Learn**

✓ What you should say in your thank you note after the interview.

✓ What makes a second- and third-round interview different from the first round.

✓ How to prepare for a demonstration lesson.

✓ How to handle references and salary discussions.

*We were undecided between two very qualified candidates. It was only during the demonstration lesson that the differences really emerged. After that, our choice was easy.*

—Principal

*It ain't over till it's over.*

—Yogi Berra, baseball player and philosopher

Phew! Your cover letter and resume piqued their interest. You felt confident in your interview because you were knowledgeable about the school's educational needs and how you would meet them in your classroom. But your campaign to land the teaching job you want is not over until they make you a job offer and your salary and benefits are decided. (And then the hard work really begins . . . teaching!)

After the interview, schools generally narrow the field of candidates down to one, two, or three finalists. Several steps lie ahead before a

> Several steps lie ahead before a final decision is made, including second- and maybe third-round interviews, perhaps a demonstration lesson, checking references, and salary negotiations. While you wait to hear whether you are a finalist, there is still time for more preparation.

final decision is made, including second- and maybe third-round interviews, perhaps a demonstration lesson, checking references, and salary negotiations. While you wait to hear whether you are a finalist, there's still time for more preparation. *Accelerate* your efforts now that you have almost reached your destination.

## Interview Information

When you arrive home from the interview, immediately complete an *Interview Information Form* (page 131), while the memory is still fresh in your mind. This form is used to record key data about the interview, including the questions asked and the names of the people present, to help you get ready for the next one. If you advance to a second-round interview, you should review these notes beforehand. It is advisable to rehearse questions from the first round because the same ones are often repeated the next time around. If they decline to invite you back, practicing the questions will still help you prepare for an interview in another school. Place the *Interview Information Form* in your *Job Find File.*

## Post-Interview Blues

Everyone experiences a tremendous sense of relief immediately after an interview. Like the joke about the person who repeatedly knocks his head against a wall because it feels so good to stop, walking out the door of a stressful interview makes you feel better. It is also common to catch a case of post-interview blues, also know as the *shouldacouldawouldas,* once the initial feeling of relief fades. Symptoms of this dreaded disease include saying:

- I should have mentioned (fill in the blank) during the interview.
- I could have answered that question better, but I misunderstood it.

- I would have spoken more eloquently if I hadn't been so nervous.

Remember, nobody is perfect during an interview, including the candidates you're competing against. Looking on the bright side, a case of the *shouldacouldawouldas* has a positive dimension because it enables you to learn from your experience and interview better next time. You can use the *Interview Information Form* to analyze your performance and set goals for improvement.

## The Thank You Note

Within twenty-four hours after the interview, job-seeking etiquette requires you to send a thank you note. Remember our guiding principle that you must target the specific circumstances of each school. For that reason, don't send a generic thank you note, simply reiterating the same information. Instead, your thank you note should follow the points listed below. Ask your *Job Find Friend* to critique what you have written, and place a copy of the note in your *Job Find File.*

- Like your cover letter, the thank you note should use formal business letter style.
- The salutation should address the interviewer by the administrator's formal title, beginning with Dr., Mr., Mrs., or Ms. If you were interviewed by a committee, the salutation should address the committee leader.
- In the first paragraph, express sincere gratitude to the interviewer or the committee for taking the time to interview you.
- In the second paragraph, briefly describe one of the school's noteworthy educational objectives that impressed you during the interview. Next, write a transition sentence in which you restate the importance of the objective. Finally, remind them how *you* can help the school achieve this educational goal.
- In the third paragraph, briefly reiterate your thanks.

**Interview Information Form**

Name of School _____   Interview Date _____

Who attended the interview?

| NAME | POSITION |
|------|----------|
|  |  |
|  |  |
|  |  |
|  |  |
|  |  |
|  |  |

What did you learn about the school from the interview?

_____

_____

_____

What did you learn about yourself from the interview that will improve your next performance?

_____

_____

_____

What did you promise the interviewer(s) you would do after the interview? For example, did you promise to send a list of references or to review an educational theory that you did not know?

_____

_____

_____

What questions were you asked? Record them on the back of this page.

- The letter should not exceed 200 words.
- Some candidates use the thank you note to compensate for perceived inadequacies of an interview. From time to time, we read thank you notes that say, "I neglected to mention the following point during my interview . . ." We advise against the practice, unless you committed an extremely serious gaffe. (A case in point: Seth once clarified the difference between **heterogeneous** and **homogeneous grouping** in a thank you letter after nervously mixing up the terms during an interview.)

## Handling Rejection

Schools use a variety of methods to deliver bad news to candidates who do not make the final round, none of them very popular. Some school districts send a rejection letter, although these "thanks but no thanks" letters may not be mailed until the Board of Education or Trustees officially hire the new teacher, a process that can take weeks. In other cases, no news is bad news: if you don't hear from them in several days, you can assume you're not a finalist.

17 Bess Lane
St. Louis, Missouri 12121
June 16, 2003

Dr. Henry Wallace
Principal
Truman High School
34 President's Way
Independence, Missouri 21212

Dear Dr. Wallace:

Thank you for affording me the opportunity to interview for the tenth grade social studies position available at Truman High School. Please also extend my gratitude to the other parents, students, and teachers who served on the interview committee.

I was fascinated by our discussion about **document-based questions**. In a social studies class, students should emulate the behavior of real historians and draw conclusions on the basis of historical evidence. During student teaching, I learned to inculcate these higher-level reasoning skills into weekly document-based lessons. For example, I excerpted statements from *The Federalist Papers* and actual editorials from newspapers of the period as we studied the Constitution.

Again, thank you for allowing me to participate in a fascinating interview. I look forward to hearing from you soon.

Sincerely,

Sally MacArthur

17 Dewey Lane
New York, New York 12121
November 16, 2003

Dr. Benjamin Bloom
Principal
Horace Mann School
34 Educator's Way
New York, New York 12121

Dear Dr. Bloom:

Thank you for affording me the opportunity to interview for the computer teacher position available at Horace Mann School. Please also extend my gratitude to the other parents, students, and teachers, who served on the interview committee.

I was impressed by the commitment of Horace Mann School to the integration of computers into the curriculum, demonstrated by the 4:1 ratio of students to computers. As we discussed during the interview, computer skills advance a number of educational objectives, such as developing lifelong learning skills. The course I completed at Teachers College titled, "Using Computers in the Elementary Classroom," and my experience as a computer counselor in a summer camp have taught me how to turn this dream into reality in a classroom.

Again, thank you for allowing me to participate in a fascinating interview. I look forward to hearing from you.

Sincerely,

Sally McIntosh

Applicants understandably feel depressed when they are rejected following an interview. Ironically, they are usually less disappointed if their candidacy is rejected early in the hiring process. Candidates feel more frustration the further they advance, even though they actually were more successful. How can you cope with the disappointment?

## Acknowledge Your Feelings

You invested hard work and dreamed of achieving deeply cherished professional goals, only to have your hopes dashed. Defeated politicians, athletes cut from teams, and half the waiters in Los Angeles (they're probably auditioning actors) will tell you that you have to express your disappointment and develop a support system among understanding friends and family members.

## Try Not to Take It Personally

Each school is seeking a candidate whose unique educational and work background closely suit its needs. Your rejection was probably influenced by circumstances beyond your control, such as another candidate whose qualifications were a better match.

## Remember The Roses of Success

In the children's movie *Chitty Chitty Bang Bang,* the song, "The Roses of Success," exudes the power of positive thinking. It is suggested humorously that successful inventions would not have been created if inventors had not experienced failure first. When earlier trials failed, inventors had an opportunity to identify flaws in their thinking, consequently opening the door to necessary improvements. Analyze your performance after every interview and ask yourself: What did I do well? What could I have done better?

One final, extremely useful tip: If you're one of two or three finalists and are not offered the job, a school administrator may call you to notify you personally over the telephone. If you receive such a call, first graciously thank the administrator. Then state, "I would appreciate any feedback, both positive and negative," and jot down notes for your *Job Find File*.

# Second- and Third-Round Interviews

Second- and third-round interviews generally serve two purposes: They enable a wider circle of stakeholders to participate in the screening process, or they enable administrators who hold ultimate decision-making authority to get to know a small number of finalists and determine which candidate will be offered the job. If you were one of ten candidates interviewed in the first round, and one of two called back for the second round, your odds of landing the job have improved considerably. Later-round interviews will pose new challenges.

## Whom Will You See?

If you were seen by one or two administrators in the first round, it is quite possible that you will be interviewed by a larger panel during your second visit. The second-round interview in this case may involve parents, teachers, and administrators (some high schools may include a student or two). If the first-round interview was conducted by such a large grassroots group, then the second round may be limited to a small number of administrators. We suggest that you ask the person who calls to arrange the appointment the names and positions of the second-round interview panel. Keep in mind that schools sometimes use a variety of titles to describe essentially the same supervisory position. For example, department chair, curriculum coordinator, and lead teacher are all roughly equivalent positions. Some schools defer a final decision until a third round involving the ultimate decision makers.

## What Will You Be Asked?

It may surprise you to hear many of the questions you were asked in the first round repeated the second time around. Although you are facing a new audience, the concerns they have may be similar to those expressed earlier. This is why we suggested you record first-round questions on the *Interview Information Form* and practice answering them. Supplement your notes with any information you gained about the school since the initial appointment.

Experience has taught us that parents, teachers, students, and administrators often ask

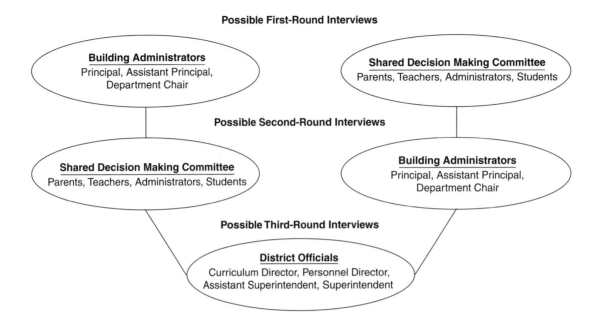

**Possible First-Round Interviews**

**Building Administrators**
Principal, Assistant Principal,
Department Chair

**Shared Decision Making Committee**
Parents, Teachers, Administrators, Students

**Possible Second-Round Interviews**

**Shared Decision Making Committee**
Parents, Teachers, Administrators, Students

**Building Administrators**
Principal, Assistant Principal,
Department Chair

**Possible Third-Round Interviews**

**District Officials**
Curriculum Director, Personnel Director,
Assistant Superintendent, Superintendent

different types of questions. Parents want to know how you will relate to children and establish lines of communication between home and school. "What did students think of you during your last teaching job?" "If a child fails a test, what will you do?" "How do you keep in touch with parents?" These are typical questions reflecting the concerns of parent members of interview panels.

Teachers frequently pose questions about classroom management, curriculum, and instructional techniques. "How do you teach fractions?" "If a child talks incessantly during class, how will you address the behavior?" "What interdisciplinary lessons have you taught?" These questions help them determine whether you and

the faculty are a good fit. At the high school level, they may also ask you very detailed questions about curriculum content.

High school students tend to ask questions directly related to their classroom experiences. Consider these examples: "What would you do if a student hands in an assignment late?" "What is your grading policy?" "What kind of homework and projects can we expect in your class?"

Administrators often ask about major issues facing the school or about newly adopted curriculum or instructional practices. For example, if voters recently approved a bond issue to fund computers in the classroom, the administrator may ask whether you have the skills to implement this schoolwide objective. If the school

---

**Questions to Ask When Arranging
Second- or Third-Round Interviews**

Be prepared! Photocopy these questions and keep them near your telephone.

1. If you did not catch the name: Whom am I speaking to?
2. Who will be present at the interview?
3. If you are speaking to a building administrator, ask: Is there anything I can bring, or issues I should address, to help the school reach a decision?
4. How many finalists are still under consideration?

Do not be alarmed if the panelists in the second-round interview appear to be reading from scripts. Some interview groups prepare questions in advance and pose the same questions to each candidate. This practice enables the interview panel to compare the candidates in a standardized, scientific fashion. Other interviews are very informal and conversational and may take place in easy chairs arranged around a coffee table reminiscent of a living room.

has experienced demographic changes—for example, an influx of new immigrants—the administrator may ask about your ability to teach an **English as a Second Language** population. Two other concerns of administrators across the country are special education and raising standardized test scores; expect questions on these topics.

### Can I Repeat Myself?

Seth attends first-, second-, and sometimes even third-round interviews with the same candidate. Often an identical topic arises, and the candidate turns to him and asks, "I discussed this in a previous round. Can I repeat myself?" Yes, it is perfectly acceptable to repeat yourself as long as there are different people in the audience. You can also include new information or additional examples, or point out a change in your views since the first interview. Seth once heard an English teacher candidate state, "In the first round, I mentioned that I would assign books written by Nelson DeMille, but as I thought about it, I realized the author is not age-appropriate for middle school students." After she left the room, the interviewers gave her credit for being reflective, an important trait in a teacher.

The steps you take to prepare for later-round interviews are similar to those for the first round, except that you have the tremendous advantage of knowing the concerns of the school *beforehand*. Here are some steps you can take to prepare:

- Review the list of interview committee members and the names of other school VIPs, such as the principal, headmaster, and district superintendent.
- Review your research from Chapter 4. Since first-round questions are the best predictor of second-round concerns, think about how

you can integrate the research into your responses next time. Also, you may have the opportunity to discuss other school goals that you identified from your homework, if these needs match your particular strengths.

- If you felt at a loss answering a first-round question, research the topic thoroughly. Second-round committees are sometimes advised to probe an issue that first-round interviewers identified as a deficiency. It is impressive when a candidate can say, "I studied this issue since the last interview because I know it is an important topic to you."
- Review the list of questions from your *Job Find File* that were asked in the first round and rehearse your answers. Practice answering questions aloud and call on your *Job Find Friend* to critique your responses.

## Demonstration Lessons

After one or two interviews, administrators may ask to observe you teaching a demonstration lesson. This is a sure sign that you are a serious candidate. From the administrator's point of view, the demonstration lesson offers a more realistic setting in which to assess a candidate's abilities. It's the same reason why the department of motor vehicles requires new drivers to take a road test after they pass the written examination.

Demonstration lessons can take place in your own school or in the school to which you have applied. Usually, candidates are not given a choice, but if you are given the option, it is more advantageous to present the lesson in your current job or student teaching placement. The exception to this rule occurs if you're applying in confidence and haven't notified your present supervisor.

---

**Preparing for the Demonstration Lesson**

Whether the demonstration lesson takes place where you are currently teaching or in the school to which you applied, planning will be the key to a successful performance. Follow these steps:

1. Make sure your objective is clear and easy to assess. The lesson should be self-contained: it should not be part one of a two-part presentation.
2. If you are not going to teach in your own classroom, include a one-sentence introduction to the students, e.g., "Hello, I am Ms. _____, and I'll be working with you today as we study the French Revolution."
3. Design a strong introduction to pique the interest of students and your observers.
4. Rehearse the lesson plan to the point where you don't need to refer to your written outline during the class. This helps you maintain momentum and control.
5. Make certain that you have all the materials needed for the lesson. If you need photocopies for distribution, make sure that you check the quality and quantity. If you will be using an overhead projector or a computer, be sure they are in working order before the class begins. Always have a back-up plan and extra materials in case the technology will not cooperate—put this plan into action quickly if difficulties arise so that you do not waste a great deal of the available time tinkering with the machinery instead of working with students.
6. End the lesson with a summary or an evaluative exercise that demonstrates student learning to your observers.
7. Thank the class for its attention and cooperation at the end of the session.
8. Leave time to talk with the observers immediately after the "demo." Ask your cooperating teacher or a colleague to cover for a brief time.

---

## Demonstration Lessons in Your School

These are the reasons why it is preferable to stage the demonstration lesson in your own school. First, administrators can witness the rapport you have built with your students. Second, they can view samples of student work posted on bulletin boards, ascertain whether you use learning centers and computers in your classroom, and assess other indicators of your teaching style. Third, if you teach a demonstration in your home school, then you know the students' capabilities and prior knowledge. It's difficult to judge the academic needs of a group that you just met. You must ask the administrator of your school for permission to have visitors in the building.

You must feel extremely comfortable with your lesson plan. The objective is to showcase your expertise, particularly those qualities that the school to which you have applied is seeking. A demonstration lesson is not the time to experiment with unfamiliar curriculum content or instructional techniques. Rob recollects visiting a teacher who wanted to use **cooperative learning** in her lesson, but since this approach was new for the class, the entire period was spent explaining procedures, and the lesson's objec-

tives were never achieved. The day before the visit, tell your class that observers will be coming, and explain the reason if you can. The next day, provide the observers with a copy of the lesson plan.

## Demonstration Lessons in the School to Which You Are Applying

The most difficult problem you will face is not knowing the students. For this reason, we suggest that you place a blank nametag on each desk before students enter the room. When the class begins, pass around a magic marker, and instruct children to write their names so you can call on them personally.

A key question is: Will they give you free rein to design the lesson plan, or will they dictate a topic? If they allow you to teach any lesson you choose, ask if you can contact the teacher beforehand to determine whether your lesson plan is suited to the group. If they assign you a topic instead, your options are limited, but you must still use instructional methods with which you are comfortable and that are aligned with the school's needs.

---

### When Should I Notify My Current Employer?

Recognizing that reference checking may jeopardize relationships with your current employer, you may decide to delay notification. School administrators are accustomed to a candidate's need to maintain confidentiality, and most schools ask before they check references. If you have very serious concerns about premature notification, you can include the following statement in the last paragraph of your cover letter: "I am applying in confidence. Please do not contact my employer at this time."

While there are understandable reasons to delay informing your current employer, springing a last minute surprise is equally harmful. Never put yourself in the position of saying, "The school I have applied to will call you later today"; untimely notification may breed antagonism.

As mentioned previously, if you are seeking to change teaching positions, ask your current school administrator for permission in advance if you plan to schedule a demonstration lesson in your present school.

---

If you can call the class's regular teacher in advance, these are some questions to ask:

- What related topics or skills have already been taught?
- Do you think my lesson plan and objectives are realistic?
- How would you characterize the class?
- What advice can you provide me about working with this group?

## References

You have made a favorable impression during interviews, and perhaps school officials have had the opportunity to observe you teaching a demonstration lesson. One piece of the puzzle remains before administrators feel comfortable offering you a job; administrators want to know about the quality of your previous work in school settings. Using the names of references you supply, they conduct telephone interviews with your current and former supervisors to investigate your character and job-related skills.

Earlier, we advised against writing the line, "References available upon request," at the bottom of your resume because most schools don't check references until the field of applicants has been narrowed down to one or two finalists. However, this practice is not universal. Some administrators begin calling references immediately if the list is supplied to them early. Other administrators do not restrict themselves to speaking with references given them by candidates. They consider any associate, current or previous, "fair game" when investigating the background of an applicant. Seth knew an administrator who boasted that he could save time by calling the most recent supervisor of candidates before interviews were scheduled, because he could save precious time if he heard the response, "Don't even bother interviewing that person!"

We suggest you prepare a page listing four to six references and place two copies, a permanent one and an additional copy to provide a potential employer, in your portfolio. Your *Resume Reservoir* from Chapter 3 lists potential references. These are some guidelines to help you with this task:

1. Write your name across the top of the page and the title, *References,* beneath.
2. Ask permission of each reference beforehand.
3. Restrict your list to supervisors, co-workers, and professors. Do not include family members or friends with whom you share strictly a social, nonprofessional relationship.
4. References from schools where you worked or colleges you attended are most preferable, followed by references from education-related organizations such as literacy volunteers, Big Brothers/Big Sisters, and summer camps. References outside these fields generally are not helpful.
5. For each reference, write the person's name, title (e.g. Principal, Cooperating Teacher, Professor of Education), the organization the individual represents, address, and daytime telephone number.

6. Recent references have greater impact. If your reference is a professor, you should have attended the school within the last three years. The same three-year rule applies to work references outside of education.

7. List the references in the order you would prefer them to be called.

8. If the second interview is drawing to a close and the employer has not requested your references, offer to provide the list, stating, "I have a list of references that I would like to leave with you."

9. If you have an extraordinary reference, you may politely ask the employer to call. Our suggested wording is, "If you are checking references, I would appreciate if you would call Dr. Nesrief, the principal where I student taught. He urged me to have schools call because he said I was the best student teacher his school ever had."

# Negotiating Salary and Benefits

## When Is It Appropriate to Discuss Salary and Benefits?

Unlike the business world, salary is rarely discussed up front in education. Public service, rather than financial compensation is deemed to be the most important incentive. Consequently, it is considered inappropriate to ask about salary, benefits, vacation schedules, and other perks during the early phases of the job search process, including the initial interview.

While discussing salary too early can make a candidate appear mercenary in an administrator's eyes, you nevertheless need to know the answers to questions about salary and benefits before you can commit to a job. Generally, the topic is raised by the administrator who has ultimate authority to make a job offer, either during

---

**Anita Job**

**References**

John Doe
Principal
Stellar School
7 Nova Drive
Frostbite Falls, MN 00001
111-516-7189

Jane Doe
Cooperating Teacher
Ninth Grade Social Studies
Happy Valley High School
16 Charming Cross Road
Frostbite Falls, MN 00001
111-516-9876

Jane Plain
Education Professor
Alumni College
Graduate Lane
Pottsylvania, PA 00002
001-631-6316

John Smith
Program Supervisor
Literacy Volunteers
1 America Alley
Pottsylvania, PA 00002
001-631-6001

or shortly after the final-round interview. In suburban or rural school districts, this responsibility may rest with the superintendent of schools or the assistant superintendent. In urban districts, the principal or director of personnel may negotiate these matters. Private school decisions are made by the headmaster or director.

We recommend that you wait until school authorities raise the issue of compensation. If you are offered the job and they don't mention salary, then you must inquire politely.

## What Should I Ask?

As administrators, we understand the importance of providing a candidate with information about salary and benefits. On the other hand, when we meet candidates who grill us with an inordinate number of questions devoted to compensation, we begin to wonder about the person's priorities. Rob recalls interviewing an excellent candidate who impressed an interview committee with his curriculum knowledge and poise. This impression was blemished, however, when he peppered the panel with a series of overly detailed questions about the benefits package.

As a rule of thumb, limit yourself to two questions about salary and benefits. Your first query should be about salary, the most critical issue. If the answer gives you enough information to make a decision, you need not ask any more questions. However, if there are other significant concerns that may influence your decision to accept a job, use the list in the box below as a guide to select your second question. As an alternative to asking these two questions, you could simply inquire, "Is there written information about salary and benefits that I could take home and review?"

Never show displeasure with a salary offer. We have often witnessed a candidate's reputation diminish in the view of an administrator, because the teacher appeared unhappy with salary or benefits. For the administrator's point of view, contracts with teachers unions may not allow a great deal of negotiation, and an administrator will begin to wonder whether you will perform your job effectively if you seem disgruntled from the start. Acknowledge the offer graciously, and then negotiate with a professional tone if you deem it important.

## What Is Negotiable?

In general, very little is negotiable. Most public schools are tied to salary scale and benefits packages that specify compensation. Private schools also try to maintain parity among their employees, so a newly hired teacher does not earn more than a veteran. If you have previous teaching or

---

**Salary and Benefits**

When considering a job offer, you may want to ask a *question or two* from the following list:

*Salary*
- What is the salary?
- Can I receive salary credit for previous teaching or military experience?
- Is there a salary schedule?
- How do I advance on the salary schedule?
- Can I receive salary credit for an advanced degree?
- What is the compensation for extracurricular activities (coaching, sponsoring a club)?

*Benefits*
- Is health insurance provided for employees and their families?
- What other types of insurance are available (life insurance, disability insurance, dental plan)?
- Is there a retirement plan?
- What other benefits are available (on-site child care, tuition reimbursement for college courses)?
- Will you cover the employment agency fee? (See Chapter 3.)

*Private Schools*
- Are travel expenses to home and back reimbursed (for international schools)?
- What is the school calendar? How much vacation time will I receive (for international schools)?
- Is housing provided? What responsibilities are associated with this benefit (for boarding schools)?

military experience, the door may be open to negotiating a higher starting salary by receiving credit for this work. For example, starting salary for a new teacher with a master's degree in a given district could be $33,000. Five years' experience could warrant an increase of $6,000 on the salary schedule negotiated with the teachers' union.

It is also possible to negotiate a higher salary if there is a shortage of qualified candidates in your teaching field. Remember the law of supply and demand. If qualified teachers are in demand and supply is low, then employers may offer higher salaries as an incentive to attract the best applicant. As we write this book, there is a dire shortage of physics teachers in our region. School districts have been known to raise salary offers dramatically to fill these positions. On the other hand, there is an overabundant supply of elementary teachers for positions in prestigious schools, so these applicants wield little bargaining power. It behooves you, therefore, to know the job market in your geographic region. This information is available from the National Center for Education Statistics <**www.nces.ed. gov**>, the American Association for Employment in Education <**www.aaee.org**>, and from our own Web site <**www.teacheredge.com**>.

## Teacher Salaries

Teacher salaries vary from state to state. In the 2000–2001 school year, according to the U.S. Department of Education, the average teacher salary nationwide was $42,898. New Jersey boasted the highest average teacher salary of $53,281; South Dakota's average salary of $30,265 was the lowest. In the 1999–2000 school year, the most recent year for which this data is available, the average beginning teacher salary in the nation was $27,989. Alaska featured the highest average salary for beginning teachers at $33,676. The lowest average beginning salary, $20,422, was offered in North Dakota (National Center for Education Statistics, 2001). Within each state, there is significant variation. In New York, for example, upstate salaries are much lower than the metropolitan area around New York City due to differences in the cost of living. Within the New York City metropolitan area, salaries also vary from school

district to school district. Teacher salaries in one school may be twenty percent lower than salaries in a wealthy suburb literally a stone's throw away. Likewise, disparities exist in many other locations across the country, a result of the financial resources available, community priorities, cost of living, and other factors.

How can you learn the beginning teacher salary in a school you are considering? You can save a great deal of time and trouble if you know early whether a school's salary is competitive. The information may even influence your decision whether or not to apply. Newspaper advertisements often note whether the school offers a competitive salary, or you may rely on your network to acquire information about starting salaries. Many teacher unions also compile this information as they assemble data for negotiations; inquiring at the local, regional, or state level may give you the information you need. As a last resort, you may also ask your *Job Find Friend* to call a school and request the information without supplying the name of the candidate.

## Still Can't Decide?

Some candidates find themselves unsure whether a particular school is the right choice, even after studying the school on-line and in print, submitting a cover letter and resume, interviewing perhaps more than once, and conducting a demonstration lesson. For some candidates, the issue is complicated because of job offers from two or more schools. How to decide?

Here are some questions to answer before you decide:

- As a new teacher, will I work alone or in will I be part of a team? You're better off if you don't feel isolated in a classroom, especially if you are a new teacher.
- What opportunities are available for in-service instruction? A school that values professional growth will provide a new teacher on the job training.
- How does the school's philosophy of education align with your own? A reading teacher, for example, might be disgruntled if the school's reading program emphasizes test preparation.

| State | Starting Salary 1999–2000 | Average Salary 2000–2001 | State | Starting Salary 1999–2000 | Average Salary 2000–2001 |
|---|---|---|---|---|---|
| United States | $27,989 | $42,898 | Montana | $20,969 | $32,930 |
| Alabama | $29,790 | $37,956 | Nebraska | $22,923 | $34,175 |
| Alaska | $33,676 | $46,986 | Nevada | $28,734 | $40,172 |
| Arizona | $25,613 | $36,302 | New Hampshire | $24,650 | $38,303 |
| Arkansas | $22,599 | $34,476 | New Jersey | $30,480 | $53,281 |
| California | $32,190 | $48,923 | New Mexico | $25,042 | $33,785 |
| Colorado | $24,875 | $39,284 | New York | $31,910 | $50,920 |
| Connecticut | $30,466 | $52,100 | North Carolina | $27,968 | $41,167 |
| Delaware | $30,945 | $47,047 | North Dakota | $20,422 | $30,891 |
| Florida | $25,132 | $37,824 | Ohio | $23,597 | $42,716 |
| Georgia | $30,402 | $42,216 | Oklahoma | $24,025 | $34,434 |
| Hawaii | $29,204 | $41,980 | Oregon | $29,733 | $42,333 |
| Idaho | $20,915 | $36,375 | Pennsylvania | $30,185 | $49,500 |
| Illinois | $30,151 | $48,053 | Rhode Island | $27,286 | $48,474 |
| Indiana | $26,553 | $43,055 | South Carolina | $25,215 | $37,327 |
| Iowa | $25,275 | $36,479 | South Dakota | $21,889 | $30,265 |
| Kansas | $25,252 | $39,432 | Tennessee | $27,228 | $37,074 |
| Kentucky | $24,753 | $37,234 | Texas | $28,400 | $38,614 |
| Louisiana | $25,738 | $34,253 | Utah | $23,273 | $36,049 |
| Maine | $22,942 | $36,256 | Vermont | $25,791 | $38,651 |
| Maryland | $28,612 | $44,997 | Virginia | $26,783 | $40,197 |
| Massachusetts | $30,330 | $47,523 | Washington | $26,514 | $42,101 |
| Michigan | $28,545 | $49,975 | West Virginia | $23,829 | $35,764 |
| Minnesota | $25,666 | $40,577 | Wisconsin | $25,344 | $41,646 |
| Missouri | $25,977 | $36,764 | Wyoming | $24,168 | $34,189 |
| Mississippi | $ | $32,957 | | | |

Source: National Center for Education Statistics, 2001

- How do the salary and benefits compare with other districts? Remember to compare starting teacher salaries and experienced teacher salaries. A district that has lower beginning salaries, but high salaries for veteran teachers, is probably more lucrative in the long run.
- How large is the school and/or school district? Some candidates prefer to be the proverbial "big fish in a little pond," or vice versa.
- How long is the commute? Be certain to drive the route at the same time you will actually commute. We know candidates who took a trial drive to school in the evening, only to learn after accepting the position that the same roads were congested during rush hour.
- Will I get along with my supervisor? For many candidates, this is the deciding factor. The right relationship with a supervisor makes the difference between success and failure.

Candidates sometimes ask us to spend a day visiting school before they make up their minds. We consider this request to be very reasonable. We understand that the choice of schools is a critical decision. We do not want a prospective teacher accepting a position still feeling uncertain. Totaling time spent in interviews and demonstration lessons, a candidate may have spent only two hours in the school. It is acceptable to ask to spend time taking a tour of school and visiting classrooms if you are a finalist.

### When Is the Decision Final?

Schools have different methods of "making it official." Sometimes you will be given a contract to sign. When both parties have signed on the bottom line, then you can start your celebration. A signed contract is not always necessary, however; some schools simply send a letter tendering you a job offer. Alternatively, the superintendent or headmaster may tell you that you will be recommended, but you must await personnel action at a meeting of the Board of Education or the Board of Trustees before you are officially hired. In these cases, you will receive a letter afterward notifying you of the appointment. The administrator should inform you which of these methods—contract, letter tendering a job offer, or notification of Board approval—applies to the particular school, and when you can expect to receive final word.

"Congratulations. You have the job." With these words, you know that your job hunt has been a success. You have worked many years to accomplish your goal of landing the teaching job you want. No longer a candidate, you are ready to make your mark in America's classrooms.

## REMINDERS

Prepare for second- and third-round interviews as intensely as you did for the initial round.

Demonstration lessons should be planned with great care. Your goal is to showcase your teaching talents, particularly as they relate to the needs of the school to which you are applying. A demonstration lesson is not the time to experiment with new techniques or unfamiliar content.

Prepare a list of four to six references. The best references come from recent supervisors and professors.

Discussions about salary and benefits should be reserved for the final interview with the administrator who makes the ultimate hiring decision.

# Epilogue

Our journey together has come to a close. We hope that our strategies have contributed to the success of your search for a teaching job, and that you will bring to the classroom the creativity, skills, and commitment that characterize the best members of the teaching profession. It is also our hope that you have realized the goal expressed in the title of our book—that is, getting the teaching job *you want*. We have witnessed the powerful synergy that occurs when there is a match between a teacher's strengths and the needs of the school in which he or she works. In these circumstances, energy and enthusiasm are unleashed, children feel motivated to learn and valued by the adults who teach them, and new heights of learning and growth are achieved.

We wish you great success and look forward to your forthcoming contributions to education.

# Further Reading

The following list of professional associations and journals will enable you to explore current topics in education. Each of the professional associations cited below publishes a journal. Reading them will lead you to even more information—helping you to build your knowledge base and become the best candidate for the job. In addition to journals produced by professional organizations, we have listed several popular magazines and a weekly newspaper for educators.

| Association | Journal |
|---|---|
| American Alliance for Health, Physical Education, Recreation, and Dance | *Journal of Physical Education, Recreation, and Dance* |
| American Council on the Teaching of Foreign Language | *Foreign Language Annals* |
| Council for Exceptional Children | *Teaching Exceptional Children* |
| Music Educators National Conference | *Music Educators Journal* |
| National Art Education Association | *Journal of Art Education* |
| National Council for Social Studies | *Social Studies and the Young Learner* (elementary) |
| | *Middle Level Learning* (middle school) |
| | *Social Education* (all levels) |
| National Council of Teachers of English | *Language Arts* (elementary and middle) |
| | *Voices from the Middle* (middle) |
| | *English Journal* (middle and high school) |
| National Council of Teachers of Mathematics | *Teaching Children Mathematics* (elementary) |
| | *Mathematics Teaching in the Middle School* |
| | *Mathematics Teacher* (high school) |
| National Middle School Association | *Middle School Journal* |
| National Science Teacher Association | *Science and Children* (elementary) |
| | *Science Scope* (middle school) |
| | *The Science Teacher* (high school) |
| American Association of School Librarians | *School Library Media Media Research* |
| American School Counselor Association | *Professional School Counseling* |
| International Reading Association | *The Reading Teacher* (elementary) |
| | *Journal of Adolescent & Adult Literacy* (secondary) |
| International Society for Technology Education | *Journal of Research on Technology in Education* |
| National Association for the Education of Young Children | *Young Children* |
| Teachers of English to Speakers of Other Languages | *TESOL Journal* |

*Education Week*

Published by Editorial Projects in Education, Inc., a nonprofit organization based in Washington, D.C., *Education Week* is devoted exclusively to education. With a circulation of 50,000, it is an excellent source of information about current practices and trends, and a place where positions are advertised.

*Educational Leadership*

Published ten times a year by the Association for Supervision and Curriculum Development in Alexandria, Virginia, *Educational Leadership* features articles about current trends in education and is read widely by school administrators. One of the largest professional education associations in the world, ASCD boasts a membership in excess of 160,000. The magazine does not list job openings.

*Instructor*

With 1.3 million readers, *Instructor* is a popular magazine for elementary teachers, containing practical ideas for classroom teachers, professional development, and think pieces on contemporary education issues.

*Teacher Magazine*

Also published by Editorial Projects in Education, Inc., the same group responsible for *Education Week*, *Teacher Magazine* covers current classroom issues and practices.

# References

American Association for Employment in Education. *2000 Educator Supply and Demand.* Columbus, OH: Author, 2001.

Bolles, Richard Nelson. *What Color Is Your Parachute? 2000 A Practical Manual for Job-Hunters and Career-Changers.* Berkeley: Ten Speed Press, 2000.

Campbell, D. M.; Cignetti, P. B.; Melenyzer, B. J.; Nettles, D. H.; and Wyman, R. M. (1997) *How to Develp a Professional Portfolio: A Manual for Teachers.* Boston: Allyn & Bacon

Cook, Donovan, and Jeanne Kessler. "The Professional Teaching Portfolio: A Useful Tool for an Effective Job Search," *ASCUS Annual* (August 1993): 15.

George, Paul S. *What's the Truth about Tracking and Ability Grouping Really?* Gainesville, FL: Teacher Education Resources, 1988.

Hunter, Madeline. *Mastery Teaching.* Thousand Oaks, CA: Corwin Press, 1982.

Hurst, Beth, Cindy Wilson, and Genny Cramer. "Professional Teaching Portfolios: Tools for Reflection, Growth, and Advancement," *Phi Delta Kappan* (April 1998): 582.

Hussar, William J., "Predicting the Need for Newly Hired Teachers in the United States to 2008–2009," National Center for Education Statistics, 1999.

Keegan, Thomas. *Boarding School Guide.* Flagler Beach Florida: Athletic Guides Publishing, 2002.

Kilbane, C. and McNergney, R. (2003) *Focus on Technology: Digital Teaching-Portfolios Build, Display Talent.* [Online] Available: www.aacte.org/research/focus_tech_digital.htm (American Association of Colleges for Teacher Education).

NAFSA Association of International Educators. *The International Educator.* New York: Author.

National Association of Independent Schools. *Independent Schools.* Washington: Author.

National Center for Education Statistics. *Digest of Education Statistics.* Washington: Author, 2001.

Peterson's Guides. *Peterson's American and Canadian Boarding Schools and Worldwide Enrichment Programs.* Lawrenceville, NJ: Author, 2003.

———. *Peterson's Private Secondary Schools 2003.* Lawrenceville, NJ: Author, 2003.

Porter Sargent. *The Handbook of Private Schools, 2002: An Annual Descriptive Survey of Independent Education.* Boston: Porter Sargent Publishers, 2002.

# Glossary: A Quick Guide to Educationese

Like other professionals, educators frequently use technical terms unique to their field or employ common words in ways that have special meanings. As we noted earlier in the book, it is not a good idea to use a great deal of jargon in your writing or in conversations with your prospective employers. Sometimes, however, only the vocabulary of education can capture the precise meaning or image you wish to communicate; on these occasions, using just the right expression may play a pivotal role in advancing your candidacy.

To help you prepare for that kind of moment, we have prepared the glossary on the following pages. Our list is by no means complete, but it does present many of the terms frequently encountered on the job and in the professional literature. To expand your educational vocabulary, we strongly suggest that you subscribe to one of the many publications designed for teachers and participate frequently in dialogues with other members of the field.

## A

**ability grouping.** A method of organizing classes in which students deemed to possess similar levels of achievement or potential are placed together, and others are excluded. Organizing elementary school reading groups on the basis of test scores is one form of ability grouping; honors classes at the secondary level comprise another. *See also* **homogeneous grouping** and **tracking.**

**acceleration.** A programming technique in which students who are considered advanced for their age or grade level are moved through course work more quickly than their peers and provided with work at a higher level, for example, when an eighth grader takes a high school math course.

**achievement tests.** These formal, standardized examinations measure how much a student has mastered in a given subject area. Popular examples include the Iowa Tests and the TerraNova tests. Scores are usually reported on the basis of *norms,* so a student's work can be compared to others at the same age or grade level. **Percentile rankings, grade equivalents,** and **stanines** are the most common measures.

**ADD/ADHD.** Attention Deficit Disorder and the related Attention Deficit Hyperactivity Disorder are problems that manifest themselves in a student's inability to concentrate and impulsiveness (ADD), often coupled with a need for excessive movement (ADHD).

**advisor-advisee** (also known as home-based advisory). A system employed primarily in middle and junior high schools in which each student is assigned to a small group that has an adult mentor. This advisor provides frequent contact with the assigned students and works with them to build self-esteem and group identity and to resolve issues often associated with the transition into adolescence.

**affective education.** Learning tasks and strategies that address the emotional component of human growth and development.

**alternative assessment.** A movement in education to evaluate student performance using nontraditional methods. *See also* **performance-based assessment, portfolio,** and **rubric.**

**alternative certification.** A process that enables aspiring educators from various educational backgrounds and work experiences to become teachers. Alternative certification route candidates generally have not completed traditional college level education programs; they complete an accelerated program of coursework and field experiences that leads to teacher certification.

**alternative schools.** Any school that is different in organization, curriculum, or teaching approaches from a traditional school. Often, alternative schools are established to address the needs of special populations, for example, former drop-outs, or students with behavior problems. Alternative schools may also be founded around a theme, as in environmental education, for example.

**aptitude tests.** These **standardized tests** are designed to measure a student's ability or potential. The most famous forms are **intelligence quotient (IQ)** tests that seek to represent a person's intellectual capacities. Other aptitude tests are used to help students select careers or to identify areas of special talent.

**at-risk.** This term is usually applied to students who appear headed for school failure. Factors that render a student at-risk include poverty, lack of proficiency in English, substance abuse, and physical abuse, among others.

**authentic assessment.** Evaluation of student achievement that is provided through a real-life task or an activity that mirrors a real-life task, adjusted for student age and developmental levels. In an authentic assessment approach, the traditional book report, for example, might be replaced by a book review; a test on the elements of harmony might be replaced by an assignment to compose music containing harmonic passages.

**B**

**balanced reading program** or **balanced literacy.** A design for instruction in reading that takes a pragmatic, rather than philosophic, stance toward program design. Balanced reading combines elements of **phonics** instruction with aspects of **whole language.**

**basal reader.** Textbooks designed to teach reading strategies, techniques, and skills as part of a developmental program used in elementary schools. Basals contain stories and accompanying exercises that aim to build mastery in a structured, carefully sequenced approach.

**bilingual education.** An instructional approach for students who speak a language other than English as their primary tongue. Bilingual classes teach students in their native language while seeking to promote competency in English.

**block scheduling.** A creative approach to scheduling classes, usually at the secondary level, in which courses are presented in extended time periods, or blocks. Thus, a student might have science for ninety minutes every other day, instead of the traditional forty-five minute daily period. In some schools, block scheduling is used so that a group of related classes are run at the same time, thereby enabling teachers to regroup students or use time more flexibly without causing havoc with the rest of the schedule.

**Bloom's Taxonomy of Thinking Skills.** Named after theorist Benjamin Bloom, the taxonomy, or classification system, identifies thinking skills in an ascending order of complexity. Beginning with the knowledge level, competent thinkers progress to comprehension, application, analysis, synthesis, and evaluation. The components of the last half of the taxonomy are often described as **higher order thinking skills.**

**C**

**career education.** Teaching students about the nature of different jobs and the skills that are required to reach career goals.

**character education.** Instruction that is specifically targeted to teach students about values that are believed to be shared by members of the community. Character education programs often focus on beliefs in the importance of honesty, responsibility, respect for others, respect for property, helping others, and citizenship.

**charter school.** A relative newcomer on the educational playing field, charters are public schools that operate under a special agreement with the state or local board of education. Charter schools are granted greater autonomy than other public schools, and they are frequently exempted from the federal, state, and local regulations applied to traditional public schools.

**child study team (CST).** A multidisciplinary group of professionals that works with teachers to identify student needs and recommend classroom accommodations and curriculum modifications designed to improve student performance. Although practices vary from school to school, child study teams frequently include a building administrator, reading teachers and/or other remedial specialists, a school psychologist and/or guidance counselor, the school nurse, and special educators. Child study teams help eliminate unnecessary referrals to **special education.**

**competency tests.** Another form of **standardized testing.** Competency tests generally attempt to certify that students possess the minimum level of skills and knowledge required by the state or local educational agency.

**conflict resolution.** Programs that attempt to teach students how to solve problems without resorting to violence or harassing the other parties involved in disputes. Conflict resolution programs may employ peer mediators, students who have been trained to help their classmates settle disputes in a nonviolent, effective manner.

**constructivism.** A pedagogical approach that is founded on the belief that students learn by constructing knowledge gained through learning experiences rather than by simply receiving information from others. Exploration, reasoning, and reflection are encouraged more than listening to lectures and memorizing material.

**cooperative learning.** An approach to teaching that requires that students work in groups to achieve common learning goals. Cooperative learning is based on the notion that humans often learn best when they work together in a collaborative manner. Socialization skills are emphasized in addition to cognitive development. The best cooperative learning programs stress both teamwork and individual accountability.

**cooperative teaching.** A model for teaching in which two teachers work together in the same classroom to achieve instructional goals with a group of students. *See also* **team teaching.**

**core subjects.** A term often used to refer to the subjects of English language arts, mathematics, science, and social studies.

**criterion-referenced tests.** *Standardized tests* that measure whether a student has reached a predetermined level of performance (the criterion). Criterion-referenced tests may be used to determine if a student has mastered a defined curriculum or has attained skills determined to be appropriate to her/his grade level, for example, a three-paragraph essay.

**critical thinking skills.** Usually employed to identify cognitive abilities that go beyond just remembering and restating. Often used synonymously with the higher levels of **Bloom's Taxonomy.** *See also* **higher order thinking skills.**

**D**

**Department of Defense Dependents School.** A school that provides education for children of members of the United States armed forces.

**diagnostic test.** A test or other evaluation instrument that enables a teacher to analyze the problems that are hampering a child's ability to learn.

**differentiated instruction.** The design of assignments that reflect an understanding of the varied learning styles and achievement levels of students in a given classroom.

**distance learning.** Using technology to enable students in one school to communicate via video/audio/computer connections with students, teachers, and other resource providers (like museum curators) in another location. Distance learning has evolved in a variety of formats, including video conferencing.

**document-based questions (DBQ).** A type of task presented in social studies in which students are required to comprehend, analyze, synthesize, and evaluate documents, charts, graphs, cartoons, paintings, photographs, and other materials presented as parts of the historical record.

**dyslexia.** A severe reading disability.

## E

**early childhood education.** The preschool to primary years, spanning nursery to grade 2 or 3.

**early intervention program.** An educational, health and family support initiative designed to provide resources, remediation, and health assistance to children between birth and age five.

**emotional intelligence.** Popularized by Daniel Goleman, the term refers to the ability to understand one's own emotions as well as those of people around you. It is deemed to be an essential ingredient of school and life success. For more information, read *Emotional Intelligence* by Daniel P. Goleman (New York: Bantam Books, 1997).

**English as a Second Language (ESL).** A program of instruction that teaches English to non-English-speaking students.

**essential question.** A question of basic importance to a unit of study that cannot be answered in a simple sentence or two. Essential questions require students to think critically about a topic and to analyze, synthesize, and evaluate information.

## G

**gifted and talented (G/T).** Students who demonstrate abilities or show the potential to perform far above the average. Some schools include in this definition only students who excel in the **core subject** areas, while others include pupils with a variety of talents including the arts and athletics. Gifted and talented programs operate in a variety of formats; options include special classes, pull-out programs, and work with a specialist within the regular classroom.

**grade equivalent.** A way of reporting scores on a **standardized test** that shows the year and month of school for which a given student's score is typical. For example, a pupil who received a grade equivalent of 3.2 on an **achievement test** received a score that is the average achieved by students in the second month of third grade.

## H

**hands on.** A teaching approach in which students are provided with learning activities where they directly encounter the concepts and skills under study. For example, students construct different types of paper triangles to learn about the relationships between angles and sides, rather than read about the properties of triangles in a textbook.

**Head Start.** A federal program designed to provide educational assistance to impoverished or disabled children from ages three to five and to their families. Head Start is a prime example of an **early intervention program.**

**heterogeneous grouping.** An approach to organizing classes in which students of varying achievement levels and talents are deliberately mixed together. It is predicated on the notions that students learn best in mixed ability groups and gain respect for others through first-hand experiences with diversity.

**higher order thinking skills.** Complex mental operations that include comparing, problem-solving, making inferences, analyzing, synthesizing, and evaluating information. *See also* **critical thinking skills** and **Bloom's Taxonomy of Thinking Skills.**

**History Alive!** A "hands-on" social studies curriculum that emphasizes **cooperative learning** and **multiple intelligences.**

**homogeneous grouping.** A form of *ability grouping* in which students are placed in classes for extended periods of time according to their achievement levels. *Tracking* is a form of homogeneous grouping often used in secondary schools to develop programs for gifted, average, or remedial students, or to develop separate classes for those bound for college and those headed for employment or vocational training.

## I

**IEP (Individualized Educational Program).** A document required for all students receiving special education services that summarizes student strengths and weaknesses and articulates an annual plan for instruction that addresses student needs. An IEP also states how much a student will be integrated with nondisabled peers.

**IFSP (Individualized Family Service Plan).** A document that describes the services and support a disabled preschool child and her/his family will receive as part of **early intervention services.**

**inclusion.** The practice of educating students with disabilities in classes with their nondisabled peers. In an inclusive classroom, all students follow the same general schedule. Support, as needed, is provided by specialists who deliver their assistance in the class; it is supplemented through collaborative planning and **team teaching** by regular classroom teachers and special educators.

**independent school.** A private school. The term "independent" is usually applied to schools that have no affiliations with religion.

**instructional technology.** A term that encompasses all the technological aids utilized in teaching and learning. Computers, of course, are an essential component of instructional technology, but the term also may refer to **distance learning,** video, graphing calculators, etc.

**interdisciplinary instruction.** A curriculum and teaching design in which the content from different areas is blended together to study themes, **essential questions,** and topics. This approach is most popular at the elementary and middle school levels. The approach may be illustrated by a unit on the environment, in which students learn science, math, social studies, language arts, and other disciplines by studying a local problem.

**international schools.** Schools located in foreign countries that provide a program much like those commonly found in the United States.

**interdisciplinary teaming.** *See* **teaming.**

**IQ (intelligence quotient).** The result of taking an **aptitude test** that is used to represent the ability level of a given student. IQ tests are used to identify disabilities and giftedness and to make decisions about class placement and *tracking.*

**L**

**learning disability (LD).** A condition that impedes a student's ability to achieve in a manner commensurate with predicted ability levels. Students with learning disabilities may demonstrate an inability to use and process language, as in **dyslexia,** have perceptual problems, experience great difficulties with

math, or lag behind peers in gross and fine motor skills (including handwriting). No cause has yet been determined.

**learning style.** The manner in which a student is most inclined to learn. Learning style theory is based on the belief that people process information and learn in different ways. Some, for example, learn best by processing visual information, while others need a more experienced-based approach. To address differences in learning styles, teachers are advised to present material in a variety of ways and provide differentiated tasks so students can acquire knowledge in the manner most consistent with their own personal profiles.

**LEP (Limited English Proficiency).** A description of students who come from non-English language background and are not yet fluent or literate in English. *LEP* students may also be known as **English Language Learners** *(ELL).* LEP students often attend *ESL* or **bilingual education classes.**

**looping.** A practice in which students are assigned to a teacher for more than one year. Teachers engaged in looping stay with their students as they move from one grade level to the next, for example, second to third, and then they return to the original grade to start the process once again with a new group. Advocates of looping believe that it enhances the continuity of instruction and helps teachers know their students better.

**M**

**Madeline Hunter Method.** An educational researcher and professor, Madeline Hunter wrote about instructional practices that are proven to be successful in classrooms. She is best known for describing a seven step lesson plan format in which new material is introduced and then students learn to apply skills and knowledge with increasing independence and mastery. More information is contained in her book titled *Mastery Learning* (Thousand Oaks, CA: Corwin Press, 1982).

**magnet school.** A school that offers a special curriculum or alternative program to attract students who would normally attend other schools. Magnet schools are often established in metropolitan areas to help schools achieve diversity among their student bodies.

**mainstreaming.** The practice in which students with disabilities are placed in general education classrooms for part of the school day. The degree of mainstreaming varies according to the needs of the individual student and is described in the pupil's *IEP*. Mainstreaming and **inclusion** are related, although **inclusion** implies a higher level of integration into the regular school setting.

**manipulatives.** Materials, usually designed for mathematics instruction, that allow students to learn about concepts through the manipulation of physical objects. Most commonly used on the elementary level, although materials exist for the intermediate and high school levels as well.

**mastery learning.** An approach to curriculum and instruction that defines discrete segments of a given unit and requires that students demonstrate competence, or mastery, of the segment before moving ahead to the next one. Students who do not demonstrate mastery are assigned additional work; they are tested again before they are allowed to begin the section of the unit that follows.

**metacognition.** The skill of being able to monitor one's own thinking. When students can "think about their thinking," they are able to determine whether they have done a thorough, high quality job with an assignment, and they are able to identify sources of error.

**mission statement.** A statement of core educational beliefs, such as "All children can learn," that guides instructional practices and policies.

**Montessori schools.** Schools based upon the work of Maria Montessori. The Montessori program emphasizes learning through all the senses, individualized instruction, and student choice of learning activities.

**multiage classrooms.** A design for organizing classes in which students of different ages are placed together in a classroom. Students may be grouped on the basis of broad categories, for example, all intermediate level pupils, or they may be organized into classes based on achievement levels, as when "advanced" first graders are placed with second graders.

**multicultural education.** A program of study that teaches students about the diverse ethnic, racial, cultural, language, and religious groups that populate our planet. The term also encompasses teaching about disabilities and gender effects.

**Multiple intelligences.** Based on the theories of Howard Gardner, the approach expands the traditional view of linguistic and mathematical-logical intelligence to include abilities described as musical, spatial, body-kinesthetic, intrapersonal, interpersonal, and naturalist (knowledgeable and perceptive about the environment). Teachers working with multiple intelligence approaches provide varied learning experiences and activities for their students as well as numerous options for the demonstration of mastery. For more information, read Gardner's book: *Intelligence Reframed : Multiple Intelligences for the 21st Century* (New York: Basic Books, 1999).

**N**

**norm-referenced test.** A **standardized test** that compares a student's performance with those who served as the sample upon which the scores are based. Normed scores include *percentiles*, *stanines*, normal curve equivalents (NCE), and age and **grade equivalents.** *See also* **achievement tests.**

**O**

**Outcome.** Another word for "anticipated result." Often used synonymously with "objective" and "goal."

**Outward Bound.** An outdoor education program that promotes cognitive and personal growth through cooperative work on challenging tasks. The program also emphasizes learning by doing and service.

**P**

**paraprofessional.** An aide to a teacher or school. **Paraprofessional** responsibilities vary by state and school; in some cases, they work directly with students, while in others, their role is limited to providing noninstructional support for the supervision of students or the provision of supplies and materials. Educational requirements vary—check with the school, district, or state. *See also* **teaching assistant.**

**parochial school.** A private school that is affiliated with, or supported by, a religious group or institution.

**percentile.** A rank in a distribution of test scores that indicates how a given point compares to other scores. For example, a test score in the 74th percentile means that the student scored higher than 74% of the students tested; 26% of the students tested performed better.

**performance-based assessment.** A method of evaluating student achievement in which students must complete an activity or solve a problem in order to demonstrate mastery of content. Performance-based assessments are designed to show how well a student can apply knowledge in a meaningful context, rather than just memorize it for a test. *See also* **authentic assessment.**

**phoneme.** A discrete unit of sound in a language. The word "cat" is composed of three different phonemes. **Phonemic awareness,** that is, the ability to hear the separate sounds in a word, is viewed as a key factor in reading achievement.

**phonics.** An instructional technique that helps student master the association between sounds and the letter or letters of the alphabet that represent them.

**portfolio** or **portfolio assessment.** As applied to students, the term refers to a collection of pupil work that documents progress over time. Portfolios are often used for diagnostic purposes, allowing teachers to determine what has been mastered and what remains to be accomplished. Portfolios can also be graded as part of the evaluation for a curriculum unit.

**practicum.** The portion of a teacher preparation program devoted to student teaching.

**problem-based learning.** This curriculum approach provides students with real-life problems for study and organizes class work around developing the solution to these problems. Material is not presented in traditional discipline-based units. Rather, students gain knowledge in content areas as they work collaboratively to solve the problem assigned to them.

**Progressive education.** Practices loosely based on the ideas of educator and philosopher John Dewey. Progressive educational practices include learning through experience, collaborative classroom work, a respect for **affective** educational goals, and the belief that teachers should serve as facilitators of growth rather than dispensers of wisdom.

**pupil personnel services (PPS).** The resources provided by guidance counselors, social workers, school psychologists, and others with special training in helping students address cognitive, social, and emotional issues.

## R

**Reading Recovery.** An intensive, one-on-one remedial reading program for first graders.

**remedial education.** Efforts that address academic deficiencies presented by students and help them catch-up with their peers. Reading and math specialist services are often provided under this umbrella term.

**resource room.** A type of **special education** class that provides students with assistance in mastering the content presented in the general education classroom or offers remedial work designed to address specific areas of difficulty. Students attend resource room classes for limited periods of time; they spend the remainder of their day with other specialists and in the mainstream.

**rubric.** A scoring guide. Rubrics come in various forms. In general, they specify what is required for specific levels of mastery on a given task. For example, pupils writing a composition may be provided with a rubric that describes levels of performance in relation to content, organization, and usage of the English language. Performance may be represented by a number, for example, Level 4, or by a descriptive term, such as, accomplished, or novice.

**running record.** A system for assessing student reading performance in which the teacher records everything a child says or does while reading a passage aloud. The record may be used to document progress, identify strengths and weaknesses, and develop plans for remediation of deficits.

## S

**school-to-career education.** A way of presenting educational material and experiences that emphasizes the connection between academic activities and the world of work or preparation for advanced studies. For example, a teacher presenting a unit on measurement might include lessons related to how architects, engineers, and carpenters use measurement to solve problems encountered on the job.

**self-contained class.** A classroom composed only of students with special educational needs.

**service learning.** The practice in which service activities, that is, tasks that help others or the community in general, are integrated into courses of study so that pupils develop better understandings of citizenship, increase their self-esteem levels, develop empathy, and learn how to apply academic knowledge in real-life situations. Service learning is differentiated from community service by its academic content and its focus on self-reflection activities that help learners assess their cognitive, social, and emotional growth.

**special education.** The services provided to students who have disabilities.

**standard.** A statement of what students "should know and be able to do." *Content standards* describe the material to be mastered in various subjects. *Performance standards* specify the levels of student achievement that are anticipated.

**standardized test.** A published test, constructed by experts, that is administered in a highly regulated fashion, so that instructions and test conditions do not vary from one setting to another. Standardized tests can be *norm-referenced* or *criterion-referenced*.

**stanine.** A rank in a distribution of test scores that indicates how a given point compares to other scores that are grouped into nine levels. For example, a test score in the eighth stanine means that the student scored in the upper end of the achievement range, while a score in the first stanine means that the student scored in the lowest possible grouping. A stanine rank of four, five, or six is generally considered in the average range.

**strategic plan.** A long-term plan for use of school resources and the development of educational programs. A strategic plan, sometimes called a five year plan, serves as a road map to guide the way to the future.

## T

**teaching assistant.** An aide to a teacher. Responsibilities may vary by school, district, and state. **Teaching assistants** usually are allowed to provide instruction to students, under the direct supervision of a teacher. *See also* **paraprofessional.**

**team teaching.** A teaching method in which two or more teachers take responsibility to work with a given group of students. Team teaching is often utilized in **inclusion** efforts. *See also* **cooperative teaching.**

**teaming.** Often called, **interdisciplinary teaming,** this middle school approach to organizing classes allows a group of teachers to share the same group of students. Teams can vary in size, with some schools using two-teacher teams, and others creating teams representing many of the content areas. Teaming allows teachers to implement interdisciplinary units and manipulate the schedule for greater flexibility.

**Title I.** A federal program designed to assist disadvantaged, **at-risk** students. Frequently, **Title I** funds are used to provide supplementary materials and remedial specialists for pupils who lag behind their peers.

**tracking.** A method of grouping students according to their achievement or aptitude levels by placing them in classes designed solely for specific groups. Tracking is most frequently found in secondary schools, with students placed into sequences of classes that prepare students for different post-secondary school paths. *See also* **homogeneous grouping.**

**trade books.** Books available for purchase "over-the-counter" that are used as curriculum resources in developmental reading programs, English language arts classes, social studies courses, and other content areas. Trade books are often used in elementary reading programs as part of a **whole language** approach, or as a supplement to or substitute for a **basal reader**.

## V

**vocational education.** Implemented at the high school level, vocational education provides training for a trade or a skilled specialization. Vocational education students may study subjects as diverse as auto mechanics and recording engineering. The term encompasses the relatively new approach known as "tech prep," in which students are prepared for additional technical training after high school graduation.

## W

**Waldorf education.** An educational philosophy based upon the child development theories of Rudolf Steinert. Students stay with the same teacher for eight years; instruction emphasizes oral communication, the arts, and crafts including knitting, weaving, and woodworking.

**whole language.** An approach to teaching reading, writing, listening, and speaking in which students learn from whole to part, rather than the reverse. Whole language emphasizes the integration of the various aspects of language arts and the reading of whole texts, rather than using the mastery of phonics skills as the prerequisite required for reading "real" books. Comprehension is stressed. Whole language also underscores the connection between reading and writing, as well as the importance of promoting a love of language among students.

**writing process.** An approach to teaching writing that encourages students to perform the sequence of steps followed by authors as they compose works of various types, namely: selecting a topic, writing initial drafts, making revisions, editing, and publishing (or sharing) the finished piece with an audience.

**writer's workshop.** A method for teaching writing that features much individualization, frequent conferences between the teacher and individual students or among small groups of students, and small mini-lessons about specific writing skills and strategies.

## Y

**year-round school.** A flexible way of organizing the calendar in which the traditional long summer vacation is replaced by a twelve month school year that features several breaks of shorter durations. Year-round schools are designed to promote the continuity of instruction and, in some formats, permit schools to accommodate increased enrollments without expanding facilities.

# Index

Advertisements
   abbreviations in, 26
   Internet, 33–36
   interpreting, 23–27
   newspaper, 22–27, 33–36
   private schools, 38–40
Alternative certification, 4, 6, 13
   cover letter, 63, 66
   definition of, 150
   resume, 89
   finding vacancies, 38, 40

bulk mailings and cold calls, 22, 34, 37–38

career changers, 4–5
   cover letters, 65–66, 72
   interviews, 104, 115–116
   percent of newly hired teachers, 3
   resumes, 85, 88
   finding vacancies, 38, 40
career services office. *See* College placement office
CD's. *See* Portfolios, digital
certification, 30, 33
   advertisement, 22, 26, 28
   job market, 6, 8
   pending, 27, 95
   portfolio, 95
   resume, 81
cold calls. *See* Bulk mailings and cold calls
college placement office, 2
   finding job openings, 28
   researching schools, 50
cover letters
   career changers, 65–66, 72
   common errors, 56–59
   format and design, 61–68
   language, 66–68
   recent college graduates, 66, 69
   returning to workforce, 64, 71

   sample cover letters, 69–72
   targeting to school's needs, 63
   transferring from one teaching job to another, 64–65, 70
creditable experiences, 20, 64

demonstration lessons, 3–4, 135–137
digital portfolios. *See* Portfolios, digital
DVD's. *See* Portfolios, digial

employment agencies, 40
electronic portfolios, *See* Portfolios, digital

*Finding Common Ground,* 59–61, 63, 102, 104

illegal questions, 123
inside candidates, 31–33
international teaching jobs, 33, 36, 38–39, 50
Internet
   cover letters, 61
   finding job openings, 22, 33–36, 39–40
   on-line applications, 27
   portfolios, 92, 97
   researching schools, 25, 44, 46–51
*Interview Information Form,* 130–131, 133
*Interview Informer,* 102–103
interviews
   arrival, 106–107, 110–112
   attire, 106
   career changers, 115–116
   controversial questions, 119–120
   "Do you have any questions for us?", 123–125
   high pressure interviews, 121–122
   illegal questions, 123
   interview kit, 105
   portfolios in interviews, 96–97
   preparation for, 102–108
   private schools, 102, 104

recent college graduates, 113

relaxation techniques, 105–107

researching schools, 102–104

returning to workforce, 114–115

second round interviews, 133–135

talking points, 104–105, 113, 115, 123–125

techniques, 117–119, 121–122

"Tell us about yourself", 113–117

thank you notes, 130, 132

*Top 100 Interview Questions,* 125–128

transferring from one job to another, 114, 116–117

types of, 112–113

using portfolios, 96–97, 104, 120–121

job fairs, 29–30

*Job Find File,* 13, 20, 25, 29, 32, 44, 53, 102, 130, 133, 135

*Job Find Friend,* 13, 16, 20, 30, 68, 78–79, 85, 104, 125, 133, 135, 140

job hunting, four basic principles

build your resume and knowledge base, 4–5, 15, 76, 102

doing your homework, 4, 29, 76

target your strengths to the school's needs, 5–6, 76, 102

be yourself, 5, 76, 120

job market, 6–8

by certification, 8

projected teacher supply, 7

seasonal projections, 40–41

by state, 7

listserves, 33–34, 37

networking

finding job openings, 30–34, 38–39, 41, 102

on-line applications, 27

researching schools, 46, 122, 140

paraprofessional, 31–32, 110, 154

*Personal Profile,* 12–13, 16, 27, 41, 58–60, 92, 104, 114

portfolios

contents, 92–95

digital portfolios, 3, 97–99

organization, 95–96

using in an interview, 96–97, 102, 117–118, 121

private schools

cover letters, 61, 65

finding job openings, 22–23, 25, 29, 34, 37, 38–39

interviews, 102, 104, 114, 116

researching on Internet, 49–51

resumes, 81

salary and benefits, 139

visiting, 53

recent college graduates

cover letters, 64, 66, 69

interviews, 113

percent of newly hired teachers, 3–4

resumes, 86

references, 137–138

portfolios, 95

resumes, 83

rejection

handling rejection, 130, 132–133

reasons for, 2–3

relaxation techniques, 105–107

researching schools

community, 46

curriculum, 44

local press, 33, 50–51

philosophy, 44

private schools, 49–50, 53

school publications, 51–52

using the Internet, 46–50

who's who, 46

*Resume Reservoir,* 12–13, 16–17, 27, 41, 58–60, 82, 104, 114, 137

resumes

attention-getting resumes, 76–78

build your resume and knowledge base, 76

career changers, 88

doing your homework, 76

format and design, 78–80

language, 84–85

neutral resumes, 76–78

recent college graduates, 86

resume rubric, 85

returning to workforce, 87

sample resumes, 69–72

sections of, 80–83

target your strengths to the school's needs, 76, 78

be yourself, 76

returning to workforce, 3–4
    cover letters, 64, 71
    interviews, 114–115
    percent of newly hired teachers, 3
    resumes, 87

salary and benefits
    negotiating, 138–140
    state-by-state data, 141
*School Profile Form*, 44, 59–60, 102
school publications
    interviews, 107
    finding job openings, 33
    researching schools, 44, 51–52
student teaching
    cover letters, 59, 63, 66, 68
    demonstration lessons, 135
    interviews, 113, 116–119, 121
    portfolios, 93–34, 97
    resumes, 76, 78, 82
    finding vacancies, 31–32

substitute teaching, 32–33
summer school teaching, 33

talking points, 104–105, 113, 115, 123–125
thank you notes
    after interview, 130, 132
    after job fair, 29–30
*Top 100 Interview Questions*, 125–128
transferring from one teaching job to another
    cover letters, 64–65, 70
    interviews, 114, 116–117
    percent of newly hired teachers, 3–4
    resumes, 87

vacancy advertisements. *See* Advertisements

writing sample, 92, 103, 108